# THE FAMILY
# Handyman.

# BEST
# TIPS
# & PROJECTS
# 2016

# THE FAMILY
# Handyman®

# BEST
# TIPS
# & PROJECTS
# 2016

by The Editors of *The Family Handyman* magazine

**THE FAMILY HANDYMAN BEST TIPS & PROJECTS 2016**
(See page 288 for complete staff listing.)
Editor in Chief: Ken Collier
Project Editor: Teresa Marrone
Contributing Designers: BatScanner Productions, LLC
Contributing Copy Editors: Donna Bierbach, Mary Flanagan, Peggy Parker
Indexing: Stephanie Reymann

Vice President, Group Publisher: Russell S. Ellis

Trusted Media Brands, Inc.
President & Chief Executive Officer: Bonnie Kintzer

*Warning: All do-it-yourself activities involve a degree of risk. Skills, materials, tools, and site conditions vary widely. Although the editors have made every effort to ensure accuracy, the reader remains responsible for the selection and use of tools, materials, and methods. Always obey local codes and laws, follow manufacturer's operating instructions, and observe safety precautions.*

ISBN 978-1-62145-316-1

Address any comments about *The Family Handyman Best Tips & Projects 2016* to:
Editor, Best Tips & Projects 2016
2915 Commers Drive, Suite 700
Eagan, MN 55121

To order additional copies of *The Family Handyman Best Tips & Projects 2016,* call 1-800-344-2560.

For more Trusted Media Brands products and information, visit our Web site at tmbi.com.
For more about *The Family Handyman* magazine, visit familyhandyman.com.

Printed in China.
1 3 5 7 9 10 8 6 4 2

# SAFETY FIRST—ALWAYS!

Tackling home improvement projects and repairs can be endlessly rewarding. But as most of us know, with the rewards come risks. DIYers use chain saws, climb ladders and tear into walls that can contain big and hazardous surprises.

The good news is, armed with the right knowledge, tools and procedures, homeowners can minimize risk. As you go about your projects and repairs, stay alert for these hazards:

## Aluminum wiring

Aluminum wiring, installed in about 7 million homes between 1965 and 1973, requires special techniques and materials to make safe connections. This wiring is dull gray, not the dull orange characteristic of copper. Hire a licensed electrician certified to work with it. For more information go to cpsc.gov and search for "aluminum wiring."

## Spontaneous combustion

Rags saturated with oil finishes like Danish oil and linseed oil, and oil-based paints and stains can spontaneously combust if left bunched up. Always dry them outdoors, spread out loosely. When the oil has thoroughly dried, you can safely throw them in the trash.

## Vision and hearing protection

Safety glasses or goggles should be worn whenever you're working on DIY projects that involve chemicals, dust and anything that could shatter or chip off and hit your eye. Sounds louder than 80 decibels (dB) are considered potentially dangerous. Sound levels from a lawn mower can be 90 dB, and shop tools and chain saws can be 90 to 100 dB.

## Lead paint

If your home was built before 1979, it may contain lead paint, which is a serious health hazard, especially for children six and under. Take precautions when you scrape or remove it. Contact your public health department for detailed safety information or call (800) 424-LEAD (5323) to receive an information pamphlet. Or visit epa.gov/lead.

## Buried utilities

A few days before you dig in your yard, have your underground water, gas and electrical lines marked. Just call 811 or go to call811.com.

## Smoke and carbon monoxide (CO) alarms

The risk of dying in reported home structure fires is cut in half in homes with working smoke alarms. Test your smoke alarms every month, replace batteries as necessary and replace units that are more than 10 years old. As you make your home more energy-efficient and airtight, existing ducts and chimneys can't always successfully vent combustion gases, including potentially deadly carbon monoxide (CO). Install a UL-listed CO detector, and test your CO and smoke alarms at the same time.

## Five-gallon buckets and window covering cords

From 1996 to 1999, 58 children under age 5 have drowned in 5-gallon buckets. Always store them upside down and store ones containing liquid with the covers securely snapped.

According to Parents for Window Blind Safety, 571 children have been seriously injured or killed in the United States since 1986 after becoming entangled in looped window treatment cords. For more information, visit pfwbs.org or cpsc.gov.

## Working up high

If you have to get up on your roof to do a repair or installation, always install roof brackets and wear a roof harness.

## Asbestos

Texture sprayed on ceilings before 1978, adhesives and tiles for vinyl and asphalt floors before 1980, and vermiculite insulation (with gray granules) all may contain asbestos. Other building materials, made between 1940 and 1980, could also contain asbestos. If you suspect that materials you're removing or working around contain asbestos, contact your health department or visit epa.gov/asbestos for information.

For additional information about home safety, visit mysafehome.org. This site offers helpful information about dozens of home safety issues.

# Contents

# 1 Interior Projects, Repairs & Remodeling

## COVER-UP FOR GRUNGY GROUT

When cleaning isn't enough, the usual cure for grimy grout is to grind it out and regrout. But here's an easier approach: DAP Kwik Seal Grout Recolor Kit (available at home centers) lets you put a fresh coating over old grout in a few hours. It's a four-step process. First, you clean and prep the grout with DAP Pre-Treat. Next, apply the Color+Seal coating. Remove the excess and then buff off the haze. The kit contains everything you need and covers about 100 sq. ft. of 4-in. tile (smaller tile will have more grout lines and require more material).

**1 Pretreat the grout.** Sponge on the pre-treat solution and let it sit for five minutes. Then scrub the grout with the supplied brush. Wipe clean with the chamois.

**2 Apply colorant.** Squirt a thin bead of colorant on the grout lines in a 2-sq.-ft. section. Then scrub the colorant with the grout brush included in the kit.

**3 Remove excess colorant.** Wipe the excess colorant from the tile using the chamois. Wipe only the tile, not the grout lines. Let dry for 30 minutes.

**4 Buff to remove haze.** Apply a light mist of glass cleaner and buff the tile with a clean rag or chamois. Let dry for a full 24 hours before exposing it to water.

## TUNE UP THE ROUGH OPENING WHEN HANGING A DOOR

Twisted or out-of-plumb rough openings raise havoc with door installations. If you install the jambs to follow the walls, the door is likely to swing open or shut on its own. On the other hand, if you plumb the jambs against the out-of-plumb rough opening, the trim will be hard to install.

As long as the bottom of the wall isn't held in place by flooring, there's a simple solution. Just move the studs on both sides of the opening back to plumb. Don't think you can do this with your trim hammer, though. You'll need a maul or a sledgehammer.

NOT PLUMB

CHECK IT

CORRECT IT

## REMOVE A BROKEN CERAMIC TILE

You can remove a cracked ceramic tile by grinding out the surrounding grout and then smashing it to bits with a hammer. However, the brute force method can also break the bond between neighboring tiles and the tile backer board. Then you have a real mess. Here's a better way.

Start by removing the surrounding grout with a grout scraper tool (**Photo 1**). Next drill holes in the tile with a 1/4-in. tungsten carbide bit (**Photo 2**). The holes loosen the tile's bond to the backer board. Then chisel out the tile (**Photo 3**). Scrape out any remaining thin-set material and install the replacement tile.

GROUT SCRAPER TOOL

**1 Remove grout.** Grind out the grout with a hand scraper or an oscillating tool fitted with a grout removal blade.

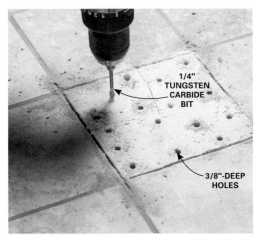

1/4" TUNGSTEN CARBIDE BIT

3/8"-DEEP HOLES

**2 Drill the tile.** Drill multiple 3/8-in.-deep holes in the tile using a tile bit. (A hammer drill will really speed this up.) Wear safety glasses.

BALL PEEN HAMMER

**3 Chisel out the tile pieces.** Tap a tile chisel or cold chisel straight into the center of a crack. Then angle the chisel to 45 degrees and chisel toward the edges.

## SAVE BY CUTTING YOUR MATTRESS DOWN TO SIZE

Many mattress stores recycle your old mattress for free when you buy a new one. But what if you just want to get rid of an old one without replacing it? Garbage haulers charge a fee per mattress and often require a special pickup. But a mattress is just fabric, springs and wood. You can chop up the mattress and box spring in less than an hour with just a utility knife, saw and bolt cutter.

Start by removing the fabric. Just cut around the edge and peel off the layers of material and foam. Then cut the perimeter wire using a bolt cutter (**Photo 1**). Cut the springs into manageable pieces (**Photo 2**) and toss them along with the fabric, foam and wood pieces into the trash.

**1 Cut around the edges.** Snip the border wire every few feet with the bolt cutters. Flip the spring over and repeat on the other side. Wear eye protection.

**2 Cut up the springs.** Cut the springs into smaller sections and feed them to your refuse hauler in batches.

# RECAULK A TUB OR SHOWER

*These tips for prep and supplies will ensure a long-lasting job*

by **Rick Muscoplat, Contributing Editor**

**A**nybody can recaulk a tub or shower. All you need is a tube of caulk and a caulking gun. But if you don't prep the surfaces properly, the caulk won't last long. And if you're sloppy, the messy caulk job will ruin the look of even the most beautiful tile job. We talked to a few experts to learn how they get such smooth, clean-looking caulk lines, and we'll show you their techniques. We'll also show you the best way to remove the old caulk and prep the surface to get a long-lasting caulk job. Finally, we'll give you a heads-up on how to avoid the most common caulking mistakes.

You can remove the old caulk, prep the surface, and recaulk a tub or shower in about four hours (including drying time). You'll need a razor scraper and single-edge razor blades, caulk remover, mineral spirits, paper towels, a utility knife, a caulk gun, and kitchen and bath caulk. An oscillating tool with a flexible scraper blade really speeds up the job of removing old caulk, but you can do the job without it. Here's how to start.

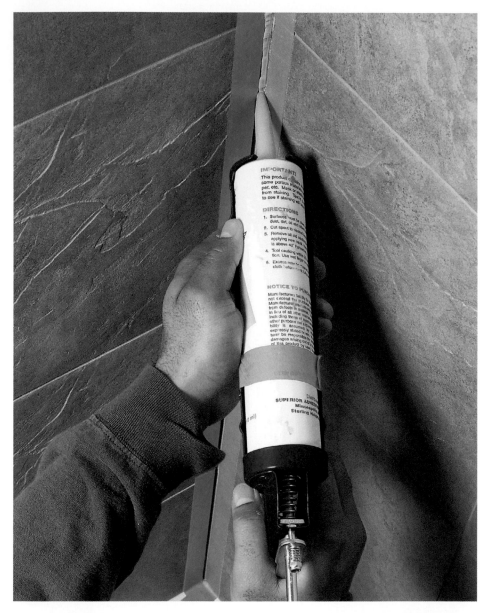

## Buy the right caulk and a quality caulk gun

Tubs and showers require a special caulk that contains mold- and mildew-prevention additives. The tubes are usually labeled "for kitchen and bath use." Most are 100 percent silicone, but you can also find some latex versions. Latex caulk is easier to tool and cleans up with soap and water. If this is your first time applying caulk, latex may be your best option. Silicone is more challenging to tool and requires mineral spirits for cleanup. However, silicone lasts longer than latex and stays flexible over its life. But it's harder to remove when it's time to recaulk. Both types can develop mold and mildew once the additives wear out.

Most home centers and hardware stores stock only three kitchen and bath caulk colors: white, almond and clear. However, ask a salesclerk whether you can special-order a custom color. And check out a paint or hardware store. Some can custom-mix colors right in the store.

A high-quality caulk gun can make a difference in your caulk job. It has a sturdier plunger mechanism to provide a smooth, even flow and a pressure release to stop the flow quickly. High-quality caulk guns cost two to three times more than a basic model, but they're worth it. Economy guns usually have a ratchet action or a sloppy friction mechanism that pushes the caulk out in bursts, so you apply too much in some areas and too little in others.

## Remove the old caulk

You can't apply new caulk on top of the old and expect it to last. So the old caulk has to go. If the old caulk was silicone, you have to devote extra effort to remove all traces of it before applying new caulk. Start by slicing through the old caulk with a utility knife or an oscillating tool (**Photo 1**). Then scrape off as much old caulk as possible. Next, apply caulk remover (3M, Goof Off, Goo Gone, DAP and Motsenbocker all make caulk remover products) to break the adhesive bond and make it easier to scrape off (**Photo 2**).

Once the old caulk is gone, remove any loose grout between the walls and the tub or shower floor. Treat any mold in the grout along the wall/tub gap with a mold-killing product (one choice is ZEP Mold Stain & Mildew Stain Remover; available at home centers). Scrub the grout and then rinse off the mold killer with water and let it dry (use a hair dryer to speed the drying). Clean the surfaces one last time with mineral spirits. Let dry.

## Mask the gap

Some pros scoff at the idea of using masking tape. But they caulk every day and can lay down a caulk bead with their eyes closed. For DIYers, we recommend masking the gap. It takes a bit more time, but you'll get much better results than caulking freehand. Start by finding the largest gap between the tub/shower and the walls. That gap dictates how far apart you must space the two rows of tape. Then apply the masking tape (**Photo 3**). If you have a fiberglass or composite tub, you should fill it with water before you caulk.

## Apply the caulk bead

There are two schools of thought when it comes to tip angle and whether to pull or

**1** **Cut and peel the old caulk.** Slice through the caulk along the walls with a utility knife, or with an oscillating tool equipped with a flexible scraper blade. Then use your knife or tool to scrape along the tub or shower floor.

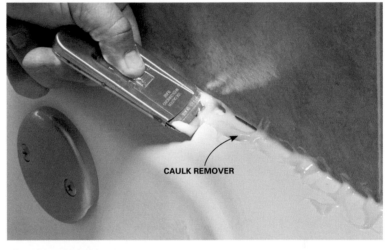

CAULK REMOVER

**2** **Loosen and remove the remaining caulk.** Squirt caulk remover on all the remaining caulk and let it do the hard work. Then scrape off all the old caulk with a razor scraper. Wipe with a rag.

**3** **Mask the gap.** Mask the wall corner gaps first. Then apply tape to the walls above the tub or shower floor. Finish by applying tape to the tub or shower floor where it butts up to the tile.

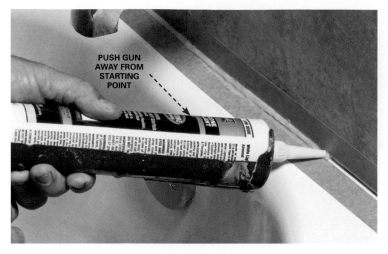

**4 Cut, push and apply.** Cut the nozzle tip to match the gap width. Hold the gun at a 90-degree angle to the gap and push a bead of caulk slightly ahead of the nozzle as you push the gun forward and continue applying pressure. Apply only enough caulk to fill the gap.

**5 Tool with your finger.** Wet your finger with water (or rubbing alcohol for silicone caulk) and start at an outer corner. Wipe your finger across the caulk to create a rounded bead and remove excess caulk from the gap.

**6 Peel off the tape.** Lift a corner of the tape along the tub and pull it off at a steep angle while the caulk is still wet. Then remove the tape along the wall. Remove the tape from the wall corners last.

push the caulk. Our experts prefer cutting the caulk tube nozzle at a blunt 20-degree angle, instead of 45 degrees. And they hold the gun at a 90-degree angle to the gap while pushing a small bead ahead of the tip (**Photo 4**). That way, they can complete the entire bead in one pass. Plus, the gun pressure forces the caulk deeper into the gap for better holding power and sealing.

If you cut the tip at a 45-degree angle and pull the gun away from the starting corner, your gun will always run into the opposite corner, forcing you to flip it 180 degrees and start the bead again. That creates a blob where the two beads meet, making tooling more difficult. Plus, pulling the gun tends to apply a surface bead that doesn't penetrate as far into the gap.

Whichever tip angle you choose, always cut the tip with a sharp utility knife rather than the guillotine mechanism built into some caulk guns. Remove any burrs with a utility knife or sandpaper before caulking—the burrs will create grooves in the caulk lines.

## Shape the bead and remove the tape

You can find all kinds of caulk-shaping tools at home centers. But if you take our advice and tape off the wall, you won't need any shaping tools. Just use your index finger to tool the caulk (**Photo 5**). After tooling, remove the masking tape while the caulk is still wet (**Photo 6**). Let the caulk cure for the recommended time before using the tub or shower.

### Avoid these caulking mistakes

■ Buying the wrong caulk. Always use kitchen and bath caulk in a tub or shower. It contains mold and mildew inhibitors that are not present in other types of caulk.

■ Caulking on top of old caulk. New caulk doesn't bond well to old caulk, especially if the old caulk contains silicone. Just like with painting, better surface prep provides better results.

■ Not removing mold on grout near the caulk areas. Grout is porous, and any mold present in the grout above the caulk line will eventually spread down into the new caulk area and destroy the bond.

■ Cutting the nozzle larger than the gap you're filling. A larger opening applies too much product, making it harder to tool and clean up.

# REPLACE A
# NOISY BATH FAN

*Don't put up with a jet engine in your bathroom*

## by **Rick Muscoplat, Contributing Editor**

**If** the bath fan in your home is more than 20 years old, chances are it's pretty loud. A loud fan may be good for masking bathroom noise, but the jet engine roar is downright annoying the rest of the time. Worse yet, your old bath fan may not be moving enough air to keep your bathroom free of mold and mildew.

Newer-style bath fans, on the other hand, are so quiet you can hardly hear them running, and they cost very little to operate. It's easier than you think to swap out that noisy, inefficient bath fan, especially if you choose one that's designed to be installed without ripping out the bathroom ceiling.

Of the many replacement models to choose from, we picked the NuTone No. RN110 Ultra Pro Series (available online) because the fan can be installed from inside the bathroom. It's not the quietest model available, but at 0.6 sones (about 25 decibels), it's a huge improvement over the old 4-sone (about 60 decibels) fan we're replacing. If you can locate a joist, cut drywall and handle basic electrical work, you can do the whole job in about two hours and save about $200 on the installation. You'll need a stud finder, a drywall saw, a drill and screws, and aluminum duct tape.

### Buy the right size for your bathroom

There's no such thing as a "one-size-fits-all" bath fan. For bathrooms up to 100 sq. ft., calculate the required cubic feet per minute (cfm) by multiplying the room's length x width x height. Multiply that result by .13 and round up to the nearest 10. Example: 10 ft. wide x 9 ft. long x 9 ft. high x .13 = 105. Round up to 110 and buy a 110-cfm bath fan. For bathrooms larger than 100 sq. ft., simply add up the cfm requirements for each of these plumbing fixtures: toilet, 50 cfm; shower, 50 cfm; bathtub, 50 cfm; jetted tub, 100 cfm.

### Turn off the power before proceeding

You'll have to remove the power cable from the old unit and connect it to the new fan. This must be done with the power off. Don't rely on turning off the fan switch; flip the breaker as well. Then double-check that the power is off with a voltage sniffer. If you're not comfortable working with electricity, hire an electrician to remove and connect the wires.

### Find the joists and duct, then enlarge the opening

Most bath fans are mounted to a ceiling joist with the duct running parallel to the joist. Start by locating the direction of your ceiling joists (**Photo 1**). Then locate the damper (you may have to remove the fan motor and blade

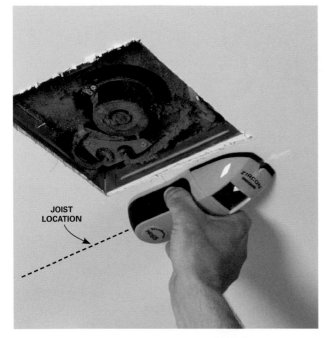

JOIST
LOCATION

**1** **Find the joists.** Slide a stud finder along the ceiling until you find the joist nearest the old fan. Mark the location. Then find the joist on the opposite side of the fan.

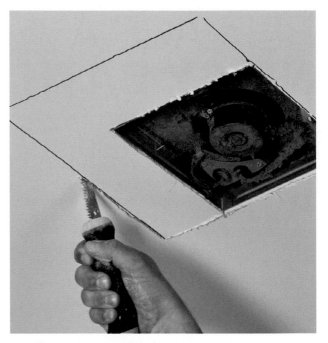

**2** **Mark and cut the ceiling opening.** Using the template provided, trace the new opening onto the ceiling. Then cut along the lines using a drywall saw. Cut shallower strokes around the flexible duct so you don't puncture it.

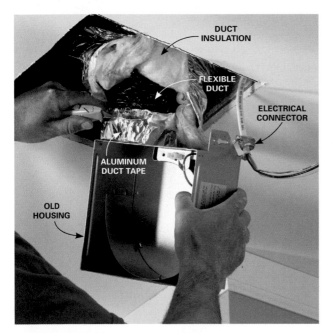

DUCT
INSULATION

FLEXIBLE
DUCT

ELECTRICAL
CONNECTOR

ALUMINUM
DUCT TAPE

OLD
HOUSING

**3** **Disconnect and remove old parts.** Unscrew the old fan housing from the joist. Then disconnect the electrical cable from the housing. Finally, slice through the duct sealing tape with a utility knife and disconnect the duct.

NEW
BRACKET

**4** **Mount the bracket.** Slide the bracket through the opening and extend it so it contacts the joists on each side of the opening. Secure both sides to the joists with drywall screws.

## You may have to go into your attic

The installation we show here is all done from inside a bath with a floor above it. However, if you're replacing a bath fan in a bathroom with an accessible attic above it, you have the option of doing some of the work from up there. Use your judgment. You may save some mess by going into the attic and moving the insulation aside before you remove the old fan. Then rearrange the insulation after the installation is done. Or, eliminate the second trip by making the electrical and vent connections at the same time.

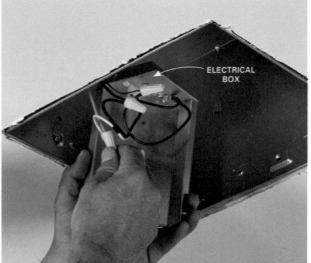

**6 Connect the wires.** Secure the hot (black), neutral (white) and ground (green/bare copper) wires with wire nuts. Then slide the metal electrical box into place in the housing and attach it with the screw provided.

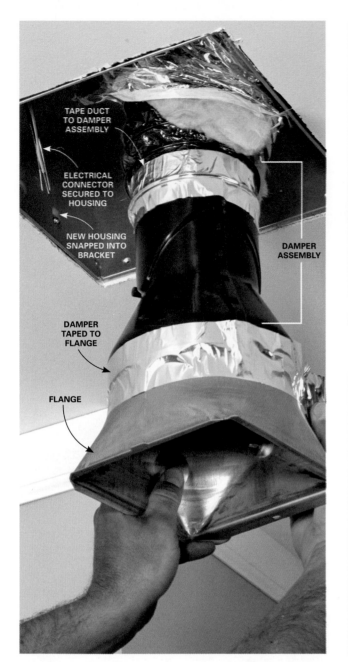

Labels: TAPE DUCT TO DAMPER ASSEMBLY; ELECTRICAL CONNECTOR SECURED TO HOUSING; NEW HOUSING SNAPPED INTO BRACKET; DAMPER ASSEMBLY; DAMPER TAPED TO FLANGE; FLANGE

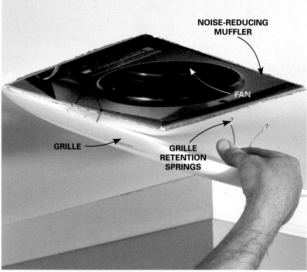

Labels: NOISE-REDUCING MUFFLER; FAN; GRILLE; GRILLE RETENTION SPRINGS

**5 Connect the duct.** Pull the old duct through the housing and into the room. Then tape the duct to the damper assembly. Slide the damper onto the flange and secure with aluminum duct tape. Push the duct, damper and flange back into the ceiling and secure the flange to the housing using the screw provided.

**7 Install the fan and grille.** Slide the fan assembly into the housing until it snaps in place. Secure with screws. Plug the electrical connector into the electrical box mounted earlier. Then screw in the noise-reducing muffler. Squeeze the grille springs and snap the grille into place.

from the housing). That'll tell you where the duct lies in the ceiling. Mark the duct location. Then enlarge the opening (**Photo 2**).

## Remove and replace the housing, duct and fan

With the opening now enlarged, you'll have room to disconnect the old duct, electrical cable and old housing (**Photo 3**). Install and secure the new mounting bracket (**Photo 4**). Connect the electrical cable to the new housing and snap the housing into the frame so the duct opening is facing the existing duct. Then connect the duct, damper and flange using aluminum duct tape (**Photo 5**). Finish the rough-in by connecting the power wires and ground to the electrical box provided (**Photo 6**).

Then simply slide the fan into the housing and add the muffler and grille (**Photo 7**). Turn on the power and test. Apply a bead of fire-resistant (intumescent) caulk around the fan housing and drywall to prevent moisture intrusion into the attic.

# SAME SPACE, MORE STORAGE

*5 simple projects that turn wasted space into storage space*

by **Spike Carlsen, Contributing Editor**

**O**ur house is done growing—no more additions, remodeling projects or storage sheds for this old girl. So when we need more storage space, we have to find it within the existing structure. I started snooping around and came up with five simple storage projects that can be carved out of—well—almost nothing. And every single one is inexpensive and buildable in an afternoon. It's what I call "bonus storage space."

**Twin closet shelves**

**Two-tier spice drawer**

"The beauty of a super-simple project? You actually wind up building it!"

**Double-decker garage shelf**

**Yard tool slant rack**

**Above-door display shelf**

"We were out of garage floor space—so I tried looking up."

# DOUBLE-DECKER GARAGE SHELF

Floor space in most garages is hard to come by—so the best place to find storage space is overhead. This project has a 16-in. top shelf for big items, a 5-in. lower shelf and plenty of hook space. Need different size shelves or more space between them? It's easy to modify this basic design. To build a saw guide like ours, search for "saw cutting guides" at familyhandyman.com.

## What it takes

**TIME:** 3 hours (per 8-ft. shelf)
**COST:** About $30
**SKILL:** Beginner
**TOOLS:** Table saw (or a circular saw and a straight-cut jig), drill, circular saw

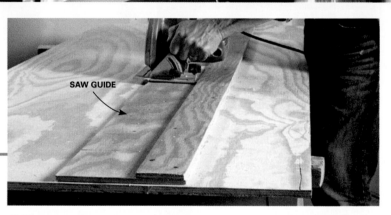

SAW GUIDE

**1** **Rip the plywood top to width.** Use a homemade saw guide and a circular saw, or a table saw, to cut the plywood for the 16-in.-wide top shelf.

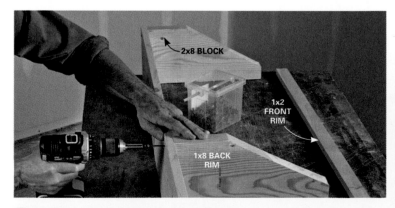

2x8 BLOCK

1x2 FRONT RIM

1x8 BACK RIM

**2** **Screw the framework together.** Use all-purpose screws to secure the 1x8 back rim and 1x2 front rim to the 2x8 support block. Space the support blocks every 32 in.

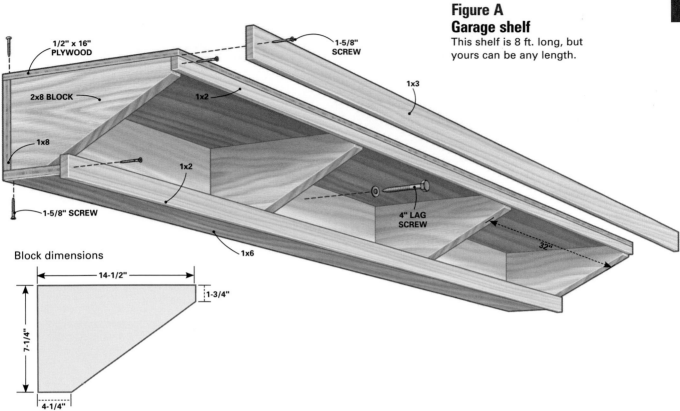

**Figure A**
**Garage shelf**
This shelf is 8 ft. long, but yours can be any length.

1/2" x 16" PLYWOOD

2x8 BLOCK

1x8

1-5/8" SCREW

1-5/8" SCREW

1x2

1x2

1x6

1x3

4" LAG SCREW

32"

Block dimensions

14-1/2"

1-3/4"

7-1/4"

4-1/4"

1x3 TOP LIP

TEMPORARY SUPPORT BLOCKS

1x2 BOTTOM LIP

1x6 BOTTOM SHELF

**3** **Complete assembling the shelf.** Install the plywood top, bottom shelf and the 1x2 and 1x3 lips. Use construction adhesive for added strength.

4" SCREW

**4** **Secure the shelf to the wall.** Use 4-in. lag or construction screws to secure the 1x8 back rim to the wall studs. Drive two screws into each stud—one high, one low.

# ABOVE-DOOR DISPLAY SHELF

Use the area above windows and doors to install display shelves. As a bonus, if you increase the height and depth of the "box" that forms the core of each shelf, these shelves can double as valances for window curtains or blinds.

Your materials will vary based on the size of your window or door. There are a few key measurements to keep in mind as you customize this design to fit:

■ Make the inside of the box 1/8 in. longer than the door or window trim. That way, the box will easily fit over the trim.

■ The height of the box should be about the same as the width of the window or door trim (or you risk having the door hit the shelf when it opens). If this is doubling as a valance, the box can hang below the trim.

■ The top shelf should overhang the three edges (the front and the two sides) of the box equally so the crown molding fits symmetrically.

Crown molding comes in a variety of styles and widths (from 2-1/4 in. to 6 in. and larger.) Mock up a small section of shelf to determine the best size and proportion of molding for your project.

Mount the completed shelf to the wall above the window or door. In most cases you'll be able to secure the shelf to the trim and framing along the sides and top of the opening. If not, use L-brackets mounted to the top of the shelf. **Note:** Use extra care if you mount this over an entry door (or one that your teenager slams a lot). Be sure all the displayed items are arranged securely behind the "lip" created by the cove molding.

**1** **Build the core of the shelf.** Build the three-sided 1x3 box so it fits over your door trim. The 1x6 shelf should overhang the ends the same amount as it does the front.

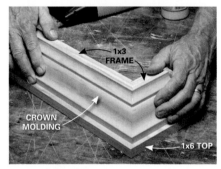

**2** **Install the crown molding.** Cut and install the crown molding. Install the 3/4-in. cove molding along the edge of the top shelf, letting it protrude 1/4 in. upward to create a lip.

## What it takes

TIME: 3 hours

COST: $20 to $25

SKILL: Intermediate

TOOLS: Miter saw, finish nailer, drill

> "Our house has a couple dozen windows and doors—which means we have a couple dozen places for display shelves."

## Figure B
## Display shelf

# TWIN CLOSET SHELVES

I tossed my hat onto the closet shelf the other day and discovered a whole lot of unused real estate up there. Made me think, if one shelf is good, two would be better. And the upper shelf could be 15 in. deep instead of 12 in. because there's no closet rod hanging out below. The deep baskets (I bought these at Michaels; michaels.com) help with the organization; cabinet knobs make for easier access. We show a two-tier shelf; you can install three if your closets (and you) are tall enough.

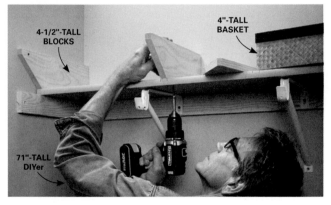

**Secure blocking to the existing shelf.** Buy your baskets, then cut spacer blocks 1/2 in. wider than the baskets are tall. Cut the ends of the blocks at an angle to accommodate the wider top shelf. Screw blocks to the bottom shelf, spacing them 1/2 in. farther apart than the baskets are wide. Then install and secure the top shelf.

## What it takes

**TIME:** 1 hour
**COST:** About $25 (including baskets)
**SKILL:** Beginner
**TOOLS:** Circular saw, drill

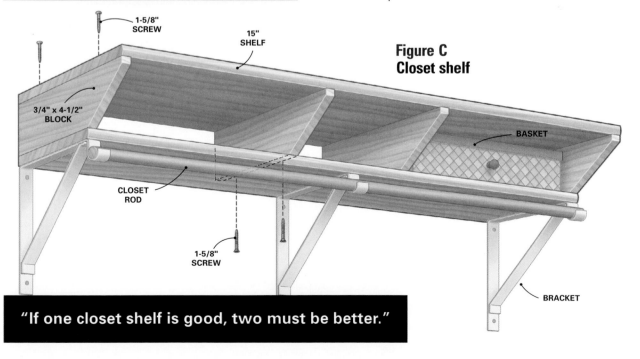

**Figure C**
**Closet shelf**

"If one closet shelf is good, two must be better."

## What it takes

**TIME:** 3 hours
**COST:** About $20
**SKILL:** Seasoned beginner
**TOOLS:** Jigsaw, miter saw, finish nailer, drill

# TWO-TIER SPICE DRAWER

Recently we remodeled our kitchen: new cabinets, countertops, appliances, the works. Yet the first thing we show off when people visit isn't the fancy new stove, but the $20 two-tier spice tray. When we open the drawer, we can slide the top tray all the way back into the cabinet to access the entire bottom layer; no need to lift out a separate tray or sort through layers of stuff. It's not only a space-saver but also a smart

organizer since all the spices are in one place, face up. We used the same basic design to make a two-tier utensil drawer too.

Do a little measuring before diving into this project. You can install the 1-3/4-in.-thick tray (like ours) if your drawer is at least 4 in. deep on the inside. Also, these trays are most useful if your existing drawers have (or you install) full-extension slides on the main drawer.

**Figure E
Spice drawer**

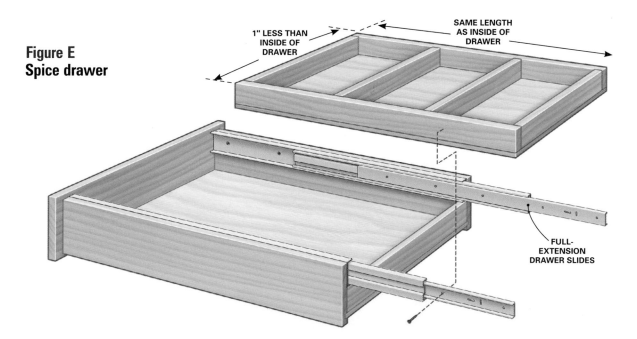

1" LESS THAN
INSIDE OF
DRAWER

SAME LENGTH
AS INSIDE OF
DRAWER

FULL-
EXTENSION
DRAWER SLIDES

**1** **Cut away the top half of the drawer back.** Use a jigsaw to cut away a little more than half of the drawer back.

DRAWER BACK

MOUNT SLIDE FLUSH TO DRAWER TOP

**2** **Install the tray slides.** Secure full-extension drawer slides to the top inside edges of the drawer. Install them "backward" so they extend toward the back of the drawer. It's OK if they run an inch or so beyond the back of the drawer; most cabinets have extra space in back.

**3** **Build the upper tray.** Since most standard drawer glides are 1/2 in. wide, build your tray 1 in. narrower (or a hair less) than the inside width of the drawer. Build your tray the same length as the inside drawer length. Install partitions according to your needs.

1/4" PLYWOOD BOTTOM

**4** **Install the tray.** Attach the plywood bottom to the tray with nails or brads. Screw the tray to the drawer slides so the top of the tray is flush with the top of the drawer. Then reinstall the drawer.

**"We doubled our spice and utensil storage in a couple of hours."**

# YARD TOOL SLANT RACK

Stashing stuff in the unused spaces between studs is a smart move; adding these slant boxes to expand the space is smarter yet. They give your tools more "headroom" and give you easier access to long- and short-handled tools.

For the tall unit, use the bottom wall plate for the bottom of your box. Attach the plywood to create a 1-in. gap at the bottom for removing dirt or dropped items. For the shorter slant boxes, install your own blocking to create the bottom; leave a gap at the bottom of the plywood for those, too. We show 48-in. and 16-in. versions; you can make yours any depth or length you want. **Note:** If your garage has a short ceiling (or your tools have extra-long handles), create a cutout in the top of the plywood face, as shown in **Figure D**, to allow more entrance and exit leeway for your tools.

**Rip a 2x4 diagonally to create the sides.** Screw each wedge to the face of a stud. Install a plywood face and you're ready to store stuff.

"This may take the record for the world's simplest storage project."

## Figure D
## Slant rack

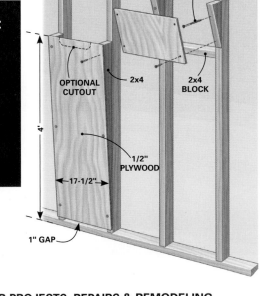

16"-O.C. STUDS

5" CONSTRUCTION SCREW

OPTIONAL CUTOUT

2x4

2x4 BLOCK

1/2" PLYWOOD

4'

17-1/2"

1" GAP

**What it takes**

TIME:
1 hour

COST: $8

SKILL:
Beginner

TOOLS:
Circular saw, drill

# HACKED!

*Customize store-bought "RTA"
furniture to fit your needs*

by **Tim Johnson, Contributing Editor**

**Modern console**

S pend a little, get a lot. That's the idea behind ready-to-assemble (RTA) furniture. But RTA furniture isn't just inexpensive. It's also super adaptable. Because you assemble it yourself, RTA furniture invites tinkering. In fact, customizing RTA pieces is so common that it has its own name: "hacking."

We used furniture pieces from IKEA. You can also find RTA furniture at discount stores and home centers.

**Craft center**

**Built-in bench**

# MODERN CONSOLE

*Mimic a mid-century modern classic by turning a simple shelving unit on its side, wrapping it with plywood inside and out, and attaching legs. Our materials cost was about $250.*

## Build it

Notice that the end panels of the original assembled Kallax shelving unit protrude beyond the sides. Remove both panels (**Step 1**) and trim off the protruding edges (**Step 2**). Then reattach both panels flush with the sides (**Step 3**). Cut hardwood plywood panels to wrap around the unit (**Step 4**). Make the top and bottom panels long enough to cover the side panels, and cut the side panels to fit tightly between the top and bottom pieces. Cut all the panels wide enough to create a 3/16-in. lip around the front of the shelving unit. Adhere iron-on edge banding to these pieces.

Fasten the panels with flat-head sheet metal screws after drilling countersink pilot holes through the unit. The unit's frames are hollow, so be careful not to punch through their thin faces when drilling the countersinks. Make sure the screw heads seat flush.

Cut plywood to cover the bottom and sides inside the unit (**Step 5**). Don't fasten these pieces with screws; instead, go for a friction fit. Apply iron-on edge banding to the exposed edges.

Remove all the plywood parts to apply finish. Finish the legs too. Reinstall the panels and inserts—tack the inserts with small nails or brads. Then attach the legs (**Step 6**).

**Basic unit**

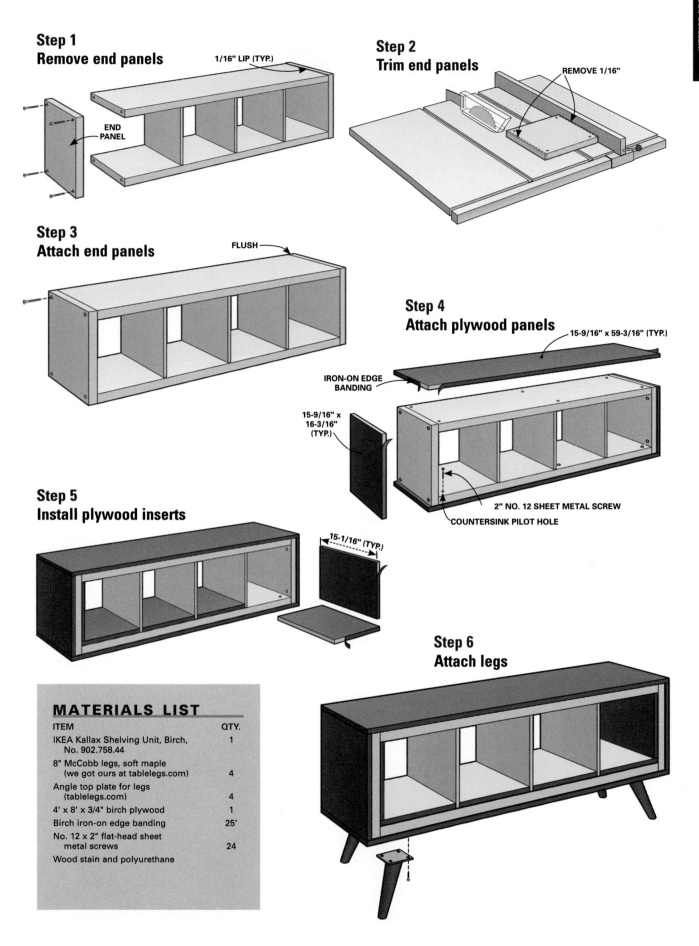

## Step 1
### Remove end panels

1/16" LIP (TYP.)

END PANEL

## Step 2
### Trim end panels

REMOVE 1/16"

## Step 3
### Attach end panels

FLUSH

## Step 4
### Attach plywood panels

15-9/16" x 59-3/16" (TYP.)

IRON-ON EDGE BANDING

15-9/16" x 16-3/16" (TYP.)

2" NO. 12 SHEET METAL SCREW

COUNTERSINK PILOT HOLE

## Step 5
### Install plywood inserts

15-1/16" (TYP.)

## Step 6
### Attach legs

### MATERIALS LIST

| ITEM | QTY. |
| --- | --- |
| IKEA Kallax Shelving Unit, Birch, No. 902.758.44 | 1 |
| 8" McCobb legs, soft maple (we got ours at tablelegs.com) | 4 |
| Angle top plate for legs (tablelegs.com) | 4 |
| 4' x 8' x 3/4" birch plywood | 1 |
| Birch iron-on edge banding | 25' |
| No. 12 x 2" flat-head sheet metal screws | 24 |
| Wood stain and polyurethane | |

# CRAFT CENTER

*Build a worktable with a huge surface, convenient storage and easy mobility by sand-wiching three small storage units between a base with casters and a plywood top with hardwood edging. We spent about $330 on materials for the table shown here.*

## Build it

Cut hardwood plywood for the top and base and install hardwood edging and iron-on edge banding as shown in **Step 1**. Position two Kallax shelving units back to back and fasten them to the base with flat-head sheet metal screws after drilling countersink pilot holes through the Kallax frames (**Step 2**). The frames are hollow panels, so be careful not to punch through their thin faces when drilling the countersinks. Make sure the screw heads seat flush.

Install the third Kallax unit across the front of the base, using the same method. Then tip the assembly over onto the top and fasten it as before (**Step 3**). Install locking swivel casters (**Step 4**). Then tip the assembly right-side up and round over all the top's sharp edges with a router and a round-over bit. Complete the job by installing Kallax drawer inserts and applying your favorite finish to the top (**Step 5**).

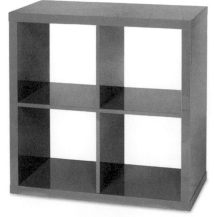

**Basic unit**

# Step 1
## Make the top and base

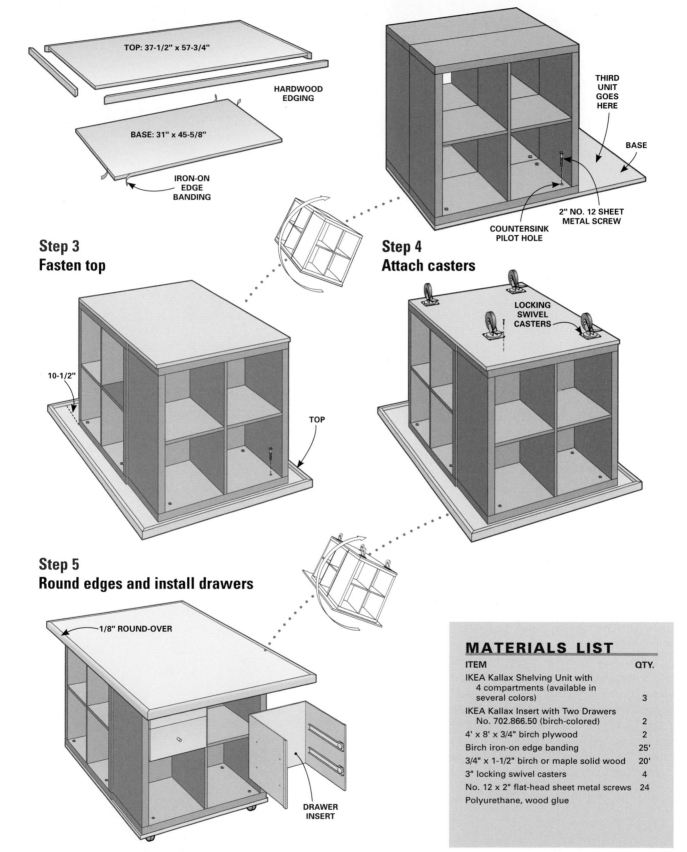

TOP: 37-1/2" x 57-3/4"

HARDWOOD
EDGING

BASE: 31" x 45-5/8"

IRON-ON
EDGE
BANDING

# Step 2
## Fasten units to base

THIRD
UNIT
GOES
HERE

BASE

2" NO. 12 SHEET
METAL SCREW

COUNTERSINK
PILOT HOLE

# Step 3
## Fasten top

10-1/2"

TOP

# Step 4
## Attach casters

LOCKING
SWIVEL
CASTERS

# Step 5
## Round edges and install drawers

1/8" ROUND-OVER

DRAWER
INSERT

## MATERIALS LIST

| ITEM | QTY. |
| --- | --- |
| IKEA Kallax Shelving Unit with 4 compartments (available in several colors) | 3 |
| IKEA Kallax Insert with Two Drawers No. 702.866.50 (birch-colored) | 2 |
| 4' x 8' x 3/4" birch plywood | 2 |
| Birch iron-on edge banding | 25' |
| 3/4" x 1-1/2" birch or maple solid wood | 20' |
| 3" locking swivel casters | 4 |
| No. 12 x 2" flat-head sheet metal screws | 24 |
| Polyurethane, wood glue | |

# BUILT-IN BENCH

Create a classic mudroom bench by fastening base molding and a new top to a cabinet designed to display a flat-screen TV. Our bench materials cost about $250, plus $50 for base molding. Your base molding cost will depend on the type and quantity you choose.

## Build it

Assemble the Hemnes TV unit through Step 27 of the manufacturer's instructions. Move it into position and shim the legs as necessary to level it. Then install a support block under the rails beneath the center divider (**Step 1**). This allows the unit to be used as a bench. Fasten the unit to the wall through its upper back rail (**Step 2**).

Build a new top by gluing hardwood edging to 3/4-in.-thick hardwood plywood and then rounding over all the sharp edges (**Step 3**). Sand the top, stain it and apply your favorite finish. Use corner brackets to fasten the top to the bench (**Step 4**). Then fasten base molding around the bench to build it in (**Step 5**). Install the drawers to complete the project.

**Basic unit**

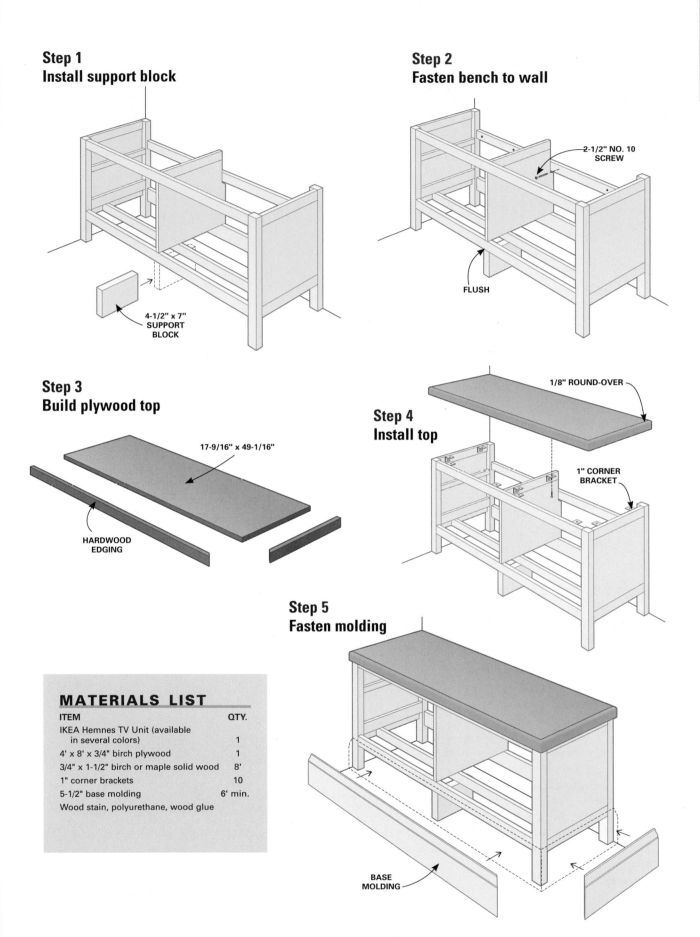

## Step 1
## Install support block

4-1/2" x 7" SUPPORT BLOCK

## Step 2
## Fasten bench to wall

2-1/2" NO. 10 SCREW

FLUSH

## Step 3
## Build plywood top

17-9/16" x 49-1/16"

HARDWOOD EDGING

## Step 4
## Install top

1/8" ROUND-OVER

1" CORNER BRACKET

## Step 5
## Fasten molding

BASE MOLDING

### MATERIALS LIST

| ITEM | QTY. |
|---|---|
| IKEA Hemnes TV Unit (available in several colors) | 1 |
| 4' x 8' x 3/4" birch plywood | 1 |
| 3/4" x 1-1/2" birch or maple solid wood | 8' |
| 1" corner brackets | 10 |
| 5-1/2" base molding | 6' min. |
| Wood stain, polyurethane, wood glue | |

# TOP 10 TIPS FOR A
# DUST-FREE HOME

*Learn how to control dust and get a healthier environment in your home*

by **Elisa Bernick, Contributing Editor**

S tudies show that the average six-room home in the United States collects 40 lbs. of dust each year. Sounds impressively awful, right? But don't confuse all that dust with dirt and bad housekeeping. It's actually a combination of dead skin, animal fur, dander, decomposing insects, dust mites, food debris, lint, fabric fibers, drywall particles, tracked-in soil, soot and pollen. It also contains hazardous chemicals that migrate from home products and enter through open doors, windows and on the soles of your shoes. Household dust can trigger allergy and asthma symptoms. While it's impossible to get rid of dust completely, here are our top tips for keeping dust at a minimum so you and your family stay healthier.

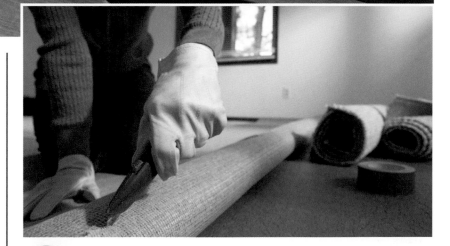

## 1 Ditch your carpeting

In most homes, carpet is by far the biggest dust reservoir. It's a huge source of fibers and absorbs dust like a giant sponge. Even the padding underneath holds dust, which goes airborne with each footstep. Although ripping out your wall-to-wall carpet may sound radical, it's the best thing you can do if you suffer from serious allergies. Replace carpeting with hard flooring like laminate, wood or tile, and wet mop it regularly (with a microfiber cloth) instead of sweeping. Sweeping is more likely to stir up dust than to remove it.

## 2 Clean with microfiber products

Microfiber products attract and hold dust with an electrostatic charge, unlike dry rags and feather dusters, which just spread dust around. Machine washable microfiber products can save you money over disposable brands because you can use them over and over. Just make sure to let them air dry (so they'll stay soft), and don't use bleach or fabric softener, which degrades the fibers and reduces their ability to attract and hold dust.

Microfiber dusting tools for blinds, ceiling fans, floors and general cleaning are available online and at many stores. Buy your microfiber cloths in the automotive section. "Cleaning" and "detailing" towels are the same as "dusting" cloths, and they're often a lot cheaper.

## 3 Bag and box it

Stray fibers from clothes, bedding and pillows are a major source of dust. The solution is to store these things in bags and clear plastic containers. You can use space-saving vacuum-seal bags, garment bags or even large garbage bags to help cut down on dust from clothes and fabrics. Clear plastic containers will lock fibers in and dust out and let you see what's inside. And because seasonal clothes shed fibers year-round, store your winter coats inside garment bags to help contain fibers and keep the coats themselves from becoming coated with dust.

## 4 Upgrade your furnace filter

Your home's forced-air heating or cooling system helps to control dust by filtering the air. A standard cheap fiberglass filter protects your furnace from large dust particles and provides maximum airflow, but it does little to reduce household dust. More expensive pleated filters usually provide a good balance between cost and filtration efficiency. These filters trap 80 to 95 percent of particles 5 microns and larger.

But if you have family members with allergies, consider spending more on high-efficiency filters, which capture 99 percent of airborne particles as small as 0.3 microns (bacteria and viruses, fumes and pollen). Be aware that you'll have to run your furnace fan full time to get the maximum benefit from a high-efficiency filter, and you'll have to change the filter frequently to prevent damage to your furnace from the reduced airflow.

If you go the high-efficiency route, install a filter monitor such as FilterScan, which automatically alerts you when your furnace filter needs changing, or the GeneralAire G99 Filter Gage, which requires you to manually check it. For more information, search "furnace filter monitor" online.

**PLEATED FILTERS TRAP MORE AIRBORNE PARTICLES THAN FIBERGLASS FILTERS**

 **Make the most of your vacuuming**

The right vacuuming technique, combined with the right filters, bags and machine, has a significant impact on how much dust remains in both your carpeting and your house. Keep the following tips in mind:

■ Vacuum entrance areas and high-traffic areas twice a week and the rest of the carpeting and large area rugs at least weekly.

■ Make numerous slow passes over the same area in all directions (fast passes stir up more dust than is being sucked up).

■ Take smaller rugs outside for a vigorous shaking every week and take large area rugs outside several times a year and beat them with a broom or tennis racket.

■ Use certified True High-Efficiency Particulate Air (HEPA) filters to remove invisible particles and allergens. Look for the word "True" on the label; otherwise you're wasting your money.

■ If you have allergies, upgrade to a sealed-body bagged vacuum with an airtight "sealed filtration" system that works together with a True HEPA filter. This means all of the exhaust will exit through the HEPA filter instead of leaking dust back into your house through the machine's housing. Sealed-body vacuums have rubber seals or gaskets around the lid and filter and will last 10 to 20 years. Brands include Riccar, Miele and Sanitaire. You can get a good bagged vacuum for $350 to $600.

■ Buy high-quality vacuum bags. Inexpensive 2- or 3-ply paper bags leak more dust. Higher-quality cotton-lined paper bags are better, and top-quality synthetic cotton HEPA bags are the best. Bag capacity matters too. Higher-capacity bags capture more, smaller particles that would have otherwise clogged the filter.

■ Clean all your bagless vacuum filters regularly and replace them every three months.

■ Turn off the agitator brush on hard flooring so you're not blowing dust into the air.

■ Maintain your vacuum: Empty the canister frequently (always outside) and change bags and belts when needed. Keep the agitator brush free of hair and other material, and check the vacuum for cracks and loose hinges and get it serviced every so often to keep it running smoothly.

**TRUE HEPA FILTER**

DAMP TOWEL

 **Dust with your dryer**

Blankets, pillows, slipcovers, drapes and other textiles not only trap household dust, but they create it as they shed and disintegrate. Curtains and drapes in particular get very dusty because they absorb moisture and dirt from the outside and act as a landing pad for dust from ceiling fans and air vents. The best idea is to buy machine-washable items and launder them twice a year (OK, at least once). For non-machine-washable textiles, throw them in the dryer on the air-fluff setting (no heat) for 20 minutes with a damp towel. The damp towel will attract pet hair, and the tumbling movement and airflow will remove the smaller particles for you.

 **7 Purify the air**

Here are four things you can do to cleanse the dusty air in your home:

■ Place air purifiers in your most-used rooms to help suck up dust before it settles. Choose units with True HEPA filters ($80 to $200 or more) rather than ionic cleaners, which release ozone, a respiratory irritant. Search online for "air purifier reviews" to find recommendations.

■ Add a plant to every room. Plants naturally absorb common indoor pollutants like benzene and formaldehyde. NASA studies have shown that many plants, including aloes, palms and ferns, can absorb as much as 80 percent of the formaldehyde in a room in 24 hours.

■ Keep the humidity in your house between 40 and 50 percent to help lower static electricity, which can cause dust to stick to surfaces and make them harder to clean. A humidifier (cleaned regularly) and leafy indoor plants will both increase humidity levels. Just don't increase the level to more than 50 percent. This will promote the growth of mold, a far more dangerous condition than dust. You can monitor humidity levels with a cheap hydrometer from a gardening store.

■ Keep your windows closed on windy days. Dust enters through doors and windows in the form of pollen, mold spores and airborne pollutants.

**8 Reduce remodeling dust**

Remodeling dust goes everywhere air flows, so the key to stopping this dust is stopping airflow. Create an airtight plastic dust barrier curtain and completely seal the top and sides with tape. If you can't seal the bottom edge with tape, lay a board across it. Light plastic (1 mil or so) is fine for most jobs. If you need to pass through the dust barrier, use heavier 4- or 6-mil plastic and add an adhesive-backed zipper.

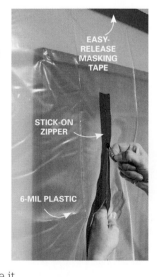

Also make sure to seal both supply and return air ducts with tape and plastic. That way you'll avoid plugging your furnace filter or coating every room in the house with a blanket of fine dust when the blower turns on. **Note:** Turn off the heating/cooling system while the ducts are covered. Operating the system with restricted airflow can damage it.

**9 Ban shoes inside (but offer slippers)**

More than half of household dust enters your home through windows, doors, vents and on the soles of your shoes. Think about where you walk all day long (restrooms, city streets, construction sites, etc.) and all the bacteria and debris your shoes collect. Do you really want to track that inside? An EPA study of homes where a doormat was added at the entrance and shoes were banned indoors showed a 60 percent reduction of lead dust and other contaminants in the home, as well as a significant reduction of allergens and bacteria.

Your first line of defense should be a coarse-fiber heavy-duty doormat placed outside exterior doors. Inside, have everyone remove their shoes at the door. Keep a bench, a shoe rack and a basket of cheap slippers available so no one has to walk around in their stocking feet on chilly floors.

**10 Clean the air while you clean the house**

Your vacuum's agitator brush and exhaust whip up dust that eventually settles on the surfaces you've just cleaned. Filter out some of that dust before it settles by switching your thermostat to "fan on." This turns on the blower inside your furnace and filters the air even while the system isn't heating or cooling. Leave the blower on for about 15 minutes after you're done cleaning. But don't forget to switch it back to "auto." Most blowers aren't designed to run constantly.

# FAST FURNITURE FIXES

*Easy repairs for everyday furniture*

by **Tom Caspar, Contributing Editor**

The creaking sound you hear each time you sit on that old kitchen chair is not a good sign. It has loose joints, and every time you sit on it, you're wearing down and further loosening them. Someday that old chair is going to fall apart.

One of these tips will save that chair—and many other pieces of your favorite furniture, too! But keep in mind that these are fast, easy, practical fixes. They are not the best repairs for treasured heirlooms or valuable antiques.

You don't need a workshop to make these repairs—a few simple tools and a sturdy table will do. And you don't need any special skills. If you know the most basic stuff—how to cut plywood and drive screws—you can do it!

## Rescue a drawer

Drawer fronts that are just nailed or stapled to the drawer box often come loose or even fall off completely. You could simply pound the parts back together, but that kind of fix won't last long. For a repair that's stronger than the original construction, add a backer to the drawer front.

Make the backer from 3/4-in. plywood and cut it to fit tight inside the drawer. Using a spade bit, drill 3/4-in.-diameter holes in the plywood so you can access the screws that hold the drawer's handle. Fasten the backer to the inside front of the drawer, then screw the drawer sides to the ends of the backer.

## Strengthen ready-to-assemble furniture

New furniture that's put together with bolts and nuts often loosens up with use. If retightening the bolts every now and then seems like too much bother, you can take the piece apart and strengthen it with epoxy.

Most RTA furniture uses loose-fitting dowels to align each part. Spread epoxy inside the dowel holes and on the dowels themselves when you reassemble the piece. (If the dowels fit nice and tight, use yellow glue instead—it's more convenient.) Don't bother spreading glue on the ends of each part. They usually butt against a finished surface, and no glue will stick to a finish for very long.

## Fix a wobbly table

If you've got a table that rocks on an uneven floor, you've probably tried wedging something under the short leg. Doesn't last, does it? Here's a better way: Use washers and nail-on glides.

First, drill holes for the nails with a 1/16-in. bit and install the glides. Then set the table in place and slip washers under the low leg until the table is steady. When you've determined how many washers are needed, pull off the glide and reinstall it along with the washers.

## Support sagging shelves

If your shelves sag, sometimes you can simply flip them over—but eventually they'll droop again. Here's a permanent solution: Add supports that fit tight between the shelves.

Pine stair tread, which has a rounded front edge, is perfect for this. It's available at all home centers (about $10 for 3 ft.). Many stores will cut it to length for you. You can paint or stain the supports to match the shelves, of course. But if the shelves hold books, consider staining them a color similar to your books. You'll be surprised at how well they blend in.

## Hide scratches with wax

To revive a finish, rub colored paste wax over the entire surface and buff. This isn't a perfect fix; heavy scratches or dents will still be visible. But light scratches and wear will almost disappear.

For the best camouflage, pick a color that's slightly darker than the finish. You can find Minwax or Briwax colored paste wax at some paint stores or order it online.

## Save it with screws

When ready-to-assemble (RTA) particleboard furniture breaks—by being pushed across the floor, for example—the original knockdown fasteners often pull out of the wood and can't be replaced. The solution is to bypass them completely and screw the piece together from the outside.

Ordinary screws won't hold in particleboard, however. You need 2-1/2-in. to 3-in. screws with coarse threads and large, washer-style heads. (Large heads prevent the screws from being pulled through the particleboard.) Many home centers carry "cabinet installation screws" that are perfect for the job. Be sure to drill a pilot hole first, even if the screws have self-tapping points. You can also buy colored self-stick caps to cover the screw heads.

DOWEL

## Inject epoxy into loose joints

When one or two joints loosen on a chair but you can't get the rest of them apart, here's an advanced repair technique to try: Inject epoxy into the loose joints using a syringe.

Once mixed, most epoxy is too thick to push through a syringe. However, an epoxy used for fiberglass boat repair (like the one shown here) has just the right consistency. To inject the glue, drill 1/8-in. holes in an inconspicuous place in line with the dowels. Aim for the cavity behind each dowel. Insert the syringe into the hole, then inject the epoxy until it runs out of the joint. Push the joint together, then wipe off the excess epoxy.

West System 101-TS packets are convenient for storing and dispensing epoxy. They're like ketchup packets—you just tear off the top and squeeze. They're available online (one source is westmarine.com), but at $25 for six packets, this epoxy is more expensive than the hardware store variety. Plastic syringes are available at many pharmacies and online for less than $2 apiece.

## 3 classic tricks

People who repair furniture for a living have all kinds of simple tricks up their sleeve. Here are a few that anybody can do at home:

■ Lubricate a sticking drawer with canning wax, which is made from paraffin. Paraffin works much better than candle wax.

■ When you're gluing a splinter or chip, use masking tape to hold it in place. A clamp isn't necessary.

■ Use steam to raise a dent. Place a wet towel on the dent, then press the pointed end of a hot iron onto the towel, right above the dent, for 10 seconds or so. Two or three applications may be necessary.

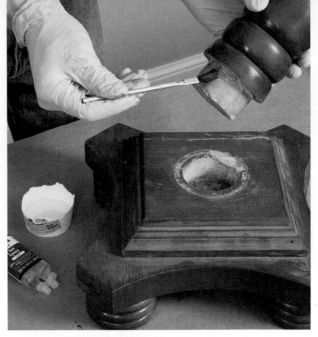

## Add metal braces

If appearance doesn't matter, screwing a brace, bracket or T-plate onto a piece of furniture is often the quickest way to fix it. Adding metal may not make the piece totally sound, but at least it won't come apart. Chair braces (above) are an easy fix for a wobbly chair. They're better looking and much stiffer than L-brackets. Most hardware stores carry chair braces in finishes like chrome, brass or bronze ($5 for a set of four); T-plates and L-brackets are also readily available, and may work better for other types of repairs. To avoid splitting the wood, be sure to drill 1/8-in. pilot holes before driving in the screws.

## Epoxy a sloppy joint

When parts don't fit tightly, epoxy is the answer. Other woodworking glues—yellow, white or polyurethane—require a snug fit. The gap between parts can't exceed the thickness of a piece of paper. Epoxy, on the other hand, bonds across a gap of any size.

Epoxy won't stick well to old glue, so remove as much of the old glue as you can with a file or coarse sandpaper. Most epoxies must be used within five minutes of mixing, but you can buy a slower-setting epoxy if you need more time. Devcon 2-Ton Epoxy gives you a leisurely 30 minutes to assemble parts and is available at many hardware stores.

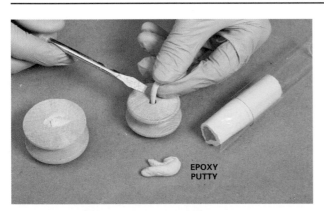

EPOXY PUTTY

## Fill stripped-out screw holes

Wooden drawer knobs tend to strip out and then come loose or even pull off. Using a fatter screw or shoving matchsticks into the hole might work, but here's a sure fix: Fill the hole with epoxy putty, then drill a new hole. Epoxy putty is available in a 2-oz. roll for a few dollars at home centers and hardware stores.

Epoxy putty is easy to use. You just cut off the amount you want, knead the piece until the inner and outer layers blend together, then roll it between your fingers to form a thin string. Push the string of putty into the hole with a screwdriver. Then scrape off the excess before it hardens.

## Shim a hinge

When a door won't close or won't align with a catch, placing a shim behind one of its hinges might solve the problem. The shim will kick out the upper or lower half of the door, depending on which hinge you choose.

Make the shim from one or more playing cards. Remove the hinge, then cut the cards to fit into the hinge's recess. Place each piece in the recess and punch screw holes in it using an awl or a small Phillips screwdriver. Remount the hinge with the original screws.

SHIM

# A BETTER PLACE **TO AGE**

*Easy upgrades make home safer for older folks*

by **Elisa Bernick, Contributing Editor**

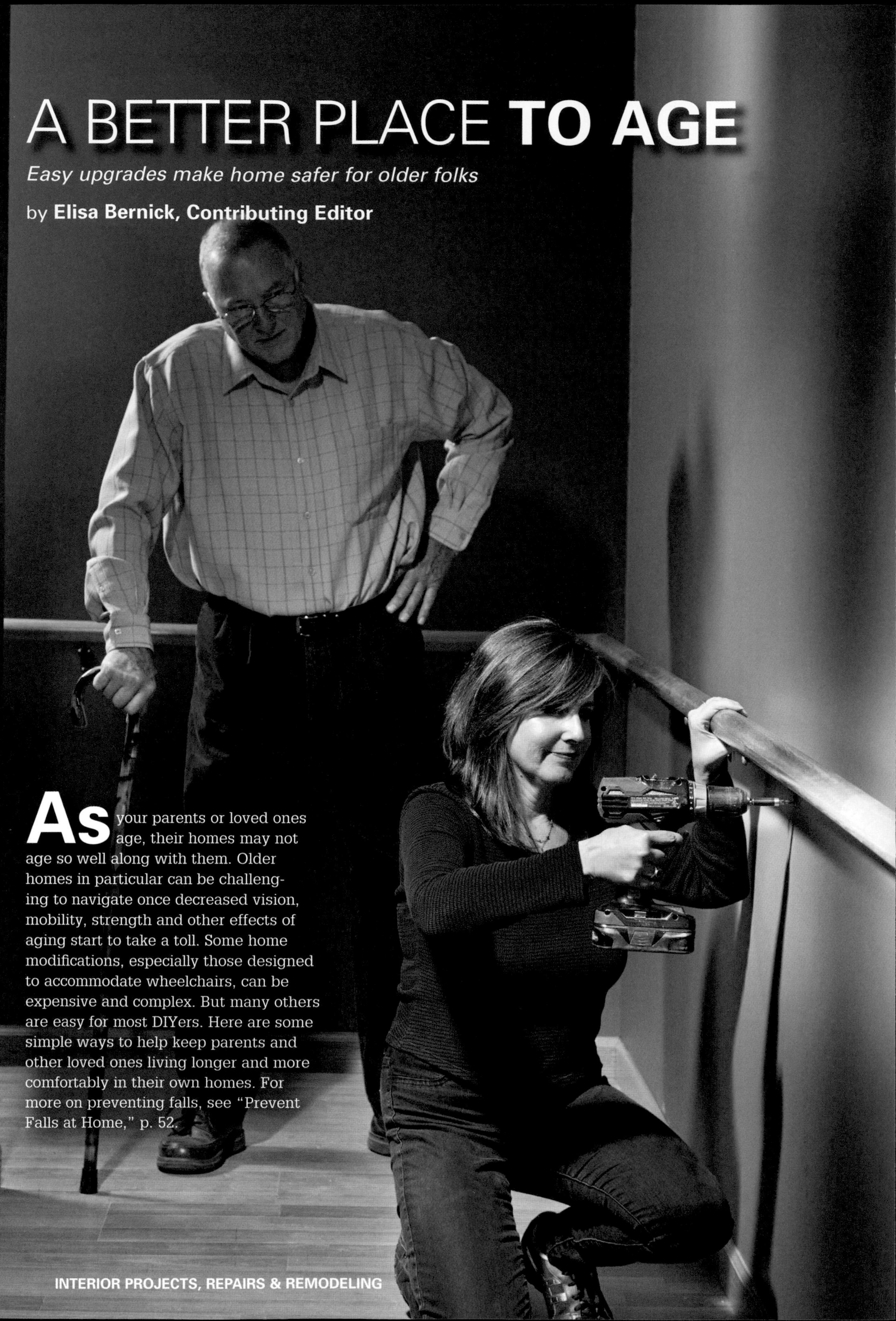

**As** your parents or loved ones age, their homes may not age so well along with them. Older homes in particular can be challenging to navigate once decreased vision, mobility, strength and other effects of aging start to take a toll. Some home modifications, especially those designed to accommodate wheelchairs, can be expensive and complex. But many others are easy for most DIYers. Here are some simple ways to help keep parents and other loved ones living longer and more comfortably in their own homes. For more on preventing falls, see "Prevent Falls at Home," p. 52.

## MEET AN EXPERT

Louis Tenenbaum is a carpenter and former contractor. He is the founder of the Aging in Place Institute and one of the nation's leading speakers and consultants on aging in place. You can visit his website at louistenenbaum.com.

*"We age most happily and inexpensively in the comfort and dignity of our own homes."*

— Louis Tenenbaum

### Expert tip

### Find out how it feels to have an old hand

Want to know what it's like to have stiff or arthritic joints? Hold a tennis ball in the palm of your hand and stick your hand inside a sock. Now walk around and try to manipulate the switches, door-knobs and cabinet pulls in your house.

## Widen doorways with offset hinges

Navigating narrow doorways is tough for someone using a wheelchair or walker. Doorways can be widened, but it's a complex and costly job. An easier solution is to replace the existing hinges with expandable offset door hinges. These special hinges are designed to swing the door clear of the opening and add 2 in. of clearance. The hinge measures 2 in. x 3-1/2 in. and wraps around the door trim. You need at least 3 in. between the inside of the doorjamb and the adjoining wall for the hinges to fit. They use the existing holes and screws and come in a variety of finishes. Available online and at many home centers for about $5 per hinge.

## Remodel with aging in mind

A kitchen remodel is the perfect opportunity to build in "universal design" components that will look great and allow the room to work well as you age in your own home. Consider incorporating:

- Rollout drawers and pull-down shelf inserts
- Appliances with touchpad controls, not knobs
- A shallow (6-in.-deep) sink, which is easier to use than a deep one
- Countertops at different levels so someone seated can work comfortably
- A side-by-side refrigerator with a long, continuous handle that can be opened by someone who is seated
- Under-cabinet task lighting
- Drawer storage rather than upper cabinetry

LUTRON

## Replace toggle switches with rocker switches

It's easier for stiff or arthritic hands to press flat, rocker-style switches than to manipulate toggles. Rocker switches feature a big on/off plate that you can operate with a finger, a knuckle or even an elbow. Some rocker switches are illuminated to make them easy to find day or night. These great little inventions use a tiny bit of electricity from the circuit they're on to light a small LED or neon bulb, and they install as easily as regular switches. For a broad selection of illuminated switches, visit kyleswitchplates.com. Prices range from $7 to $40.

## Replace cabinet knobs with handles

Arthritis and stiff joints make grabbing small round knobs on cabinet drawers and doors difficult too. Replace these small knobs with C- or D-shaped pulls, which let you tuck your fingers around them, making it easier to open the door or drawer. Consider this for your own kitchen too. Adding new pulls and handles is a quick, inexpensive way to update a kitchen while making it more comfortable and convenient to use over the long term.

## Install "invisible" grab bars

Sometimes people are reluctant to add grab bars because they think it will make their home look institutional. But you can find stylish and sturdy grab bars in many

shapes, sizes and finishes, and some, like those in the elegant Invisia Collection, serve double duty as towel racks, toilet paper holders, corner shelves and more. Search "designer grab bars" and "specialty grab bars" to find sources and various options.

### Scary!

One in three seniors will fall this year and 20 percent of those falls will contribute to their deaths.

SIMPLIFIED BUILDING

## Extend stair rails

The handrails for exterior stairs typically end at the bottom step. But stepping off the bottom step (or preparing to step up on it) is actually when someone is the most off balance and likely to fall. Simple Rail handrail kits from Simplified Building make it easy for DIYers to build an extended handrail that fits any stairway. The kits use Kee Klamp pipe fittings and come with all the components you need (such as fittings, pipe, connectors and railings) at reasonable prices. Visit simplifiedbuilding.com to see exactly what you need to accomplish your project and a gallery showing hundreds of customer-built projects.

MAYTAG

## Raise your washer and dryer

To make it easier on aging backs and knees, set your front-loading washing machines and dryers on pedestals 12 to 15 in. above the floor. To find out how to build a simple washer/dryer pedestal, visit familyhandyman.com and search "DIY washer pedestal."

## Put a bench near steps

This allows people to steady themselves after they climb up or down. It's also a good idea to set a chair at the end of a long hallway for resting. Just make sure it's placed so that it's not a tripping hazard.

## Add shower grab bars and do the yank test

A securely fastened grab bar can be the difference between a momentary slip and a hip-breaking fall. The best location for grab bars depends on the needs of the person who'll be using them, so ask before you install them. General guidelines call for a vertical bar at the tub edge and an angled bar on the long back wall of the tub.

A 24-in. grab bar positioned at a 45-degree angle will attach easily to wall studs. If you can't anchor to a stud, you can secure wood blocking between the studs. If you're lucky, you'll be able to go through a closet or storage area behind the tub so the wall patch won't have to be perfect.

After you're done installing a grab bar, do the yank test by pulling on the bar with all your strength. Make sure the bar will hold up when it's really needed. For detailed grab bar installation instructions, search "install grab bars" at familyhandyman.com.

## Replace doorknobs with levers

Gripping and twisting a doorknob can be hard for people with arthritis or a loss of dexterity in their hands. Lever handles solve that problem. You simply press down on the lever to release the door latch without gripping anything. In fact, an elbow or forearm will work too, which is nice when you're carrying things. Many lever handles are reversible, which means they'll fit both a right-handed or left-handed door. (Handedness is determined by which side the door hinges are on when you stand outside the door as it swings away from you into the room.) But check the handle requirements before you buy so you get the right handle for your situation.

JOHN BOOS

## Add a rolling cart to the kitchen

A rolling cart is helpful in any kitchen, but it's especially helpful for older cooks. It's a convenient prep center, and models with drawers or shelves allow someone to store frequently used items and roll it around so their tools are always close at hand. And it can be extremely useful for someone with diminished strength or dexterity to ferry items to and from the table without the risk of dropping things or injuring themselves.

## Add grab bars near exterior doors

Grab bars aren't just helpful in the bathroom; they're also useful near exterior doors, inside and out. For people who are unsteady on their feet, the simple act of opening a door can be difficult. A grab bar gives them something to hang on to near house and garage entrances and steps. The Prima Outdoor Grab Bar is made of weatherproof plastic with an aluminum core and special soft grip moldings that reduce the risk of a user's hands slipping even when it's wet. It can be mounted horizontally, vertically or diagonally. Look for it online.

PRIMA

## Install low-pile carpet

Thick carpet pile over a thick pad is the worst for anyone who is unstable walking—it increases the likelihood of tripping and falling. It also makes it more difficult to push and maneuver wheelchairs and walkers. To make getting around easier, consider installing a low-profile commercial-grade "level loop" or "cut pile" carpet with a pile height of no more than 1/2 in. and a 1/4-in. (10-lb. density) pad.

## Install handrails in hallways

Long hallways can be tough on people with limited mobility, which is the reason so many senior care centers have continuous handrail systems. Consider adding the same safety feature at home. You can install a simple wooden railing (see the lead photo, p. 42) or consider the PromenAid handrail system, a problem-solving product that has a unique bracket that slides along an open channel in the bottom of the handrail. This lets you locate the handrail anywhere and slide the brackets to wherever studs are located without adding extra blocking. The brackets also pivot so you can install the handrail vertically or at an angle. These elegant handrails have snap-on end caps and returns, and the articulating joints allow them to go around corners or along stairs. You can buy complete kits or individual components at promenaid.com. Just make sure any handrail you install has returns.

◄ RETURN

## Get LED lightbulbs

The average home has 40 lightbulbs. Changing a burnt-out bulb often involves climbing a ladder or step stool and risking a nasty fall. If you replace those lightbulbs with CFLs, or even better, LEDs, there's a good chance they'll never have to be changed again in that homeowner's lifetime.

## A showerhead grab bar is a big help

For people with limited mobility or who prefer to shower while seated, a handheld showerhead is a terrific help. And even better is a handheld showerhead on a sliding rail that allows for individual adjustment. But because those rails are often flimsy, grabbing one could be a disaster. Delta's Adjustable Hand Shower Grab Bar Shower Head is the best of both worlds. It's an ADA-compliant grab bar with a sliding handheld showerhead in one attractive package (available at various online retailers).

## A bargain?

Aging-in-place modifications can be pricey. Installing an elevator can run $35,000, a chair lift $6,000, and adding a bedroom or bath to the main floor can be costly. But consider the alternative: A nursing home averages $90,000 a year for a private room, and assisted living runs about $45,000 a year.

## Resources:

**For more information about aging in place, including helpful products, safety checklists and resources to help you pay for home modifications, visit:**

- rebuildingtogether.org/wp-content/uploads/2012/06/RT-Aging-in-Place-Safe-at-Home-Checklist.pdf
- homemods.org
- livablehomes.org/checklist.html
- abledata.com
- ageinplace.com/aging-in-place-basics/home-remodeling-basics/
- aarp.org
- ncoa.org

## It helps to plan ahead

"Some years ago, I had the foresight to build two railings—one leading to the side yard and the other to the front steps of my home. Now I need and use them daily."
–Richard Vasek, Field Editor

# DIY **UPHOLSTERY**

*Anyone can make a nasty seat nice—
in just a couple hours*

### by **Spike Carlsen, Contributing Editor**

**Y**ou know the chairs I'm talking about—the ones you sat on for 4,122 dinners, the vintage ones inherited from Grandma, the dusty ones picked up at the garage sale, the ones your aunt spilled wine on. THOSE are the chairs I'm talking about.

Reupholstering is a great way to bring tired-looking chairs— even tired-looking rooms—back to life. The materials are relatively inexpensive, the tools are simple and it's a project almost anyone can tackle with success. Here's how.

**BROKEN SEAT**

**1** **Remove the old upholstery.** Pry and yank the staples with a screwdriver and pliers or side cutters. Remove the upholstery and cushion material.

**NEW PLYWOOD SEAT WITH BEVELED EDGES**

**OLD SEAT**

**3/4" PLYWOOD**

**2** **Make a new seat.** If the old seat is in bad shape, cut a new one from plywood. Trace around the old seat, then cut with a jigsaw or circular saw. Bevel or soften edges with a sander or router to match the old contour.

## Chairs are not all created—or upholstered—equally

Here we'll show you how to reupholster a chair with a "drop-in" or "screw-on" seat—a style shared by many benches and stools. Seat bases can be constructed from a variety of materials: solid wood, plywood, pegboard and others. The seats are normally screwed on but can also be glued on or dropped in. The cushions can be foam, cotton or other natural materials.

Our seats, for example, were made from a pegboard-like material secured to a 1x3 framework, covered with horsehair padding. Someone had already reupholstered the chairs, going directly over the old fabric. Expect the unexpected and adjust your game plan accordingly.

## Round up your materials

When you shop, buy "upholstery grade" fabric for its strength and stain resistance. Fabric prices vary wildly; you might find

**What it takes** (per chair)

**TIME:** 1 to 2 hours
**COST:** $20 to $50
**SKILL LEVEL:** Beginner
**TOOLS:** Scissors, bread knife, stapler, basic hand tools

## Which stapler works best?

All the staplers shown will do the trick. The question is: How hard do you want to work—and squeeze—to get the job done? Your stapler buying decision may also hinge on a few other factors, including how often you'll use it, what else you might use it for—and whether you need a good excuse to buy an air compressor.

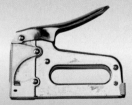

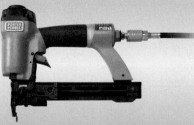

### Hand stapler
**Cost: $15 to $30**
It will give your hand a workout, and you may have to occasionally use a hammer to drive the staples all the way in, but you can still get good results. Make sure you hold the nose of the stapler firmly against the seat base when you pull the trigger.

### Electric stapler
**Cost: $25 to $75**
We used one for our project and it worked flawlessly. You still need to firmly press the nose against the fabric and plywood to get a well-seated staple—but it's way easier on the hand. As a bonus, some models also shoot 3/4-in. and shorter brad nails.

### Pneumatic stapler
**Cost: $40 to $150**
**(plus air compressor)**
If you're going to be stapling for hours on end, invest in a pneumatic stapler. These drive the staples flush with the pull of a finger and allow you to be extremely accurate in the placement of your staples. Some tools also drive brad nails up to 1-1/4 in.

BREAD KNIFE

1" HIGH-DENSITY FOAM

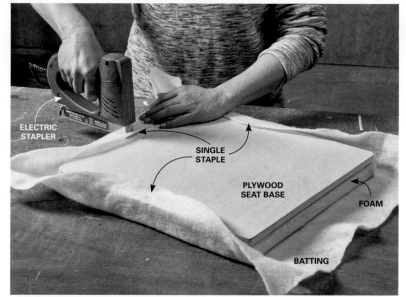

ELECTRIC STAPLER

SINGLE STAPLE

PLYWOOD SEAT BASE

FOAM

BATTING

**3** **Cut the foam.** Trace the outline of the seat onto 1-in.-thick foam. Cut the foam with a bread knife. To avoid tearing the foam, pull the knife toward you, using light pressure and short strokes.

**4** **Add the batting.** Cut the batting so it overhangs all sides of the seat by about 4 in. Then drive a single staple on each side to hold the foam in place.

## MATERIALS LIST
(per typical chair)

1/2" to 3/4" plywood (if needed)
30" x 30" quilt batting
1" x 24" x 24" high-density foam
30" x 30" upholstery fabric
24" x 24" landscape fabric (optional)

**5** **Center the pattern.** Determine the best layout for your material; make sure any patterns or stripes align correctly. Hang the edge of the seat over your work surface then drive a staple, from below, in the centers of the front and back.

something for $5 in the bargain bin or spend 10 times as much. We bought our fabric, foam and batting at a fabric store. For the dust cover, we used landscape fabric from a home center.

## Remove the old and get ready for the new

If you're re-covering more than one chair, number each chair and seat; that way, the screw holes will line up properly when you reinstall the seats. There are special tools just for yanking upholstery staples or tacks, but you can get by with basic hand tools (**Photo 1**). **Tip:** Old, dull side cutters are perfect. They grip staples well but don't cut them off.

Remove the padding and inspect the seat. If the wood base seems solid, reuse it. If it's cracked, use it as a template to make a new one (**Photo 2**). We used a

sander to taper the edges to match the profile of the old one. Plop the seat on top of the foam and outline it with a marker. Use a serrated bread knife (**Photo 3**) to cut just inside the line.

## Install the new fabric

Place a section of batting—4 in. wider in all directions than the size of your chair seat—on a flat work surface, then set your foam and seat on top. Lightly stretch the batting and drive one staple (**Photo 4**) along each edge.

### Don't worry about mistakes

Upholstery work is forgiving. If you make a mistake, just yank out the staples and try again.

**6** **Staple the front edge.** Working from the center outward, install staples along the front as you lightly tension the material with your hand. Stop 2 in. from the corner. Flip the seat over several times to check the pattern as you go. Repeat the process along the back edge and sides.

**7** **Trim the corners.** Cut off the excess batting and upholstery so you don't end up with ugly lumps at corners.

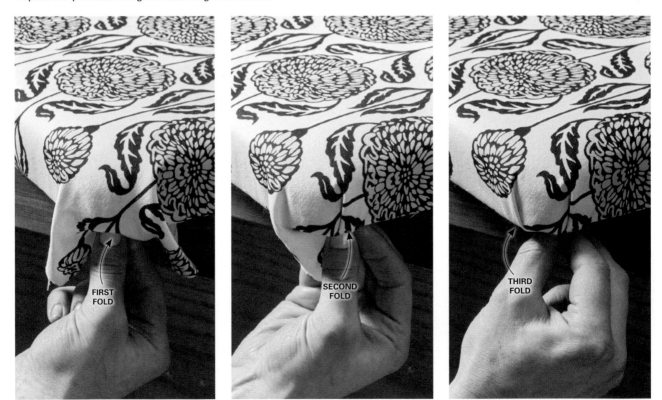

**8** **Wrap the corners.** Create a "butterfly corner" by first tucking the center under, then folding and tucking the material to each side. Flip the seat over and drive staples to hold the corner tight.

## Match the pattern

Make sure the fabric pattern is cut and laid out the same on each seat if you're doing a set of, for example, dining room chairs.

Flip the seat over, then center your material on top (**Photo 5**). Cut the material so you'll be able to wrap it up onto the chair bottom at least 4 in. in each direction. With the seat facing up and the front edge overhanging the work surface, drive one staple through the bottom to hold the material in place. Rotate the seat 180 degrees, then tack the back the same way.

Check your pattern alignment one more time, then flip the seat upside down. Starting at the front middle staple and working toward the corners, use the palm of your hand to lightly stretch the material, then drive a staple every 2 in. (**Photo 6**). Keep the staples within an inch of the edge, and secure the batting and fabric at the same time. Use your entire hand, not just fingertips, to tighten the material. This way you'll avoid little dips and puckers in the pattern.

Repeatedly flip the seat over to check the pattern for straightness; it's easier to keep flipping and checking than to go back and pull staples. Our expert flipped the seat over and checked the pattern a dozen times while stapling each edge. Stop stapling 2 in. from each corner.

Secure the back edge in the same way, stretching the material lightly as you work. Then complete the sides, again repeatedly checking the pattern.

## Corners are the key

You can make simple, single-fold "hospital corners" if the edges of your seat are concealed by a frame. But in most cases, the front corners will be exposed and will look better with a "butterfly corner."

Remove excess batting and material from the corners (**Photo 7**) then flip the seat right side up and experiment with a few corner tucks. Fold the center inward, then overlap each side onto that fold (Photo 8). When the corner looks symmetrical and tight, flip the seat over and staple the folds in place.

DUST COVER

**9** **Install the dust cover.** After you trim the excess fabric and batting, staple on a dust cover—we used landscape fabric. A dust cover neatly hides the exposed fabric edges.

When the corners are done, flip the seat over and cut off the excess material. Staple on a dust cover (Photo 9).

### MEET THE PRO

Lacey Brooker has been reupholstering chairs and repurposing furniture for half a decade. She's the owner of Piccadilly Prairie, a Minneapolis antiques shop specializing in shabby chic furnishings and accessories.

# PREVENT FALLS AT HOME

*Tips to keep both young and old safe at home*

## by **Elisa Bernick, Contributing Editor**

Falls are the No. 1 cause of injuries at home, and they can happen to anyone at any age. They're the most common cause of visits to the emergency room for young children, the leading cause of nonfatal injuries in people ages 25 to 54, and the most common cause of injury in adults age 65 and older.

We used statistics to compile this top ten list to help protect you and your loved ones from falls, emergency room visits and even lawsuits. For more tips on preventing falls, see "A Better Place to Age," p. 42.

### Just the facts

In 2012, the direct medical cost of falls in the U.S., adjusted for inflation, was $30 billion.

### Keep emergency lights handy

Uneven or unfamiliar footing is a prime cause of falls in the dark, and during an emergency even familiar surfaces can become treacherous. Keep a flashlight with extra batteries near your bed in case of a power outage. Also carry a small LED flashlight on your key ring. It's perfect for walking to and from the garage as well as in unfamiliar places like hotels and city streets. If you have a smartphone that includes a flashlight, use it. If your phone doesn't, there are many free flashlight apps available (but read the fine print about whether these apps may be able to access data from your phone once downloaded).

## Night-lights inside and out

Twenty percent of falls happen at night. Fatigue and alcohol can be contributing factors, but poor lighting also plays a role. You can easily make outdoor steps and walkways a lot safer by adding inexpensive solar-powered path, deck and porch lights.

Inside, line your hallway and stairs with LED battery-powered night-lights. The system shown is the PathLights Automatic Lighting System (available online), which includes wireless LED lights that "communicate" with each other when they detect motion up to 6 ft. away. You can find a huge variety of LED battery-powered, motion-activated lights and solar-powered lights at home centers or by searching online.

## Make your home a no-slip zone

According to the National Safety Council, there are 12,000 deaths each year from stairway accidents. Wooden stairways in particular can be very slippery. You can help prevent slips and falls by installing attractive skid-resistant carpet treads. These are available at carpet stores, online retailers and home centers in a variety of colors and styles.

Make sure to install the carpet treads using high-quality double-sided tape so they don't slide around even under heavy traffic. And get rid of small throw rugs that can easily bunch up and trip you. If you can't part with a favorite rug, put double-sided tape under it to keep it from sliding, and never put a rug at the top or bottom of stairs.

## Ice grips work...to a point

If you live in ice and snow country, get some ice grips for your boots and shoes. These cleats provide traction in mud, snow, ice and other conditions. They come in lightweight coil versions for paved roads and sidewalks, and heavy-duty spike models for hiking trails.

A word of caution: Don't ever rely completely on an antislip device to protect you from a fall. Feeling invincible in slippery conditions is never wise. And make sure you remove ice grips immediately when you step inside (even if you're only inside briefly). These products can be very slippery on tile and stone surfaces. Ice grips are available at sporting goods stores and online retailers.

## Pets can be hazardous...

Tripping over the family pet causes more than 86,000 fall-related injuries each year. We're not suggesting you get rid of Rex or Patches, but keep them in mind when you're hoofing it around the house.

## Add friction to slippery surfaces

Prevent outdoor falls by eliminating the slippery conditions on steps, ramps and decks. Temporary solutions include grit additives for paint and adhesive grip strips. These screw-on, durable aluminum plates, from Handi-Treads, are a more permanent option. They are available online in several configurations and finishes.

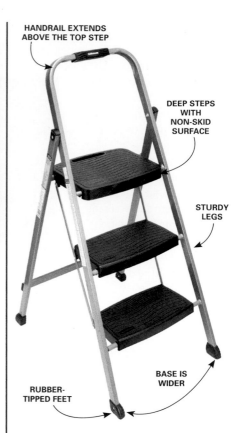

HANDRAIL EXTENDS ABOVE THE TOP STEP

DEEP STEPS WITH NON-SKID SURFACE

STURDY LEGS

BASE IS WIDER

RUBBER-TIPPED FEET

## Install hardware-mounted safety gates at the top of stairs

Every six minutes, a child under the age of 5 falls down the stairs and is rushed to the hospital—that's nearly 100,000 kids per year. Prevent this by using a hardware-mounted safety gate bolted to the wall studs at the top of the stairs. Just make sure it doesn't swing in both directions or have a trip bar at the bottom of the frame.

Pressure-mounted gates are more convenient, but they should be used only between two rooms, never to block off stairwells. Buy a safety gate certified by the Juvenile Products Manufacturers Association, which means it meets international safety standards. And be aware that nearly half of all injuries associated with safety gates happen when adults trip or fall trying to step over them. Buy a gate that's easy for you (but not your kid) to open so you won't be tempted to climb over it.

## Use step stools safely

Step stools may seem innocent enough, but they cause 160,000 injuries each year. Some of these occur because the stool itself isn't safe; more than a million folding step stools have been recalled recently because of design flaws. Injuries happen when the stool collapses or tips over or when someone loses their balance because there's nothing to grab onto.

Avoid these sorts of falls by making sure your step stool is well designed with safety features that include deep, nonskid steps and a handrail that extends above the top step. You should be able to stand on the top step and still have a firm grasp on the handrail. When you use a step stool, make sure it's sitting on a flat surface and that it's tall enough and strong enough for the job. And even if your stool has a handrail, leaning too far in any direction is a good way to become a statistic. By the way, never use an upside-down 5-gallon pail for a step stool. You're bound to go down!

## Use a wall-mount soap dispenser

The bathroom can be a hazardous place for any age. According to the Centers for Disease Control and Prevention, injuries around the tub or shower are actually most common among those ages 15 to 24.

Believe it or not, many bath falls are caused by reaching for dropped soap! So do two things—use a slip-proof bath mat and install a wall-mounted soap and shampoo dispenser. There are many different models available, and most install quickly with adhesive strips and silicone glue. Look for models with easy to fill dispensers. Available at bath stores and online retailers for $30 and up.

## Ditch the clutter, especially on stairs

Nearly half of all falling deaths occur on steps and stairways. Keeping the steps clutter-free seems obvious, but take a look at your own steps (especially those leading down to the basement). Who hasn't set something on the top step "temporarily" with a plan to take it down on the next trip? It's easy to use the steps as semipermanent storage, but it's a very dangerous habit. Odds are that eventually someone is going to trip over something and break an arm or leg (or neck). Don't set anything on the steps. Ever.

MANUFACTURER PHOTO

## Make windows safe for kids

Each year in the United States nearly 15,000 children are injured because of falls from windows. Window screens are not strong enough to prevent falls. In rooms on upper floors, install window guards with quick-release mechanisms (in case of fire) to prevent windows from opening more than a few inches. And keep furniture away from windows so kids aren't tempted to climb near them.

Window guards are available from safebeginnings.com and other online retailers, home centers and department stores. Prices range from $30 to $120.

# BASEMENT FINISHING TIPS

*Slick solutions from remodeling pros*

by **Mark Petersen, Associate Editor**

Finishing a basement is a dream project for many DIYers. You can add beautiful living space and save thousands of dollars in the process. But you're also guaranteed to run into unusual problems.

We met with pros from all the trades and asked how to solve some of the problems you're likely to encounter when working in the basement. They gave us some great quick-fix tips as well as helpful strategies for conquering major hurdles. Our goal is to help you avoid unforeseen pitfalls and assist you in creating a comfortable, high-quality space that will last a lifetime.

## Boost the airflow

The coldest room in the basement is usually the room farthest from the furnace. Boost the airflow on long duct runs with an in-line duct fan. These fans are easy to install, but they do require a power supply. Some are hardwired and some plug into an outlet, but either way you'll need to leave an access to the junction box, which can be accomplished with a panel or a cover plate. In-line fans can run 24/7 or be installed with an optional thermostat or be wired to turn on when the furnace fan does. Expect to pay about $30 at home centers for a 6-in. fan like the one shown here; 4-in. and 8-in. fans are also available.

IN-LINE
DUCT FAN

## Build walls on the floor

If you have enough space, it's easier to build the walls on the floor and then tip them up into place, but you need to plan ahead. Build and install all the perimeter walls first, and then build all the interior walls, stacking them in some out-of-the-way corner as you go. Don't install any interior walls until they've all been built; that way you won't frame yourself out of open floor space.

## Hide the service panel

Sometimes the electrical service panel is located on a wall that will eventually be in a finished living space. Instead of paying big bucks to move it, simply hang a photo, painting or other piece of art over it.

## Run pipes behind walls

It's a lot easier to run plumbing behind a new wall before it's nailed into place. That way you don't have to drill a bunch of holes through studs. Assemble the pipes and tape them to the foam insulation temporarily. Tip up the new wall, and hang the pipes on studs before nailing the wall permanently into place. That will make it easier to attach the hangers. The downside of this method is that you do lose a little floor space.

VENT
PIPE

J-HOOK
PIPE
HANGER

DRAIN-
PIPE

## Plane down any sagging joists

Hold a straightedge across joists to make sure they form a flat surface for the ceiling. If any joist sags 1/4 in. more than the one next to it, you'll end up with a noticeable bump in your basement ceiling. Snap a line from the bottom edge of one end of the joist to the other and use a power plane to shave the board straight.

Before you start, make sure there are no nails or screws embedded in the wood. Make several passes, each shorter than the next, until you cut down to the line. Power planers are loud, so wear hearing protection along with a dust mask and safety glasses. Planers cost $70 to $170, or can be rented for about $20 for a half day. If you have several sagging joists or joists that bow upward, see "Form a Flat Ceiling" on p. 61.

DRYWALL SHIMS

BOWED IN

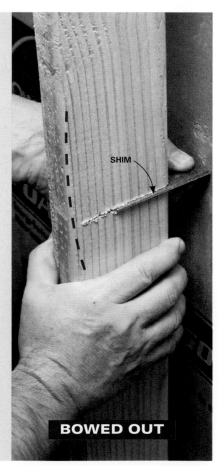

SHIM

BOWED OUT

## Straighten bowed studs

Use a 4-ft. level or some other straightedge to check for bowed studs. Even if you personally checked every stud in every wall when you built it, new lumber can twist and bow as it dries. If a stud is bowed in, fill the gap with drywall shims made from paperboard (think cereal box) like the ones shown here. (A bundle of 100 shims typically costs less than $10 at home centers.) Start with longer strips and add layers of shorter strips until the gap is filled.

If the stud is bowed out and you can get to the back side of it, use a reciprocating saw to slice into the side that's bowed in. Cut far enough so the back side opens up when you press on the front side. Insert a shim in the kerf to hold the stud where you want it. Drive a nail through the separated area to keep the shim in place and add a little strength to the stud.

## Test the airflow

It's a lot easier to troubleshoot poor airflow problems before you hang the drywall. That's why our pros recommend using an anemometer to check the airflow at each register first. This ABM-100 Airflow Anemometer is made by AAB and connects to the headset jack on your smartphone. It costs about $45 online. After downloading the free app, all you do is answer a few simple questions about your ducts and hold it in front of the register box. The numbers, which tell volume and velocity, will depend on the size of the room and the size of the ducts.

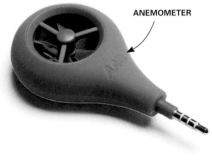

ANEMOMETER

## Don't insulate over a heated floor

In-floor heating systems are great for heating a basement, but installing thick, heavy carpet and heat-resistant padding over them is a sure way to reduce their efficiency. High R-values are a good thing for walls and attics, but when you're covering in-floor heating, lower is better.

Most carpeting is made of similar materials, so the type isn't as important as the thickness—thinner is better. Carpet padding, however, is made up of different materials with different insulating properties. Waffle rubber padding is a good choice, with an R-value of 1 for a 3/8-in. pad. Urethane is a poor choice, with an R-value of 1.62 for a 3/8-in.-thick pad.

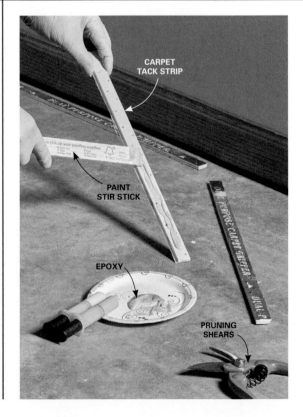

CARPET TACK STRIP

PAINT STIR STICK

EPOXY

PRUNING SHEARS

## Glue down the carpet tack strip

Ready to install carpet? You can buy a tack strip made specifically for concrete, but it's always hit-or-miss whether the nails in the strip will penetrate. For a guaranteed solid connection, pull the nails out of the strip and glue the strips down with epoxy.

It's rare for both the floor and the strips to be perfectly straight, so cut the strips into halves or thirds (pruning shears work well). It's easier to get smaller pieces to lie flat. Wipe the floor clean before you start. Construction adhesive will also work, but you'll need to wait a couple days before installing the carpet.

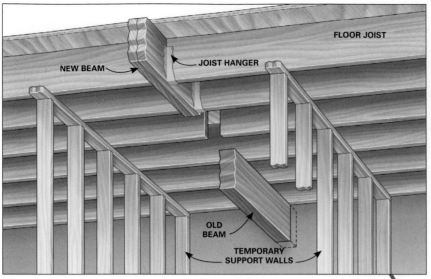

NEW BEAM

JOIST HANGER

FLOOR JOIST

OLD BEAM

TEMPORARY SUPPORT WALLS

## Raise a beam

Is that head-bonkingly-low beam stopping you from finishing your basement? You may be able to get it mostly out of the way by raising it to the same level as the floor joists. You'll need an engineer to tell you whether you can reuse the existing beam or need a bigger one. A lumberyard will be able to refer you to an engineer. Build temporary walls to support the joists before you remove the existing beam. Cut out a space in the joists for the new beam. Slide in the new beam and support each end. Finish by attaching the floor joists to the beam with hangers.

## Use screws on hard lumber

Old lumber gets hard and brittle, so nailing into it can be extremely frustrating, even for the pros. A pneumatic nail gun will penetrate old wood, but it also tends to split it. If you need to connect new walls to old existing walls or attach soffits to old floor joists, make sure you have some self-tapping construction screws on hand before you start. Screws work better on old wood and create a super-strong connection. However, you might still have to predrill screw holes when you're working with really brittle wood.

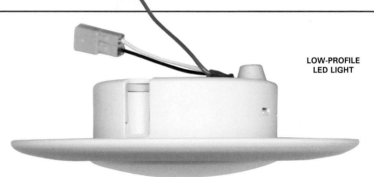

LOW-PROFILE LED LIGHT

## Install skinny lights

Many basements have low ceilings, which is why recessed lights work so well. But sometimes ducts, pipes or beams get in the way, leaving no room for the cans that house the lights. That's where LEDs come in. You can buy low-profile LED recessed lights that look like typical recessed lights but fit into standard round electrical boxes. They cost about $45 each at home centers.

## Fill the low spots

No matter what type of finish flooring you choose, the floor underneath must be smooth and flat. You don't want to feel bumps under the carpet or hollow spots under plank flooring. And an uneven surface is a common cause of cracked tiles, especially large tiles. Holes deeper than 1 in. and large cracks need to be patched, but uneven sections and low spots can be filled with self-leveling underlayment.

Vacuum and then mop the floor first; let it dry, and then roll out the recommended primer. Unless you have less than 10 sq. ft. to fill, get a helper so you have one person to mix the underlayment and the other to work it around with a squeegee. Don't do the mixing right next to the area you're working on; the dust could interfere with adhesion.

SELF-LEVELING UNDERLAYMENT

## Let a pro plan the ductwork

A poor heating and cooling design could seriously reduce the comfort of your new basement space, so don't guess at the number, size or placement of new ducts. Instead, hire a professional HVAC contractor to draw up a plan. There may be a local contractor who can supply you with a comprehensive custom plan. The ones we spoke with charge about $200.

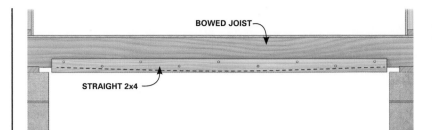

BOWED JOIST

STRAIGHT 2x4

## Form a flat ceiling

The bottom edges of floor joists are not always on the same plane, especially in older houses. You could spend two days trying to plane them all into alignment, or you could sister new lumber onto the existing joists. Make sure the flooring system is structurally sound and doesn't need additional bracing before establishing the new basement ceiling height (search for "structural repairs" at familyhandyman.com).

Install a straight 2x4 on the worst joist, and use that as a reference to snap lines on walls. Nail on new, straight boards to the sides of the joists even with the lines on the wall. To work in large rooms, pull a string tight and use it as a guide. It's easier to avoid ducts, plumbing pipes and electrical wires if you nail up 2x4s. Use larger-dimension lumber if the joist spaces are relatively uncluttered and you want a stiffer floor on the first level.

CARPET PAD

DUCT TAPE

## Quiet noisy pipes

If you've never spent much time in your unfinished basement (why would you?), you may have really noisy drainpipes but not even know it. Before you bury them behind drywall, have a helper run water, drain bathtubs, empty a washing machine and flush toilets while you hang out and listen for loud swooshing noises. If you do have a noisy pipe, wrap it with carpet padding. Use a quality duct tape or zip ties to hold it in place. If the home center near you doesn't sell carpet padding by the foot, stop by your local carpet store, which may be able to give you some free scraps.

GRAY-WATER PUMP

## Pump waste water away

Running supply lines to a basement wet bar is easy, but sometimes there's not an easy way to install a drainpipe. The solution: Get a gray-water pump and direct sink water wherever you want. These pumps are easy to install and small enough to fit inside a cabinet. They will work for dishwashers and laundry sinks as well. But they're not made for solids, so always keep a strainer in the basin. The one shown here is a Saniswift made by Saniflo. Expect to pay about $235 at home centers.

# HandyHints®

**FROM OUR READERS**

## FIX FOR NOISY FLOORS

Here's a simple fix for squeaking floor joists: Screw a 1-1/2-in. corner bracket to the joist about 1/8 in. below the subfloor. Then when you drive a screw up into the subfloor, it's pulled tight against the joist. No more squeak.

–Charles J. Long

## STOOL LEG PROTECTOR

The legs on my stool have sharp ends that slice through the plastic caps. To solve this problem, I place a washer the same diameter as the pipe into the plastic cap and then fit it onto the leg. Now the stool is no longer marring the floor.

–Peter Trivilino

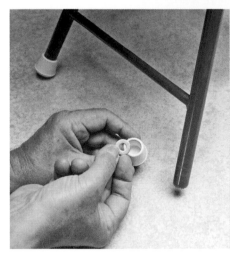

## FREE FUNNELS

I use common plastic bottles for large-mouth or very-fine funnels instead of store-bought ones. These funnels are disposable/recyclable when no longer needed. When I find an unusual bottle, I cut the top off and store it for future use. I have a collection in a box in the garage.

–Aaron Bennett

## PET HAIR REMOVER

When we were moving my daughter from her apartment, I wore my nonslip rubber-dipped gloves that I had gotten at a hardware store. While lifting her upholstered chair, I brushed some dog hair off with my gloves and noticed the hair rolling up into a bunch, leaving the upholstery virtually lint-free.

Seeing it work so well, I kept at it, and in just a few minutes the whole chair looked great. I left the gloves as a housewarming gift for my daughter's new apartment!

–Cheri Hildebrandt

## ELEVATED DOG DISH

I read in an article not long ago that some larger dogs have difficulty eating from dishes that are on the floor. To give my dog a break, I cut a plastic pail in half and then glued her dish to the bottom of it with adhesive caulk. She seems even more enthusiastic about eating than ever.

–Randy Roush

## OVERHEAD STORAGE SPACE

The space between the floor joists in my unfinished basement is the perfect spot to store leftover trim and boards. I bought some chain, S-hooks and eye screws and made some corrals to hold the stuff in place. It's easy now to see my inventory and slip a piece out or remove the chain to sort through the entire bundle.

–Les Beekman

## UNDER-SINK ORGANIZER

To tame the clutter under our sink, I made this organizer from scraps of 3-in. PVC. I cut the pipe into short lengths and then glued them to 1/2-in. plywood with polyurethane construction adhesive. I spaced the pipe pieces to accommodate liquid soaps, shampoos and other bottles and left spaces between the pipe sections for odd-shaped spray bottles. Now things are organized and don't topple over every time we reach for something.

–Dan Nashold

## EMERGENCY MIXING PADDLE

I needed to mix up some joint compound but couldn't find my mixing paddle. Then I looked up and saw a bike hook screwed into a joist. I removed the hook, chucked it into my drill and was pleasantly surprised how well it blended the mix!

–Al Herrero

# HandyHints®

## HIGH AND DRY

We keep our wet boots in a boot tray by the door. The boots used to sit in water all day and never really got dry. Then we decided to elevate them from the tray using some old cookie cooling racks. Now they're dry when we put them on, and the water evaporates from the tray more quickly.

**–Robert Henikman**

## SPRING-LOADED HINGE PIN REMOVER

I've messed up the trim around my doors a number of times by using a screwdriver and a hammer to pound out stubborn door hinge pins. I now use my spring-loaded nail set to do the job with perfect results. It takes about three shots and the pin is out. Search online for "spring-loaded nail set."

**–Matt Seery**

## DUST CATCHER

Whenever I have small repairs to make on wall surfaces, I use wide masking tape and fold it back to catch the dust. It saves on cleanup and helps keep the airborne dust down slightly.

**–Erin Kotas**

## LIGHTED SAFETY GLASSES

I was working under the kitchen sink and couldn't see what I was doing, so I used zip ties to attach mini flashlights to a pair of safety glasses. Now I use this pair whenever I climb into the attic or do any repairs in unlighted spaces. Everywhere I look is illuminated.

**–Nathan Rodgers**

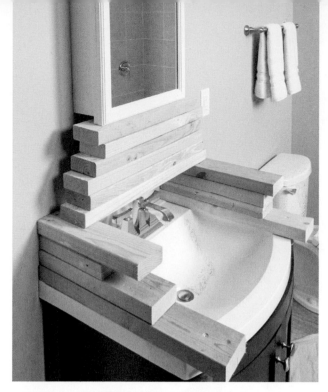

## JUST THE RIGHT HEIGHT

When I had to position, adjust and fasten a heavy medicine cabinet by myself, I came up with this solution. All it took was a stack of wood scraps!

–John Engeriser

## GENTLE HANDCART

I often use my handcart to move furniture, so I upgraded it with pipe insulation and duct tape. Now my delicate wood finishes are protected.

–Paul M. Johnson

## SAVE THOSE CAPS!

Instead of throwing away old aerosol can caps, I save them to use as mixing containers for epoxy. Once the epoxy hardens, I can usually reuse the caps a couple times because the epoxy peels away from the slick surface.

–Noel Hansen

## RENEW OLD EPOXY

Awhile back, I reached for my two containers of epoxy and noticed that the resin in one container had crystallized exactly like honey that's been in the cupboard too long. The solution is exactly the same too: Set the container in a bowl of hot tap water. After about 15 minutes, I emptied the container and refilled it with hot water. After about a half hour, the epoxy regained its normal consistency. Good as new!

–Ken Holte

# CABINET
# DOOR RACK

*A super-simple solution for cabinet chaos*

by **Spike Carlsen, Contributing Editor**

ome people think black holes exist only in outer space. Not true. There's probably one under your kitchen sink. Place detergent, cleaners or sponges under there and they disappear forever—or at least become really, really hard to find.

Here's a simple project to bring order to the chaos: a door-mounted storage rack. You can modify this basic idea to organize other cabinets too.

## What it takes

TIME: **2 hours**
COST: **$10 to $20**
SKILL LEVEL: **Beginner**
TOOLS: **Circular saw, miter saw or jigsaw, drill**

## Planning and materials

As you plan your rack, consider building multiple racks. Building two or three doesn't take much more time than building one. Also think about (and measure!) the items you want your rack to hold. You may want to mount the upper shelf a little higher or lower than we did.

Most home centers carry everything you'll need, including 1/4-in.-thick wood strips in species like pine, oak and poplar. If you don't find thin material alongside the other lumber, look for "mull strip" or "mullion" in the millwork aisle. The wood quantities on our Materials List will yield a rack sized for most cabinet doors, but you may need a little more or a little less.

## How to do it

Begin by looking inside your cabinet. With the door closed, this rack will project 3-3/4 in. into the interior. Make sure the installed rack won't bump into your sink, pipes, garbage disposal or other fixed object.

Measure the cabinet door and opening to determine the measurements of the sides and shelves (**Photo 1**). Mark the position of the upper shelf on the sides: We positioned ours 12 in. from the bottom, but you can adjust the location based on your needs. Secure the shelves to the sides using 2-in. screws and finish washers (**Photo 2**). Drill holes in the four cross slats 3/8 in. from the ends and fasten them to the sides with 3/4-in. screws.

With the rack assembled, we gave it two coats of lacquer. Lacquer is a durable finish, dries in minutes and comes in spray cans for quick, no-mess application.

After the finish dries, screw the four L-brackets to the sides of the racks, making sure to position them so they won't interfere with the door hinges. Clamp the rack to the door, predrill mounting holes using the L-brackets as guides, and secure the rack to the door (**Photo 3**). Put a strip of tape on the floor of the cabinet, 4 in. back from the door, to indicate a "No Parking" zone for items stored inside.

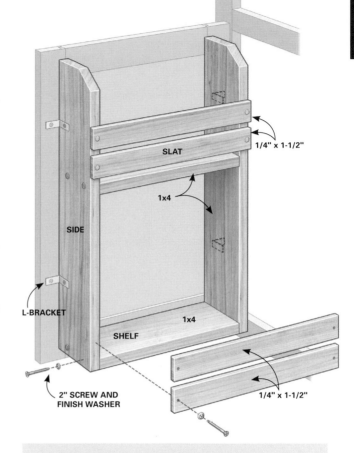

## MATERIALS LIST

1x4 (6 ft.)
1/4-in. x 1-1/2-in. strip (6 ft.)
1-in. L-brackets (4)
3/4-in. screws
2-in. screws
Finish washers
Spray lacquer

**1 Measure to size the rack.** Measure the width of the door and cut the rack shelves 4-1/2 in. shorter than that measurement. Measure the height of the cabinet opening and cut the rack sides 1 in. shorter.

**2 Build the rack.** Mark the location of the top shelf on the sides. Drill screw holes and fasten the sides to the shelves using 2-in. screws and finish washers. Add the slats, apply a finish and screw brackets to the rack.

**3 Mount the rack.** Center the rack on the door and drill screw holes. Wrap tape around the drill bit to act as a depth guide so you don't drill through the door. Clamps aren't absolutely necessary for this step, but they're a big help.

# CHOOSING FLOORING:
# LAMINATE VS. BAMBOO

*Both are easy to install—learn which is right for you*

by **Travis Larson, Senior Editor**

## LAMINATE FLOORING

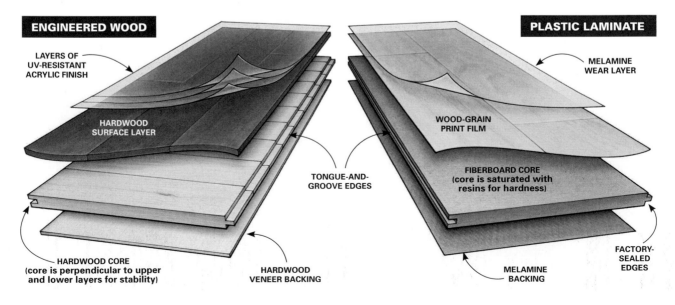

Laminate flooring is one of the great developments in home improvement of the past 50 years. It's inexpensive, durable and prefinished, but best of all, an intermediate DIYer can install it with just a few tools. Most of the various styles are installed by just snapping together the planks—no glue or fasteners required. In fact, the trickiest part is choosing the product! That's what we'll tell you about.

### Two styles: Engineered wood and plastic laminate

There are two types of laminate flooring. Both come in packages of snap-together planks about 1/4 in. thick. But here's the difference. Engineered wood is made from layers of real wood glued together with each layer perpendicular to the one below and above it for better stability. The top layer is a high-quality thin layer of hardwood coated with acrylic finish. Plastic laminate, on the other hand, is completely artificial, with a layer of melamine on the bottom, a resin-saturated fiberboard center, and a wood-grain print on the top that's protected by a layer of clear hard plastic.

Engineered wood is for purists who prefer the look of natural wood. But you pay for reality. On average, it's about double the cost of plastic laminate flooring. Its thin top layer of actual hardwood makes it more susceptible to dents, scratches and staining. But unlike plastic laminate flooring, it can be rejuvenated up to three times with careful sanding and refinishing. Because of that, you can expect it to last longer than plastic laminate—if you locate it away from water-prone and high-wear areas. If you're planning to sell your house in a few years, consider that buyers may appreciate and pay more for the look of real wood.

Plastic laminate is for those who want the look of wood flooring in a place that gets wet or seriously abused. The bulletproof topcoat and plastic internal components make laminate floors extremely durable. They stand up to moisture, pet claws, in-line skates and sand-infested flip-flops much better than engineered wood floors. Manufacturers have come light-years in making the wood-grain print look very realistic. Most people can't even tell it's not real wood.

**ENGINEERED WOOD**

LAYERS OF UV-RESISTANT ACRYLIC FINISH

HARDWOOD SURFACE LAYER

TONGUE-AND-GROOVE EDGES

HARDWOOD CORE
(core is perpendicular to upper and lower layers for stability)

HARDWOOD VENEER BACKING

**PLASTIC LAMINATE**

MELAMINE WEAR LAYER

WOOD-GRAIN PRINT FILM

FIBERBOARD CORE
(core is saturated with resins for hardness)

MELAMINE BACKING

FACTORY-SEALED EDGES

## Avoid wide planks unless the substrate is perfect

The directions will tell you the amount of slab or sub-floor unevenness tolerated by the brand and type of flooring you buy. Over an uneven floor, wider planks will be harder to snap together, end joints won't stay flush with one another and there will be more gaps beneath the planks that you'll feel when you walk across the floor. So if your concrete or wood subfloor is quite uneven, you're better off selecting a narrower plank style, and being thorough when you apply the floor leveling compound (**photo left**).

## Choose a finish based on lifestyle, not just looks

If you lead a quiet life, choose whatever flooring style appeals to you. But if you have one of those crazy households with kids, pets and lots of visitors, be a bit more careful. Flooring with a varied grain pattern, a low-gloss finish or distressed or hand-scraped patina will look much better, much cleaner, much longer than floor-ing with a glossy, monolithic grain pattern.

## Don't forget the underlayment

All laminate flooring needs foam underlayment. Don't skip it. Underlayment prevents the floor from clicking on the subfloor as you walk across it and makes it feel a bit softer. It also makes the planks easier to install because it evens out small inconsistencies in the subfloor. Some underlayment has self-adhesive tape to join one row to the next. Others call for separate tape. Be careful to use whatever is required. Go ahead and buy the special lami-nate and wood flooring instal-lation tool as well. You'll need it to pull together flooring ends where each row abuts a wall.

## Don't forget LV flooring!

Laminate floors aren't the only option for durability and ease of installation. Next time you're at the home center, take a gander at luxury vinyl (LV) flooring. There's luxury vinyl tile (LVT), which looks like ceramic tile, and luxury vinyl plank (LVP), which mimics wood (shown here). Both types are extremely resilient, about the easiest flooring in the world to install and completely waterproof. Since luxury vinyl is so pliable, it's a great choice over uneven subfloors. Prices start at $2 per sq. ft.

# BAMBOO

**STRANDED, CLICK-TOGETHER**

**STRANDED, NAIL-DOWN**

**HORIZONTAL, CLICK-TOGETHER**

**COMPOSITE, CLICK-TOGETHER**

**B**amboo flooring has evolved into one of the biggest segments of the wood flooring industry over the past 10 years. That's because it's much cheaper and more durable than most wood flooring options out there. Is it for you? Here's a bamboo flooring primer.

First of all, bamboo isn't wood at all. It's a type of grass, the biggest grass in the world, and there are dozens of varieties. The one most often used for flooring, called Moso bamboo, is from China and other parts of Asia.

Bamboo is processed in a few different ways to make flooring. "Stranded" bamboo is by far the biggest section of the bamboo flooring market. It's made by shredding the stalks into long strands and then compressing them into the final solid form using heat and plastic binders. It's available as tongue-and-groove flooring that's nailed down, or the click-together style, the same choices for most laminate and engineered plank floors. The hardness and durability of stranded bamboo flooring exceed that of any domestic solid wood flooring available. The dozens of colors available allow you to choose flooring that's shaded like cherry, ash, oak or just about any other wood species. However, since stranded bamboo doesn't have natural wood grain, few would mistake it for the real deal.

If you want the actual look of bamboo, choose "horizontal" bamboo flooring. Instead of being shredded, the bamboo stalks are cut into thin strips, which are then laminated together to form the planks. You can see the grain and nodes (the "knuckles" on bamboo stalks) in the flooring. However, horizontal bamboo flooring isn't nearly as hard as stranded, so it isn't the best bamboo choice if your floor will get heavy use or abuse.

The least expensive bamboo option is engineered bamboo flooring. It has a thin layer of bamboo laminated onto plywood, the same type of construction used for other engineered flooring. (You won't find too many choices in this category.)

Bamboo does have a couple of downsides. Because it's grass, not wood, it's more affected by moisture than other flooring choices. It will swell substantially more than wood or other types of flooring, so avoid installing it in damp areas and use care when mopping. And unlike wood flooring, bamboo can never be sanded down and refinished.

You can find bamboo flooring at home centers, specialty lumber liquidators (search online for "lumber liquidators"), or places that specialize in builders' overstock.

# PEGBOARD PALOOZA

*Ordinary material— extraordinary possibilities*

by **Spike Carlsen, Contributing Editor**

**A** funny thing happened when I began thinking about writing this article: I started noticing pegboard *everywhere*—panels, hooks, doodads, you name it. Every hand tool in the hardware store was hanging on pegboard. Every bag of bolts, roll of duct tape and tin of Tic Tacs at the checkout counter—pegboarded. Even the pegboard hooks were hanging on pegboard hooks.

But I guess that should come as no surprise. Retailers want a display system that's sturdy, easy to rearrange and adaptable—the same qualities we need in our work spaces at home.

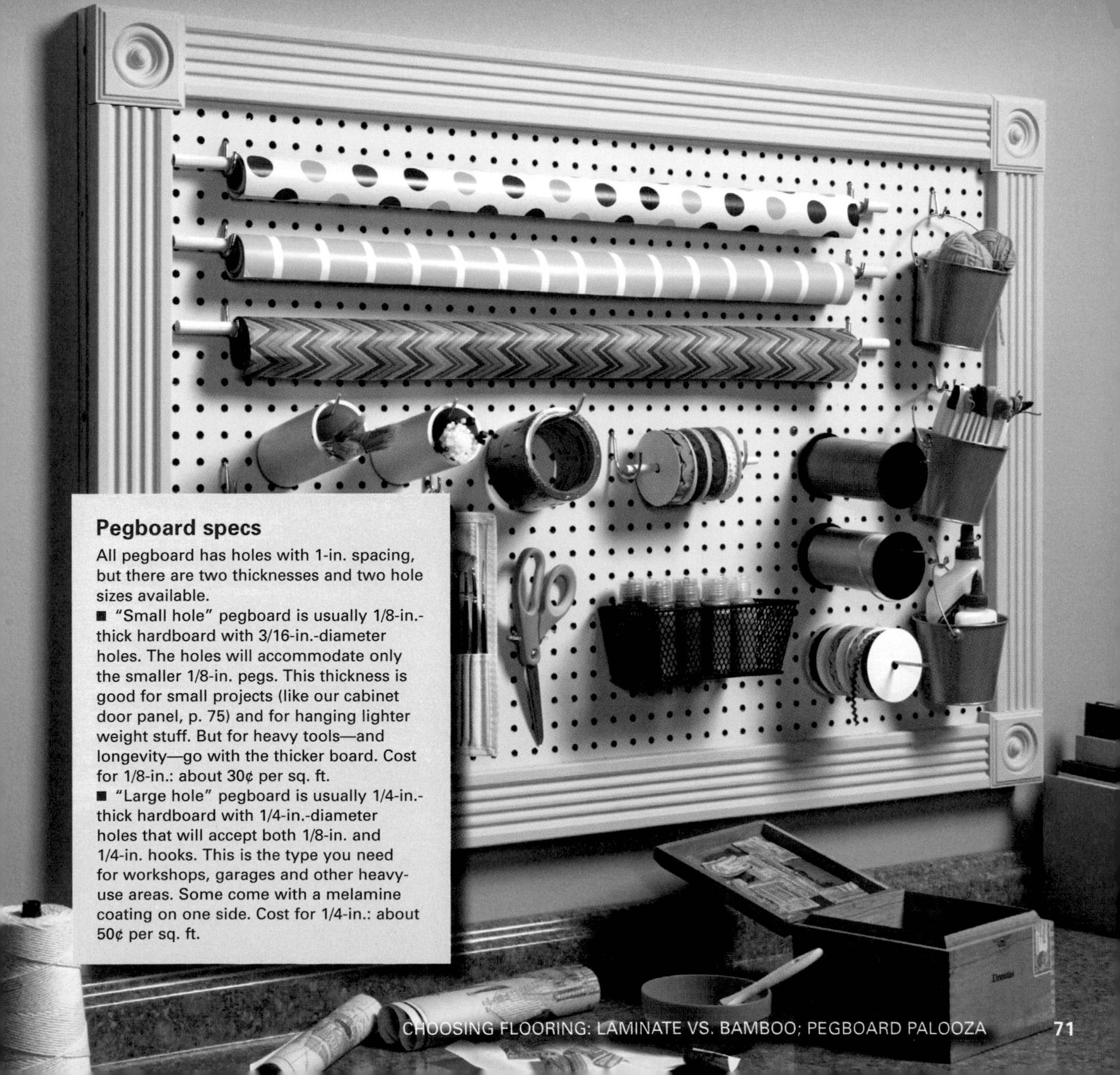

## Pegboard specs

All pegboard has holes with 1-in. spacing, but there are two thicknesses and two hole sizes available.

■ "Small hole" pegboard is usually 1/8-in.-thick hardboard with 3/16-in.-diameter holes. The holes will accommodate only the smaller 1/8-in. pegs. This thickness is good for small projects (like our cabinet door panel, p. 75) and for hanging lighter weight stuff. But for heavy tools—and longevity—go with the thicker board. Cost for 1/8-in.: about 30¢ per sq. ft.

■ "Large hole" pegboard is usually 1/4-in.-thick hardboard with 1/4-in.-diameter holes that will accept both 1/8-in. and 1/4-in. hooks. This is the type you need for workshops, garages and other heavy-use areas. Some come with a melamine coating on one side. Cost for 1/4-in.: about 50¢ per sq. ft.

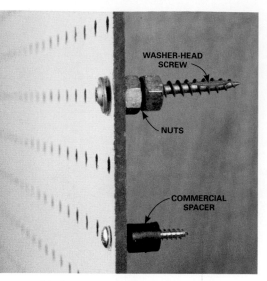

WASHER-HEAD
SCREW

NUTS

COMMERCIAL
SPACER

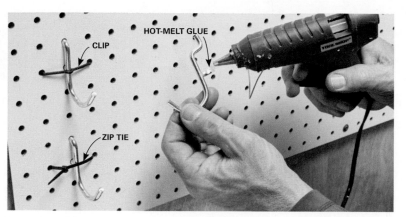

CLIP

HOT-MELT GLUE

ZIP TIE

## Hefty standoffs

Pegboard needs about 1/2 in. of "stand-off" space behind it so the hooks can be inserted. Plastic and metal pegboard panels have this space built in, created by the L-shape flanges at the edges. But you can also create this standoff space in several ways:

■ Install **screw-in standoffs with spacers** (photo above). The store-bought versions often have short screws with small heads and wimpy plastic spacers. Make your own using beefier washer-head screws and nuts for spacers. On larger panels, install standoffs in the center to maintain space and add support. Tip: Use hot-melt glue to hold these mid-panel spacers in place before you install the pegboard.

■ **Create a frame** for the back of the panel using 1x2s or 1x3s (**see photo**, p. 73). For panels wider than 3 ft., add a 1x2 rib to the back every 2 ft. to support the weight of the tools and take the flex out of the panel.

## Hooks are available in two sizes

Pegs and hooks come in two thicknesses: 1/8 in. (which will fit in any pegboard) and 1/4 in. (which fits only "large hole" pegboard). Both can bear the weight of any hand tool, but since the cost difference is negligible, go with the 1/4-in. hooks because they're less likely to pop out of the holes. The one drawback to the 1/4-in. size is that they're difficult to bend and modify for custom uses.

## Lock 'em in

The No. 1 complaint about pegboard? Hooks falling out when you remove a tool. The solution? Lock 'em in place. **Zip ties** are an inexpensive, sure-shooting way to go—but you need to have access to the back of your pegboard (or plan ahead and install the pegs and zip ties before you mount the board). **Pegboard clips** (about 20¢ each) have small barbs that lock into holes on both sides of the hook to keep them in place. Another approach is to add a dab of **hot-melt glue** to the lower leg before slipping the peg into the hole. The glue will hold well enough to keep the hook in place, but it will be removable later with a light tug.

CLIP

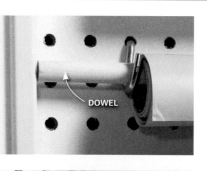

DOWEL

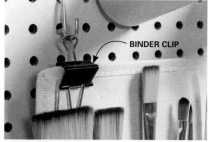

BINDER CLIP

PVC PIPE

## Make hooks hold more

Some items won't hang directly on pegboard hooks. But with a little ingenuity, you can make hooks hold just about anything. Here are three ideas:

■ **Hooks and 1/2-in. wood dowels** organize wrapping paper—no more digging through a stack of unraveling rolls.

■ **Binder clip**s grab items that can't hang on hooks. The clip shown here, for example, holds a canvas tool pouch.

■ A section of **PVC pipe** slipped over a long hook is a great nook for skinny stuff: pencils, brushes, zip ties....

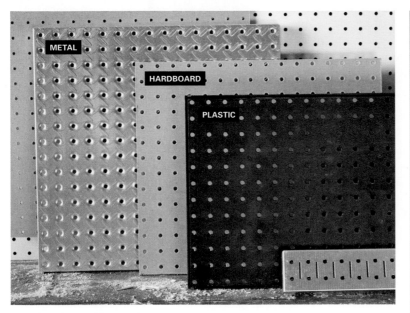

METAL

HARDBOARD

PLASTIC

## Beyond hardboard

Most home centers carry only hardboard pegboard, but you'll find other materials by searching online for "metal pegboard" or "plastic pegboard."

■ **Metal pegboard** has 1/4-in. holes and L-shape edge flanges that create built-in standoffs. The panel sizes are normally in 16-in. and 24-in. increments. Metal pegboard has a cool industrial look and is darn near indestructible. Cost: $5 to $7 per sq. ft.

■ **Metal pegboard strips** are ideal for situations where you need a single, sturdy strip of pegboard—like in the garage for hanging long-handled tools. The strips have 1/4-in. holes and built-in edge flanges for standoffs, and they're outrageously sturdy. Cost: $3 to $4 per lin. ft.

■ **Plastic pegboard** has 1/4-in. holes, folded edges to create standoffs and center ribs for rigidity. Many systems come with slide-in connectors for joining panels. It's at least as sturdy as hardboard pegboard. Cost: $4 to $5 per sq. ft.

## Go hookless

You can craft your own hooks using stuff from the hardware aisle. Clip the tips from No. 6 hollow wall anchors, drive them into 1/4-in. pegboard holes, then secure your custom tool holder by driving screws into the anchors. Short 5/16-in.-diameter lag bolts fit snugly into 1/4-in. holes to create inexpensive hangers for lightweight objects.

LAG BOLT

ANCHOR

WALL ANCHOR

BASE FRAME

## Dress it up

Most pegboard comes in two colors— boring white and boring brown. But it doesn't have to stay that way. Roll on a coat of primer followed by gloss or semigloss paint (glossy paints are easier to wipe clean). Apply light coats so you don't clog the holes. Then snazz it up with a frame. After we attached our pegboard to a 1x3 frame, we added corner blocks and trim with hot-melt glue—no fancy miter cuts or fasteners needed.

**1/4" HOLE**

**CABLE STAPLE**

## Custom shelving

Standard pegboard hooks can accommodate most tools—but sometimes you need a special place for special stuff.

Drill 1/4-in. holes in the backs of homemade shelves, then use those holes to slide the shelves over L-hooks. Or use cable staples to attach plywood shelves to standard pegboard shelf brackets. The staples allow you to slide the shelf back and forth so you can easily fit the shelf bracket "legs" into the holes.

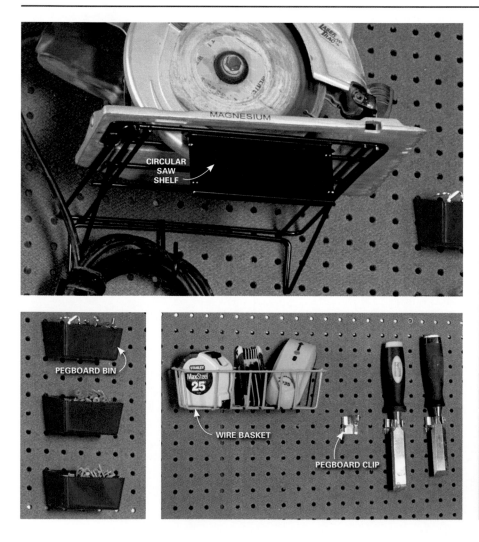

**CIRCULAR SAW SHELF**

**PEGBOARD BIN**

**WIRE BASKET**

**PEGBOARD CLIP**

## Hang anything

Most hardware stores and home centers carry standard hooks for basic hand tools, but specialized hangers are available too. The circular saw shelf, cordless drill holder, wire basket, bins and other doodads can help organize hard-to-hang tools. Search online for "pegboard" followed by the type of hanger you're looking for, such as "pegboard circular saw shelf."

**CORDLESS DRILL HOLDER**

STRIP

1x3 STRIP

## Pegboard walls

Create pegboard walls by running 1x3 strips horizontally at the top and bottom of the panel and every 16 in. or 24 in. between. Use 1/4-in. pegboard and attach it to the strips with washer-head screws. The strips will also allow you to mount screw-on hooks to the wall for very heavy items like bikes and wheelbarrows.

RABBET BIT

RABBET

## Storage behind closed doors

Pegboard is great for organizing kitchens, laundry rooms and bathroom cabinets. Rout a groove in a 1x2 frame using a rabbet bit, attach the pegboard with glue and brads, then mount it to the door. The frame helps support the edges of the pegboard and creates a 1/2-in. space behind the board so pegs can be inserted.

# GreatGoofs®

## Indoor waterfall

My wife and I decided to refinish our aging kitchen cabinets instead of getting new ones. We masked off the counters and the walls and spanned the double sink with a piece of plywood so we'd have a place to kneel while working on the upper cabinets. I put on my hearing protection and dust mask and started sanding. After several minutes I felt a tug on my shirt. I looked down and saw my wife motioning for me to stop.

I set the sander on the counter, and as the dust cleared, I could see water everywhere on the floor! My knee had bumped the sink faucet, turning it on, and the water was running onto the plywood, down to the

floor and then even into the basement. Luckily our floor survived the soaking. We did finish the sanding that day—after we turned off the faucet valves below the sink!

–Debra and Mark Pettijohn

## Raindrops keep falling ...

After I left for college, my father decided to empty my water bed. Unable to get a good siphon going, he gave up and dropped the hose on the floor and left the room to take care of other chores. Hours later he noticed water dripping through the ceiling below. The siphoning had started after all. When I went home that weekend, I saw several garbage cans in the living room. He had drilled holes all over the ceiling to let the water out. Poor Dad. I'd never seen him more frustrated or forlorn. I don't think we'll be shopping for another water bed anytime soon!

–Karin Carr

## Drill first, think later

While redoing our family room, I used an air nailer to attach baseboard trim pieces to a wall that contained a water supply line. A couple of days after installing the trim, I noticed some water on the basement floor and thought: "How long were those nails?" As soon as I pried off one of the trim pieces, water began spraying all over my new hardwood floor.

By the time I got the water shut off, it was puddled all over the floor. I was afraid of the floor getting warped, so I decided to drill a hole through the floor to drain the water into the basement. Well, of course I managed to drill through the same pipe that I had already nailed through! The plumbers had to make one cut in the family room and one in the basement to replace the damaged section. They then informed me that had I left the two pinholes, it would have been much easier to fix.

–Calvin English

### Ladder shuffle

Last fall, I remodeled an upstairs bathroom. I planned to keep the house clean by accessing the room with a ladder from outside instead of tracking through the house. The ladder rested on the first-floor deck and against a small upstairs deck. Halfway up, I felt the bottom of the ladder start to slip. The faster I scrambled, the faster it gained speed on a light coat of frost that had formed on the lower deck overnight. Just before the ladder crashed to the deck, I bailed off to the side. I suffered a few bruises but no broken bones.

–Will Vance

**Editor's note:** Screw a cleat down on wooden surfaces—and never set up a ladder in frost!

### Where there's sawdust...

When I was installing cabinets in a small room at our church, I had to start by removing a windowsill. I fired up my circular saw, and after a few minutes, the room was completely clouded with sawdust. Suddenly the smoke alarm went off and automatically alerted the fire station. The church secretary called to explain the situation, but the firefighters came anyway. When they arrived, I had to tell the whole story. My face was redder than their truck! Next time I'll open a window and use an exhaust fan.

–Howard Martin

### A bit too close

Our new patio door looked great, but I wanted to add some security hardware. Easy enough, except that I drilled my first hole too close to the glass. When the drill bit hit the glass, the entire pane shattered into thousands of pieces. All I could do was watch in horror as the fragments fell like rain. I thought I would have to replace the entire door assembly. Fortunately, the store where I bought the doors just happened to have a set of doors with no frame. The manager gave me a deal. I also purchased a different security lock!

–Lloyd Lehn, Ph.D.

# COVE LIGHTING

*Soft light and rich drama for any room*

by **Mark Petersen, Associate Editor**

**B**ored with your living space? Cove lighting can add an understated elegance and breathe life into the most uninspiring room. We'll show you how we built ours using LED strip lighting and demonstrate how to wire it up. We'll also give you the lowdown on this type of lighting and share other cove and lighting options that might be a perfect fit for your budget and décor.

## Is cove lighting right for you?

You may think your ceiling looks good now, but when the cove lighting rakes across the surface, you may discover seams and nail pops you never knew existed. Stand on a ladder and shine a flashlight across the surface of the ceiling. If your ceiling is super ugly, you may want to abandon the idea or build a cove that washes the walls with light instead.

## Our cove lighting design

Our cove is built from crown molding and set 2 in. down from the ceiling. We installed the crown on top of a baseboard to create a wider space for the light, and tacked a small cove molding onto the bottom of the base to finish it (Figure A). We fastened the light strip to the wall so the lights would rake across the ceiling, and in order to maximize the light, we kept the strip as high as we could without it being visible from the ground.

Make a small mock-up and experiment with different positions for the cove and lights. Every room is different, and the cove we made may not be the best style for your room. Check out "Design Your Own" on p. 82.

### What it takes

**TIME: 3 hours (per 8-ft. shelf)**

**COST: $30**

**SKILL: Beginner**

**TOOLS: Table saw (or a circular saw and a straight-cut jig), drill, circular saw**

## Paint first

It's easier to paint all the cove parts before you install them. Touching up a few nail holes after installation is a lot easier than taping off entire walls. Painting the part of the wall that will be seen above the cove will help tie everything together. Choose either the color of the ceiling or the color of the cove. Lighter colors reflect more light, so paint the back of the cove components as well.

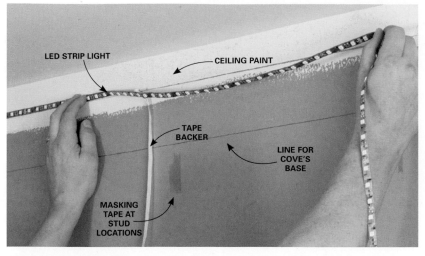

**LED STRIP LIGHT**

**CEILING PAINT**

**TAPE BACKER**

**LINE FOR COVE'S BASE**

**MASKING TAPE AT STUD LOCATIONS**

**1** **Stick on the strip lights first.** If you plan to attach the lights to the wall, it's easier to install the lights before you build the cove.

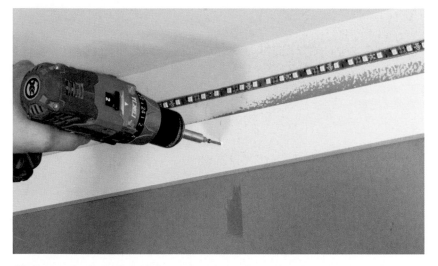

**2** **Fasten the base.** Drive 2-in. screws through the base into each stud. Sink the screws flush and place them high enough to be covered by the crown molding.

**BLOCK FLUSH WITH TOP OF BASE**

**3** **Attach the support blocks.** Cut blocks to support the crown molding. Fasten them into place with 2-in. 18-gauge brads. Mark them so you don't confuse which way is up.

## Mark the wall

Draw reference lines to indicate the bottom of the light strip and the bottom of the base. Don't worry whether the lines are level. Instead, measure down from the ceiling in several places and connect the dots to achieve a consistent distance between the cove and the ceiling. Years of settling can throw a ceiling out of level. A cove not in line with the ceiling will create a noticeably uneven gap. Save time by cutting a couple blocks of wood to use as marking gauges.

## Install the light strip

When you're placing the LED strip on the wall rather than inside the cove, it's easier to install most of it before the cove is up. Begin at the point of the room where the transformer will be installed. Leave the tape backer on the first few feet of the LED strip so it can be pulled away from the wall when it comes time to connect it to the transformer.

The tape on the back of the strip is super sticky. Once it's on the wall, it's tough to remove without pulling off the paint along with it. To start, press the strip to the wall in one spot, hold it there, pull the tape out a couple feet, and press it to the wall at that point as well (**Photo 1**). Do this a few times in a row, and check to see if it's straight. If it is, go back and press the

## Figure A
## Cove design

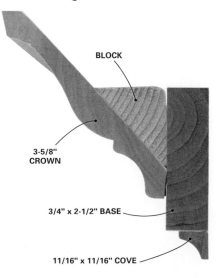

**BLOCK**

**3-5/8" CROWN**

**3/4" x 2-1/2" BASE**

**11/16" x 11/16" COVE**

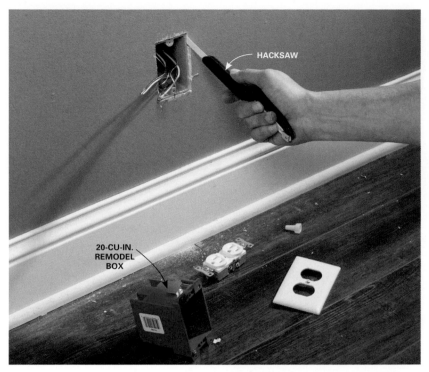

HACKSAW

20-CU.-IN. REMODEL BOX

**4** **Cut out the existing outlet box.** Pull the power for the lights from an existing box on an interior wall. Cut out the nails and remove the existing box. Replace it with a larger box to make room for the new wires. Removing the existing box will also simplify fishing in the new cables.

rest of the tape tight to the wall. Strip lights like these can be cut to size but only in certain intervals, usually 2 to 4 in. There will be clearly marked cutting lines on the strip.

## Build the cove

Secure the base to the wall with 2-in. screws into every stud (**Photo 2**). Self-tapping trim-head screws work great. Keep the screws high enough so they get covered by the crown. Depending on the size of the transformer, you may need to notch out a section of the base to make room so it's not visible from the floor (**Figure B**, p. 83).

Cut blocks to support the crown. One easy way to figure out the angle for the blocks is to hold a section of crown next to your table saw blade and adjust the blade to the same angle as the crown. Rip a 2x4 at that angle. Before installing the blocks, indicate with a marker which way is up. Stagger the blocks about every 16 in. or so, and fasten them with 2-in. 18-gauge brads (**Photo 3**).

Working with cove molding can be tricky, and in this article, we don't cover all the techniques for measuring, cutting and coping. For more information, search for "crown" at familyhandyman.com or go to the DIY University, mydiyuniversity.com, and take a course on crown molding.

Finish up by installing the small cove at the bottom. Fasten the cove with 1-1/4-in. brads angled up into the base (**Figure A**).

## Fish the new cables

Pick an existing outlet on an interior wall to pull power from so you don't have to deal with insulation when you fish the new cables. There's a good chance the existing electrical box may not be big enough for additional wires, so plan to replace it with a larger 20-cu.-in. remodel box (sometimes called an "old work" box). Removing the existing box also makes it easier to fish in the new

## Other lighting options

LED lighting isn't cheap. A system like we installed costs $9 to $14 per ft. for 22 ft., but less expensive options are available:

### Plug-in LED strip lighting

Home centers sell strip lighting with a prewired transformer. These would work well for shorter runs but need to be plugged into a receptacle hidden behind the cove. They can be wired to a regular switch, but the dimmer is located on the transformer, which won't be easily accessible. Cost: About $8 per ft. for 8 ft.

### LED rope lighting

The cheapest option by far is to install an LED rope light. Rope lights are not low-voltage, and they can be run long distances and dimmed with a regular dimmer. On the downside, they cannot be cut to size or split off in more than one direction and it's harder to direct the light. The light is about one-third as bright and may be a little blotchy depending on where it's placed. Rope lighting also requires a receptacle behind the cove. Cost: About $2.75 per ft. for 13 ft.

cables. Shut off the power, then poke a hacksaw blade on either side of the existing box to find which side the stud is on, and cut out the nails that hold it in place (**Photo 4**). If this kind of electrical work is intimidating, you could learn all you need to know by taking a few electrical courses from *The Family Handyman*'s DIY University (mydiyuniversity.com).

Use the remodel box as a template to cut a hole in the wall for the new light switch. There's no need to cut the hole next to the stud. Remodel boxes are held in place with wings that clamp onto the back of the drywall. Cut the hole for the switch box with a jab saw or utility knife at the same height as the other switches in the room. Fish the new cable from the switch box hole down and out through the existing hole below it (**Photo 5**). Put a slight bend on the cable so it hugs the back of the drywall, which makes it more easily accessible.

In this article, we used a transformer that is hardwired, so an outlet box wasn't necessary. We just had to drill a 3/4-in. hole in the drywall above the cove and run a cable down to the switch (**Figure B**, p. 83). There are other lighting options that may require an outlet above the cove. The procedure is the same as the next step; just be careful to place the

HOLE FOR THE NEW SWITCH

**Want to build your electrical skills before you tackle this project? Check out the "Electrical Basics" course at mydiyuniversity.com.**

**5 Fish the cable.** Cut a hole in the wall for the switch box, and run a cable down through the outlet box hole below it.

## Design your own

You don't have to build your cove exactly the way we did. Here are a couple alternative styles:

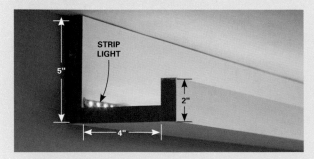

STRIP LIGHT

5"

4"

2"

### A simple cove

This easy-to-build, easy-to-install cove is made from 3/4-in. MDF ripped to size on a table saw. Countersink the screws. Fill the holes and touch up the seams with wood filler or surfacing compound.

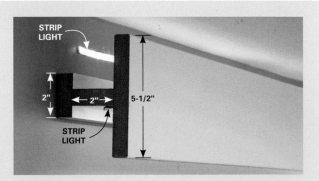

STRIP LIGHT

STRIP LIGHT

2"

2"

5-1/2"

### Valance style

Shine light both on the ceiling and down the wall with this valance-style cove. This one is made from straight 3/4-in. clear pine. The sharp edges of the valance have been softened with a router fitted with a 1/8-in. round-over bit. Install the T-shape base to the wall first and then fasten the valance to the base. Plan to buy twice as much lighting.

new outlet so it's completely hidden behind the cove. It will also help to install a recessed outlet box for the light's power cords.

Whether or not you install an outlet, leave a few feet of cable sticking out of the wall at the top. That will make it easier to wire the transformer. The excess cable can be pushed back into the wall cavity after the connections have been made.

Be generous and remove 10 in. of the cable's sheathing and strip the end of each wire before pulling them into the box. Make sure there's at least 1/4 in. of sheathing extending into the box and 3 in. of wire length extending beyond the face of the box (Photo 6). Don't overtighten the box onto the drywall or you could strip the screws or damage the portion of the drywall that holds it in place.

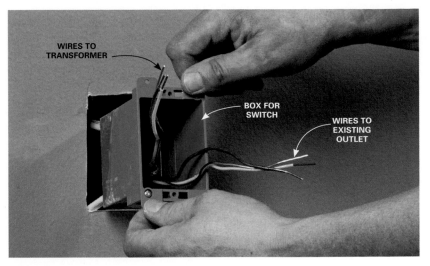

**6** **Install the new boxes.** Pull back the sheathing, strip the end of the wires, and pull wires into the remodel boxes before inserting them in the holes and clamping to the drywall.

## Choosing LED lighting

It's very important to think of low-voltage LED lighting as a "system." Transformers are available in 12-volt, 24-volt, magnetic, nonmagnetic, dimmable and nondimmable. The transformer, strip lighting and dimmer switch all need to be compatible.

You'll also have to consider how much lighting you need. Two transformers may be required for large rooms because each transformer can only provide power for a specified length of strip lighting. The lights at the end of a long run will be dimmer than the others if hooked up to an undersized transformer.

White light is most often used in commercial settings or outdoors, while warmer colors are preferred for homes. Brighter (more lumens) strip lighting costs more but is a good option. Strip lighting that is run at less than full power will last longer. Some lighting systems can last up to 50,000 hours.

Your best bet is to stop in at a lighting store. You could also call an online retailer, and explain the dimensions and layout of your room exactly.

## Figure B
## Wiring diagram

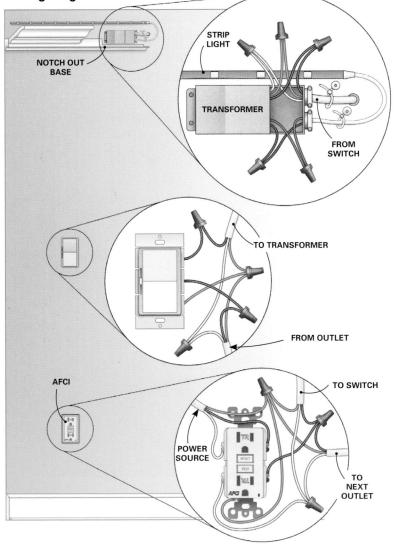

## Complete the connections

The existing receptacle will need to be replaced with one that is both tamper resistant (TR) and protected with an AFCI (arc fault circuit interrupter). AFCI interrupters protect homes from fire and are now required in most locations of the home. The AFCI has "line" and "load" terminals and cannot be connected with "pigtail" wires like the existing outlet may have been (Figure B).

It's extremely important for the dimmer switch to be compatible with the LED light strip you install. You need a "low-voltage" compatible switch, not an "LED" compatible switch. The wrong switch will cause the lights to flicker or not work at all. We used a Lutron switch recommended by the lighting supplier.

Transformers come in many shapes and sizes. Follow the wiring directions on your particular transformer. Once the transformer is connected, slide the excess cable back into the wall cavity and finish securing the strip light (Photo 7). Stick the transformer to the wall with Velcro strips if it won't stay in place, and install cable straps with drywall anchors.

## Install the crown

Fasten the bottom of the crown to the base every 16 in. with 1-1/4-in. 18-gauge brads. Secure the center of the crown to the blocks with 2-in. brads (Photo 8). To avoid nailing through the tops of the blocks, aim the gun straight in toward the wall rather than angling it up toward the ceiling. You don't want to poke yourself on an exposed brad or damage the light strip with a wayward shot.

All that's left is to flip the power back on and plan that dinner party so you can show off to all your friends.

Need help with trim projects? Check out our "Mastering Trim" course at mydiyuniversity.com.

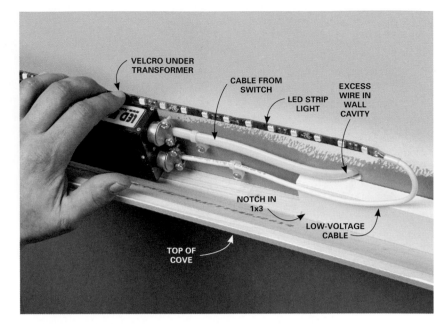

**7** **Connect the transformer.** Leave extra cable up top so the transformer can be pulled away from the cove to be wired. The excess cable can be pushed down into the wall cavity. Notch out the base so the transformer can sit lower in the cove.

**8** **Install the crown.** Tack the bottom of the crown to the base with 1-1/4-in. brads and to the blocks with 2-in. brads.

# GET SMART ABOUT
# SMOKE ALARMS

*They can save your life—but only if they're functioning properly, set up correctly, and adequately maintained*

by **Mark Petersen, Associate Editor**

**S**moke alarms may be the cheapest, easiest and most effective means for protecting your family and your home from a fire—as long as they're functioning. According to the National Fire Protection Association, three out of four in-home fire deaths occur in homes without a working smoke alarm. We've gathered some great information to help you avoid becoming a tragic statistic. You'll learn where to put your smoke alarms, how to maintain them and when to replace them. We'll also show you some cool new options available.

## Write down the install date

Smoke alarms should be changed every 10 years. Most manufacturers list the date a smoke alarm was made on the back. That's helpful information if you remember to look for it. Give yourself a proper reminder, and write the date you installed the alarm in big, bold letters on the base plate so you'll notice it every time you change the batteries.

### Three things you need to do
- Check smoke alarms once a month.
- Change batteries once a year.
- Replace alarms every 10 years.

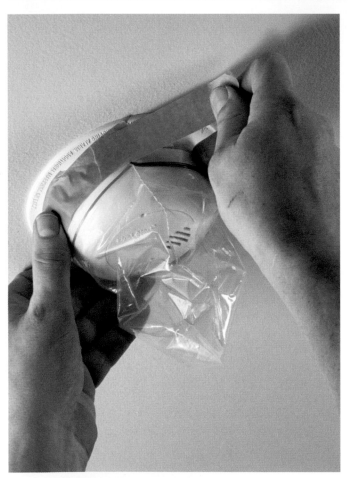

## Protect smoke alarms from dust

Excessive dust and paint overspray can wreak havoc with a smoke alarm's sensors. Before starting that messy remodeling project, temporarily cover or remove any alarm in harm's way. And if you are painting the ceiling, don't paint over the alarm—that will probably destroy it.

## Connect alarms wirelessly

If a fire triggers an alarm in the basement, will you be able to hear it from your second-story bedroom? Interconnected alarms provide better protection because if one goes off, they all go off, and early detection is key to safely escaping a house fire.

Smoke alarms in new homes are required to be hardwired and interconnected, but now you can get the same protection in your old house with smoke alarms like this one that speak to one another wirelessly. They cost more than a standard alarm, but they're a much cheaper option than installing new wires throughout the house.

## Save the instructions

Not all smoke alarms operate the same. Three chirps every minute may indicate "low batteries" for one unit and "end of life" for another. Save the instruction manual so you won't have to guess what your alarm is trying to tell you. Keep the manual in a place you'll remember. If you don't have a file or drawer for manuals, start one. If you have an unfinished basement, nail one up right next to the alarm itself.

## Where to install smoke alarms

- At least one on every level
- Bedrooms
- Outside of bedrooms (hallways, etc.)
- Kitchen (at least 10 ft. away from stove)
- Living rooms
- Basement
- Ceiling near the bottom of stairs leading to the next level

## Positioning is critical

- Walls, 4 in. to 12 in. from the ceiling
- Near the peak of a vaulted ceiling (within 4 in. to 3 ft.)
- In accessible areas (for easy battery replacement)
- Not in the garage
- Not in the attic
- Not in the utility/furnace room

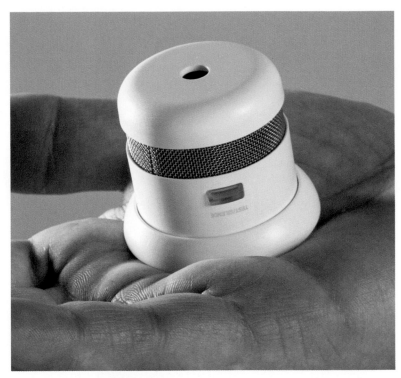

## Downsize if you prefer

If you don't like the look of smoke alarms, then smaller is better. Smoke alarms don't have to be big to be effective. This little guy from First Alert is called the Atom. It's a fraction of the size but performs just as well as its larger cousins. The Atom is available singly or in two-packs.

## Install strobe lights for the hearing impaired

People who can't hear an alarm need an alarm they can see. Some strobe alarms include smoke detection; they work great but cost two to three times as much as a regular smoke alarm. Less expensive models are available that are strobe lights only and need to be connected with a compatible smoke alarm.

## Keep the sensors clean

Dust can cause a smoke alarm to malfunction. Run a vacuum fitted with a soft brush over them every time you change the batteries, at least once a year.

## Buy a compatible replacement

Wiring up a smoke alarm is pretty easy, but connecting it in a harness plug is even easier. When you need to replace your hardwired alarms, take along an old one to the store. Save a bunch of time and buy new alarms that will accept the wiring harness on the old ones. That way all you have to do is plug in the new ones and maybe replace the base. Some new models come with wiring harness plug adapters, which makes matching easier. If your alarms are interconnected, never mix alarms made by different manufacturers.

## Wiring and connections: What's the difference?

### Hardwired

Hardwired smoke alarms operate off a home's electricity, but still rely on batteries as a backup if the power goes out.

### Battery-operated

These units work on battery power alone. Some newer models have batteries that last 10 years.

### Interconnected

Most hardwired alarms are interconnected, meaning if one goes off they all do. Battery-operated models can now be wirelessly interconnected (see "Connect Alarms Wirelessly" on p. 86).

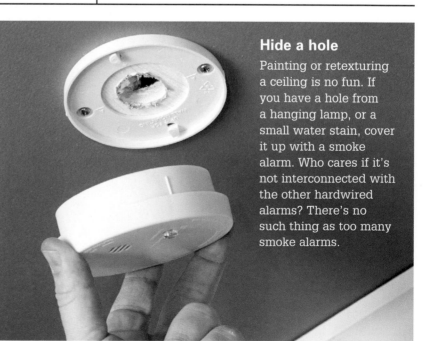

### Hide a hole

Painting or retexturing a ceiling is no fun. If you have a hole from a hanging lamp, or a small water stain, cover it up with a smoke alarm. Who cares if it's not interconnected with the other hardwired alarms? There's no such thing as too many smoke alarms.

## Quiet nuisance alarms

Kitchens are particularly susceptible to "nuisance" alarms. The horn on a typical alarm won't stop sounding until there's no more smoke to detect, which in a kitchen could take a while. Nuisance alarms are one of the main reasons people disable smoke alarms, and that's not a good idea, especially in the kitchen where the majority of fires start. Now there are smoke alarms available that have a "hush" button on them. Pushing it will kill the noise long enough for you to air out the room.

Some sensors are more sensitive than others, even if they're the same model. Before you go buy an alarm with a hush button, try swapping out the one in the kitchen with one from another part of the house.

**TEST BUTTON**

**HUSH BUTTON**

# GreatGoofs®

### Recessed lighting

During our recent bathroom makeover, my husband replaced the outdated bath fan. That meant turning off the power to the bathroom, so he hung his new cordless LED work light between the joists and got to work. After installing the new fan box, he put up new drywall, taped, primed and painted. The bathroom looked fantastic.

His next project was in the basement and one day I found him searching frantically for the work light. So I asked him the standard question: "Where did you use it last?" I could see the "LED" flash on in his head. He had left it in the ceiling above the drywall!

–Julie and Scott Ortman

# Tips for Fussy Painters

## STIR IT UP

I buy a lot of quart cans of paint, and eventually the pigments settle to the bottom of the can. To speed up the mixing, I use a paint can opener chucked into my drill. I cut and straightened the bent prying end and ground it flush with the shaft. Now whenever I have paint that needs mixing, I tighten the modified opener in the drill chuck and stir away!

–Ron Nitchie

## SKIM-COAT BAD WALLS—ESPECIALLY FOR DARKER COLORS

Lighter colors are more forgiving in terms of showing wall imperfections; darker colors show more detail. If you're set on using a

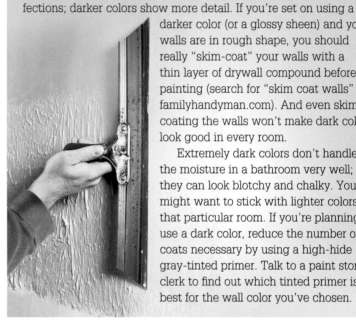

darker color (or a glossy sheen) and your walls are in rough shape, you should really "skim-coat" your walls with a thin layer of drywall compound before painting (search for "skim coat walls" at familyhandyman.com). And even skim-coating the walls won't make dark colors look good in every room.

Extremely dark colors don't handle the moisture in a bathroom very well; they can look blotchy and chalky. You might want to stick with lighter colors in that particular room. If you're planning to use a dark color, reduce the number of coats necessary by using a high-hide gray-tinted primer. Talk to a paint store clerk to find out which tinted primer is best for the wall color you've chosen.

## A PAINTBRUSH'S BEST FRIEND

Keep a jug of citrus-based stripper with your painting supplies. It works well for stripping furniture, but is also great for cleaning paint

and varnish from your good brushes. After a quick soak in the stripper, the dry paint and varnish loosen up and wash right out. This babying helps keep your high-quality brushes going a long time. A nice bonus: Unlike other strippers, citrus-based stripper smells great!

# SPRAY-PAINT PERFECTION

## by Gary Wentz, Senior Editor

You've most likely never heard of Bonnie Seymour, but she did you a huge favor. In 1949, she suggested that her husband try putting paint in an aerosol can. He did, it worked, and painting got a whole lot easier. Here are some key tips for success with Bonnie's brilliant invention.

### Nozzle cleaner

When you're done spray-painting, pour a couple ounces of paint thinner into a small container. Remove the nozzle, shake it in the covered container, then reattach the nozzle to the can.

### Plastic paint works!

Conventional spray paints just won't stick to plastic. Now paint manufacturers offer paint just for that application. These paints don't just stick; they fuse with the plastic surface to form a super-strong bond. Krylon Fusion for Plastic and Rust-Oleum 2x are two common brands.

### Overlap 50 percent

If you overlap just a little, you'll get stripes of heavy and light coverage. So instead, aim for 50 percent overlap, with each pass overlapping the previous pass about halfway.

# Tips for Fussy Painters

## SPRAY-PAINT PERFECTION continued

Do this

Not this

### Don't swing an arc

It's the most natural motion for your arm, but swinging gives you heavy coverage in the middle of the project and light coverage at the ends. So move the can parallel to the surface, concentrating on straight, steady motion.

### Two cans are faster— and sometimes better

Spray-painting a big surface isn't just slow; it can also lead to texture trouble. In warm, dry conditions, spray paint dries almost instantly, so very light "overspray" may land on nearby paint that's almost dry. When that happens, you get inconsistencies in the surface texture.

Here's how to get paint onto the project faster and get a consistent finish: Just hold a can in each hand. If you move each hand independently, one hand will stray off course. But if you hold the cans together, creating a single spray pattern, it's easy to stay on track. Keep in mind that this trick can lead to drips on vertical surfaces. Make faster passes and try a practice run on a scrap of cardboard.

## Light coats and patience prevent runs

The only sure way to avoid runs on a vertical surface is to spray on a light coat and give it a little drying time before the next. That's hard to do if you spray the surfaces in random order, but easy if you have a strategy. Start by coating each vertical surface. Spray lightly to avoid runs. Then hit the horizontal areas before starting the second round. Repeat each round in the same order. That way, each surface will get maximum drying time before you return to it. If any vertical surface still looks wet, stop and remember this: An extra five minutes of drying time now is better than sanding out runs and respraying later.

### Elevate your work

Don't set your project directly on a workbench or newspaper; the paint will glue it to the work surface. The best way to prop up wood furniture is to drive screws into the legs.

### Wear a respirator

Spray cans fill the air with fine mist and solvents. That's bad—really bad—for your lungs and nervous system. Working outside is the most effective way to avoid inhaling fumes, but a breeze may blow away most of the paint before it reaches the surface, while bugs and falling leaves wreck the finish. So it's often best to work indoors with doors and windows open. Most important, wear an organic vapor respirator ($25 at home centers). It will protect you, and you won't even smell the fumes.

### Get a handle

If you've ever sprayed a project that required several cans of paint, you already know about finger strain. For less than five bucks, a trigger handle not only prevents the pain but also gives you better control of the can.

# Tips for Fussy Painters

### Smooth a rough surface

If you want a smooth finish, pick the right primer. Some are formulated to fill pockmarks and scratches. Plus, they're sandable so you can smooth the surface before top-coating with paint.

### Spin and spray

On some projects, you can walk miles circling the item to spray all the surfaces. Instead, pick up a lazy Susan at a discount store and save some legwork.

### Start before; stop after

Spray nozzles often spit out a few large droplets when you start spraying and again when you stop. To keep sputter spatter off your project, pull the trigger before you're over the target and release the trigger after you're past the edge.

## GreatGoofs®

### A horse of a different color....

Last summer, after much debate about color selection, we were finally ready to paint our kitchen cabinets. I removed all the doors and hardware, and since it was a nice day, I decided to paint the doors and drawer fronts out by the driveway while my wife worked on the cabinet frames inside. After a couple of hours, my wife came to check the progress. "That's not the right color!" she shrieked. I had mistakenly grabbed one of the quarts we had rejected from our testing and was nearly halfway through painting the doors. "Well, it's only paint," I told her as she handed me the right color. Sheepishly I finished up the next day— after double-checking with her first!

–Dan Doshan

# 2 Electrical & High-Tech

# ADD
# KITCHEN OUTLETS

## Run new wiring without wrecking walls

by **Mark Petersen, Associate Editor**

Not that long ago, the average kitchen counter was home to a toaster, coffeemaker and maybe a blender, but things have changed. We now have juicers, bread makers, TVs, gourmet pizza ovens, computers and charging stations for a half-dozen mobile gadgets. It's not surprising that it's getting harder to find an available outlet to plug in all that stuff. Extension cords and power strips are unsightly and can be dangerous. The only real solution is to add more outlets.

### What it takes

**Time:** About 4 hours

**Cost:** About $80

**Tools:** Screwdriver, wire stripper/cutter, jab saw, hacksaw, drill, 1-in. spade bit

**Skill level:** Intermediate

We tracked down an electrician who, not surprisingly, adds kitchen outlets all the time. He showed us how he adds an outlet to a kitchen backsplash by running conduit through the back of the cabinets. This method is fast,

inexpensive, super simple, and best of all, doesn't require a whole bunch of wall repairs or painting. This article shows how to install one new outlet, but you can add several by following similar steps.

### Before you get started

Kitchens need to be on a dedicated 20-amp circuit and require 12-gauge wire. Today, 12-gauge wire is wrapped in a yellow sheath, but your old cable may be white. New circuits in kitchens need both arc fault and ground fault circuit interruption (AFCI, GFCI) protection. In this article,

### MEET AN EXPERT

**Tim Johnson works for Norske Electric in Savage, MN. He works on both commercial and residential projects, and even spent a few years wiring wind turbines 265 ft. in the air!**

we're adding an outlet to a kitchen that already has GFCI protection, which has been required for many years. If your kitchen is not on a 20-amp circuit, or doesn't have GFCI protection, you'll have to install a new circuit or circuit breaker. For more information, go to familyhandyman.com and search for "new circuit." Also, discuss your project with your local electrical inspector when you apply for a permit. If adding a circuit still seems above your pay grade, then call an electrician.

## Remove the existing box

The first step is to shut off the power. If your breaker panel is poorly labeled, plug a radio into the outlet you plan to pull power from, and start shutting down breakers until the music stops. There may also be wires from other circuits in the junction box, so probe the box with a noncontact voltage tester ($10 at home centers) before you disconnect any wires. Cover the ends of the existing wires with wire nuts as an additional precaution. **Caution:** If you discover aluminum wiring, call in a licensed electrician who is certified to work with it. This wiring is dull gray, not the dull orange that is characteristic of copper wire.

It's easier to fish the new cable if you remove the existing box in the wall. Fiberglass boxes can be broken out with a hammer and a chisel or sturdy screwdriver. It's best to cut the nails on plastic boxes with a hacksaw. Start by probing with a screwdriver to find which side of the box the stud is on. Then pry the screwdriver between the stud and the box to make room for the saw blade (**Photo 1**).

Metal boxes are difficult to remove without creating some drywall repairs. Before you attempt it, see if you can fish the cable down through the existing metal box into the hole in the cabinet.

## Cut a hole for the new box

There's no rule mandating the height of the new box, so just match the height of the existing one. The code for kitchens states that there must be an outlet within a 2-ft. reach from anywhere along the countertop, excluding those areas where there's a sink or stovetop. This means there should be an outlet every 4 ft. If you're just adding one outlet, you probably won't be subject to this rule, but if you're

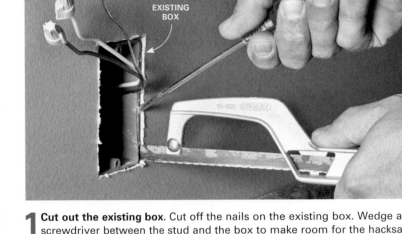

**1** **Cut out the existing box.** Cut off the nails on the existing box. Wedge a screwdriver between the stud and the box to make room for the hacksaw blade.

**2** **Cut a hole for the new box.** Trace the outline of the box on the wall at the same height as the existing box, and cut out the drywall with a jab saw. Keep the hole an inch or more away from any studs.

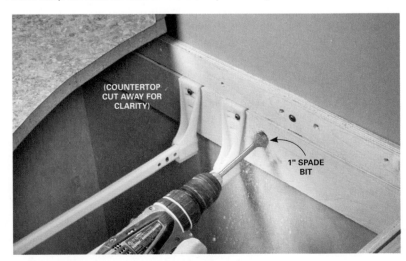

**3** **Drill holes for the cable.** Drill 1-in. holes through the back of the cabinet and drywall. Beware of hidden cable, ducts and pipes; when the bit breaks through the drywall, stop.

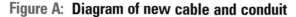

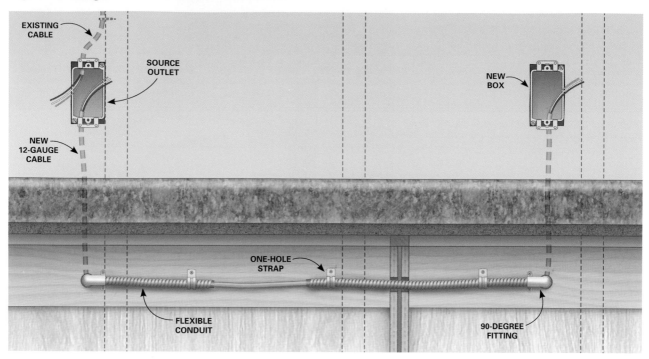

remodeling the entire kitchen, you probably will. It's best to check with your local electrical inspector.

Before cutting the hole, go to the floor below and, if possible, check to see if there are any pipes or ducts running through the wall you plan to cut into. Or go outside and see if any vents are sticking through the roof in that area. If you're not sure, make a small exploratory hole that can be easily patched.

The new box does not have to be right up against a stud. In fact, it's easier to install if it's not. Trace around the new box, and cut the hole with a jab saw (**Photo 2**). Don't shove the saw all the way into the wall cavity, just in case there's a wire or pipe hidden behind the wall.

If your backsplash is tiled, use a rotary tool fitted with a diamond tile-cutting bit. Set the depth of the bit so it cuts through the tile only. Finish the cut with a jab saw. Whenever possible, use the grout lines for two sides of the hole because cutting will be much easier. Drill starter holes in two opposite corners with a glass-and-tile drill bit.

## Drill the holes and fish the new cable

Empty the cabinets, and pull out the drawers to get better access. Lying on your back halfway inside a cabinet is not the most comfortable position, so throw down a couple of couch cushions before you get started. And be sure to wear eye protection. Drill a 1-in. hole for the new cable in the cabinet—near the top (**Photo 3**). Don't let the bit travel too far into the wall cavity, or the insulation may twist up like cotton candy on a stick and make it difficult to pull the bit back out. Drill through the sides of the cabinet near the back for the conduit to pass through.

Measure the distance the new cable will travel both horizontally and vertically, and then add several feet before cutting it—it's better to throw out a few feet of cable than end up short.

Shove one end of the cable through the hole up toward the box hole (**Photo 4**). It doesn't matter if you start at the new or the existing outlet side. Our expert puts a slight bend on the end of the cable so it hugs the back of the drywall. This will help keep it from getting hung up on insulation.

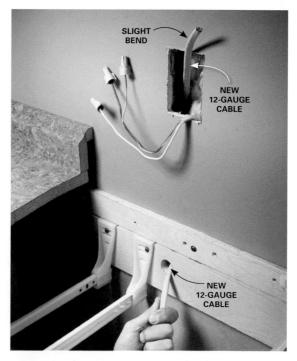

**4** **Fish in the new cable.** Slide the new cable through the drilled hole, then up and out through the electrical box hole. Put a slight bend on the cable so it hugs the wall and doesn't get hung up on insulation.

## Install the conduit

Measure the length of the flexible conduit by sliding a tape measure through the holes in the side of the cabinet. Have a buddy hold the end of the tape in the hole or secure it with masking tape (**Photo 5**).

Cut the conduit to length and attach a bushing or fitting to the side you plan to push the wire through. Bushings and fittings protect the cable from getting damaged on the sharp edges of the conduit. Our expert likes the 90-degree fitting because it results in a nice "finished" look with no cable exposed. A standard bushing will result in a small section of exposed cable at the ends, but that's acceptable.

Push the cable through the conduit so it sticks out a few inches on the other side, and then slide the conduit through the holes in the side of the cabinets (**Photo 6**).

Once the conduit is through, install the bushing/fitting on the other end of the conduit, and pull the cable the rest of the way through the conduit.

Push the cable up through the second hole in the wall the same way you did the first, and then secure both sides of the conduit with straps near the hole (**Photo 7**). If the conduit travels more than halfway across the length of the cabinet, add another strap halfway between the end of the conduit and the hole in the cabinet.

## Install the new boxes

It's easier to remove the cable sheathing before installing the new "old work" boxes, but make sure to leave enough on the cable so about an inch of sheathing pokes into the box. Once the sheathing is removed, pull the wires into the box, slide it into place and secure it (**Photo 8**).

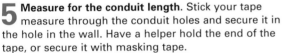

**5** **Measure for the conduit length.** Stick your tape measure through the conduit holes and secure it in the hole in the wall. Have a helper hold the end of the tape, or secure it with masking tape.

**6** **Slide the conduit into place.** Feed the new cable through the conduit, and then push the conduit through the 1-in. holes drilled into the sides of the cabinet.

### Planning to tile?

If you plan to tile your backsplash, adding outlets is even easier than we show in Photos 1 – 9. Just run the new cable through a channel in the drywall. A channel is easier because you don't have to empty out the cabinets or mess around with conduit, and the wall can be quickly patched. Make the channel with a jab saw. Cut it a bit higher than the boxes so there's room to bend the cable down into the hole. Install a steel nail plate to protect the cable from future nails or screws.

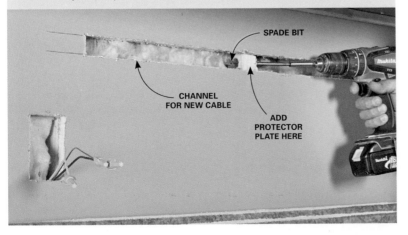

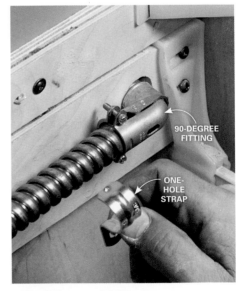

**7** **Secure the conduit.** Hold the conduit in place with straps. Place straps near the 90-degree fittings and one more in the middle if the conduit travels more than halfway across the length of the cabinet.

There are several kinds of "old work" boxes, sometimes called "remodel boxes." "Old work" boxes don't get nailed to a stud but instead are secured with wings that clamp onto the drywall as a screw is turned. The type shown here is made from sturdy fiberglass and is available at most home centers.

In this wiring scenario, five individual 12-gauge wires are occupying the source box (all grounds count as one), so the 18-cu.-in. box shown here is large enough to handle all the wires and receptacle without crowding. You may need a larger box if there are six or more wires.

### Wire the new receptacles

All outlets in a kitchen require AFCI and GFCI protection. In this example, we're working with a kitchen circuit that already has GFCI protection at some point upstream, which means that we only need to install a receptacle that has AFCI protection (for more details, see "Dual-Function Breakers," below). One properly wired AFCI outlet will protect all the other 20-amp outlets downstream. Virtually all newly installed receptacles need to be tamper resistant, so look for the "TR" before you buy.

All the line (incoming) and load (outgoing) wires need to be in their proper places (**Figure B**). If you've wired receptacles before, you may have used "pigtails" to

## Figure B: Wiring diagram for AFCI receptacle

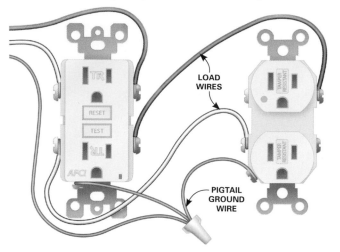

LOAD WIRES

PIGTAIL GROUND WIRE

connect them. That's where the hot, neutral and ground wires run continuously with small pigtail wires pulled off and connected to each receptacle. Using pigtails is a great way to ensure that if one receptacle goes bad, the rest downstream stay operational. But when wiring GFCI and AFCI receptacles, only the ground wires can be hooked up with pigtails; otherwise the outlets downstream will not be protected (**Photo 9**).

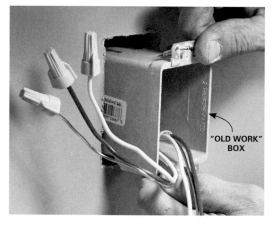

**8 Install the new boxes.** Cut the sheathing off the cable before pulling the wires through the remodel boxes. Slide the boxes into the holes and fasten them to the drywall.

"OLD WORK" BOX

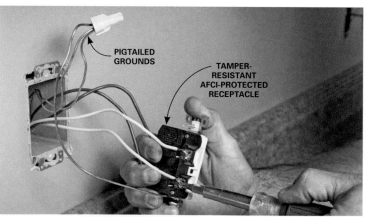

PIGTAILED GROUNDS

TAMPER-RESISTANT AFCI-PROTECTED RECEPTACLE

**9 Wire the receptacles.** Install a tamper-resistant AFCI receptacle at the source outlet as shown in Figure A. The outlets downstream can be standard tamper-resistant receptacles.

## Dual-function breakers

A ground fault occurs when electricity travels outside its intended path (wires), and seeks the shortest route to the ground (you). Water is often the cause of a ground fault. That's why, for many years, kitchens, baths and outdoor outlets required GFCI protection, which shuts down the power before injuries occur.

An arc fault occurs when electricity jumps from its proper conductor to an unintentional conductor. Common causes are pinched wires, frayed or cracked wire insulation, and wires damaged by screws, nails or staples. An arc fault can cause a fire, which is why AFCI protection has recently been mandated by the new electrical code for most of the house.

Until recently, the only way to achieve both GFCI and AFCI protection on the same circuit would be to install one form of protection in the panel and the other in the first available receptacle. Now there are dual-function breakers available that offer both types of protection. The 20-amp breaker shown here costs about $50 at home centers. Look for dual-function outlets in the near future.

# GET **FASTER BACKUPS**
# WITH YOUR DESKTOP COMPUTER

Make your old machine play nice with a fast, new backup hard drive

by **Rick Muscoplat, Contributing Editor**

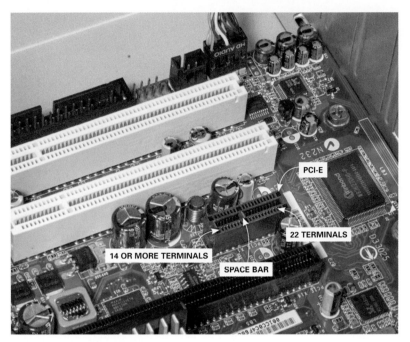

**1 Identify a PCI-E slot.** Find an empty slot and count the number of terminals in front of the spacer bar. If the slot has 22 terminals, a space bar and is followed by at least 14 more terminals, it's a PCI-E slot.

**If** you buy a new backup hard drive, chances are it'll have an ultra-fast USB 3.0 interface. But if you plug it into your old desktop PC with a USB 2.0 port, it'll run at half speed and your backups will take longer. The good news is you can probably upgrade your desktop to USB 3.0 for about $30. Here's how.

Open the computer and look for an empty PCI-E slot (**Photo 1**). If you find one, buy a USB 3.0 PCI-E peripheral card (one choice is the Anker Uspeed PCI-E to USB 3.0 with 20-pin connector; about $20 online). If you want to access the high-speed ports from the front of the machine and have an empty drive bay, buy a USB 3.0 front panel (such as the Anker 3.5 inch Front Panel 2 USB 3.0 Ports; about $10 online).

Install the PCI-E card (**Photo 2**) and the USB front panel (**Photo 3**). Then fire up the computer and install the software drivers that came with the card.

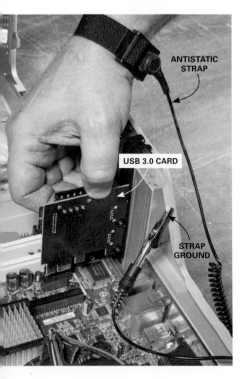

**2 Install the USB 3.0 card.** Connect an anti-static strap between your wrist and the computer chassis. Then remove the metal slot "blank" from the rear of the case. Next, slide the USB 3.0 card into the slot and secure the metal card bracket to the chassis with a screw.

**3 Install the front panel.** Pop out the plastic filler plate from the front of the computer. Then slide in the new panel and secure with screws. Connect the cables to the USB 3.0 card and reinstall the side cover.

# WORKING WITH
# METAL-CLAD CABLE

A pro shares some tips and hints

by **Mark Petersen, Associate Editor**

When electrical wiring needs extra protection, metal-clad (MC) cable is a great solution, and is often required by electrical codes. MC cable is easier to work with than rigid conduit, and it too offers protection from fire, vibration, gnawing pests and physical harm in general. The wiring methods are mostly the same as for nonmetallic-sheathed cable (such as Romex), so we've focused on how to work with the cable itself. These tips aside, you still need to consult your electrical inspector about whether you can, or should, use MC cable on your next project.

### What is MC cable?

Metal-clad cable comes in several varieties, but the type you'll find at most home centers is three insulated wires (two circuit conductors and a green equipment grounding conductor) protected by a flexible armor usually made from aluminum. MC cable is identified by the gauge of the wire, not the diameter of the armor. The most common sizes are 14 gauge, 12 gauge and 10 gauge.

## Metal boxes only!

Plastic or fiberglass boxes aren't designed to be used with MC cable. Even if you're able to rig up a connection to a plastic box, you *will* fail the electrical inspection. Make sure the metal box has knockout holes located where you need them, and don't rely on the spurs on the bracket to hold the box in place—add a couple screws as well.

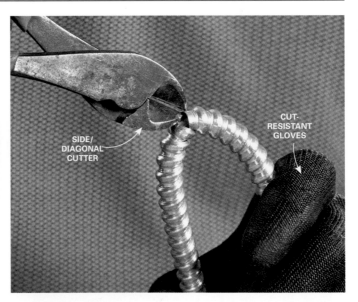

## Use FMC for multiple circuits

Flexible metal conduit (FMC) is commonly called "Greenfield." The main difference between MC cable and FMC is that FMC doesn't have the insulated wires preinstalled; you have to pull them through instead. This requires more work but gives you the option of pulling, and protecting, more than one circuit in the same conduit. It also allows you to add wires in the future, something you can't do with MC cable. FMC is identified by its diameter. The most common sizes are 1/2 in., 3/4 in. and 1 in.

## Use 'liquid-tight' outdoors

Install liquid-tight flexible conduit wherever the wiring will be subjected to wet conditions. Liquid-tight flexible conduit is water resistant and is available without the wires installed and in short lengths (whips) that come prewired. There are two common types: liquid-tight flexible metal conduit and liquid-tight flexible nonmetallic conduit. Ask your electrical inspector which is approved for your project.

## Bend and cut

If you just have one or two cuts to make and don't want to invest in a cutting tool (p. 105), bend the MC cable sharply until the armor pops open, and then use that opening to start the cut with a side/diagonal cutter. You only need to cut through one section in the armor. This method will leave a jagged edge that will need to be trimmed after the armor is separated. The cut ends of MC cable are sharp, so be sure to wear cut-resistant gloves.

## Save time with a whip

Fixture, appliance and air conditioner whips are short sections of cable or flexible conduit that have not only the wires installed, but the connectors as well. Whips cost a lot more per foot but are a huge time-saver because you don't need to mess around with cutting the armor. Whips are usually available in 4-ft., 6-ft. and 8-ft. lengths.

## Twist and pull

When removing a section of armor to expose the wires, twist the short end of the cable counterclockwise as you pull the cable apart. If it feels like it's taking too much pressure to separate, double-check that the cut went all the way through the armor. Don't pull too hard or the armor could separate farther down the line. That's a problem because damaged armor shouldn't be installed, and you'd have to start over.

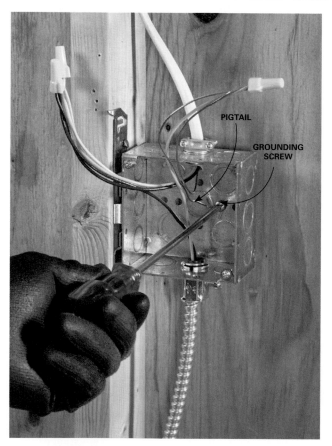

PIGTAIL

GROUNDING SCREW

## Ground the box

Whether it's the first box in a line or the only one on an entire circuit, every metal box needs to be grounded. Grounding a box is as simple as connecting the incoming and outgoing ground wires to a pigtail, and then connecting the pigtail to the box with a grounding screw.

SINGLE-HOLE STRAP

## Screw the straps

Single-hole straps make for easy and sturdy supports. Avoid connecting them with nails or you'll risk smashing the cable with a hammer. Install a strap within 12 in. of each box. All subsequent straps need to be within 6 ft. of each other. When you're routing cables, be sure to avoid sharp bends that could damage the cable sheath or the conductors.

### A rotary cutter works best

Cutting the armor without damaging the wires is probably the trickiest part of working with MC cable. The best method is to use an armored cable rotary cutter (about $30 at home centers). This tool uses a small cutting wheel powered by a hand crank and will cut only through the armor, leaving the wires undamaged every time. Apply firm pressure to the handle, but don't squeeze too hard or the crank will be difficult to turn.

ARMORED CABLE ROTARY CUTTER

CUTTING WHEEL

### Install the connector into the box first

You *can* attach a connector to MC cable, then join it to the box, but it's easier to mount the connector on the box before feeding the wires through. Connectors like the one shown here (Speed-Lock is one well-known brand) are popular with electricians because the one screw secures both the connector to the box and the MC cable to the connector. There should be a minimum of 6 to 8 in. of exposed wire inside the box.

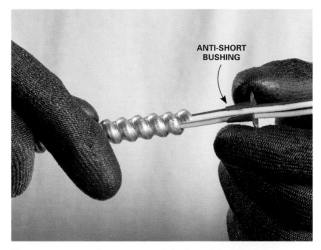

ANTI-SHORT BUSHING

### Protect conductors with bushings

Plastic anti-short bushings protect the wires from being damaged by the sharp edge of the armor when the cable gets clamped down into a connector. And even if the connector you're using has its own bushing, make sure to add a bushing like the one shown here. It's a cheap and easy way to achieve an extra level of protection. Some manufacturers supply a bag of anti-short bushings when you buy the cable, or you can buy a pack for a couple bucks.

**MEET AN EXPERT**

Rune Eriksen installed miles of MC cable during his 31 years as an electrician at the VA Medical Center in Minneapolis.

ELECTRICAL & HIGH-TECH

# HandyHints®

## CORD CLIP

A paper binder clip works great to manage small electrical cords. I use one to keep my long headphone cords neatly wound and tangle-free.

–Michael Johnson

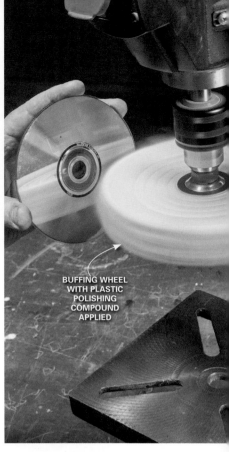

BUFFING WHEEL WITH PLASTIC POLISHING COMPOUND APPLIED

**Buff the scratches**
Press the disc against the buffing wheel and rotate it in a circle, not toward or away from the center.

## NEW LAPTOP FOOT

While typing on my laptop keyboard, I noticed that it rocked slightly. I checked out the bottom and saw that one of the hard rubber feet was missing. Not one to spend a lot on computer repairs, I grabbed my caulk gun and a tube of black silicone and squeezed out a small amount at the missing foot location. Then I leveled the caulk with a toothpick and let it set overnight. The next day, the silicone was hard and worked perfectly. A couple months later, it's still attached!

–Charles Crocker

## WIRE CHASE

I decided to hang my flat screen TV on the wall and place the game components below on a low table. The only downside was the bunch of unsightly cords coming down the wall. To hide the cords, I built a chase from plywood and painted it to match my walls. I used 1/2-in. plywood for the back and sides and hardboard for the front panel.

–John Fontaine

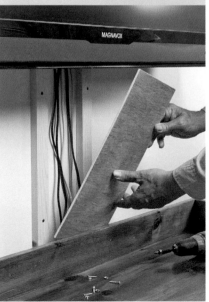

## FIX A SCRATCHED DVD

Just sliding a DVD across a table is enough to scratch it. You can usually remove light scratches by swirling cream plastic polish around the disc with a micro-fiber cloth. However, if the disc still doesn't play and you own a drill press, you've got one more chance to save it. Pick up a buffing wheel and bar compound (one example is the Assorted Polishing and Buffing Kit, No. 67259; $8 at Harbor Freight).

Chuck up the buffing wheel and set the drill press to its highest speed. Start the drill press and rub the least abrasive compound onto the wheel. Then lightly buff the disc as shown. Wash the disc with dishwashing detergent and dry it. Then test the disc. If it works, you're all set for movie night. If not, you gave it your best shot.

–TFH Editors

# ROUGH-IN
## WIRING

Proper rough-in makes inspection easy

by **Mark Petersen, Associate Editor**

**W**hether your project is finishing a garage or a basement or building an addition, it's important to get the rough-in wiring done right the first time. We talked with several pros and got advice on drilling holes, installing boxes and pulling cable. With these tips in hand, you'll work faster, avoid disasters down the road and put a smile on the face of your electrical inspector.

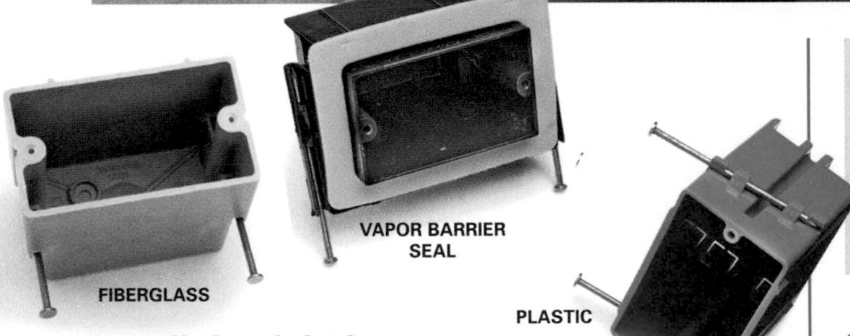

**FIBERGLASS**

**VAPOR BARRIER SEAL**

**PLASTIC**

## Use the proper cable

| Wire gauge | Amps | Uses |
| --- | --- | --- |
| 14 | 15 | Common living spaces |
| 12 | 20 | Kitchens and bathrooms |
| 10 and up | 40-plus | Large appliances |

## Install the right box

Either plastic or fiberglass boxes will do the job, and each is completely code compliant. Some electricians prefer fiberglass ones because they're tougher, but others prefer the plastic ones because they're cheaper.

Whatever style you choose, pick box sizes that have a volume of at least 20 cu. in. Dimmer switches and other smart devices are common these days and take up more room in the box than the simple devices of the past. Plus, bigger boxes just make wiring easier, especially if they're crammed full of wires and connectors. Boxes destined for exterior walls and ceilings must be equipped with a vapor barrier seal.

## Use special staples for stacking cable

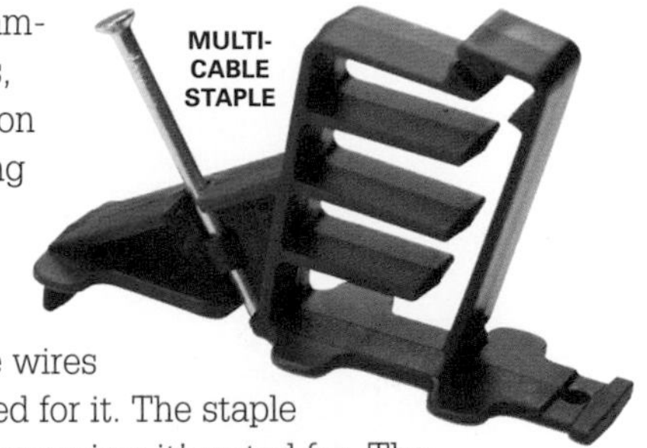

Staples (and drilled holes) need to be at least 1-1/4 in. away from the edge of a framing member. In some cases, that means stacking wires on top of one another and using one staple to secure them. Most standard staples can handle two wires. Never install staples over multiple wires unless the staple is approved for it. The staple package should list how many wires it's rated for. The staple shown here is good for up to four wires.

**MULTI-CABLE STAPLE**

## Auger bits and angle drills work best

A 3/4-in. spade bit will work OK for drilling the holes, but auger bits drill faster and require less effort. Choose a bit like this Milwaukee ship auger bit that will chew through nails. It's easier to drill straight holes through the studs with a right-angle drill. Right-angle drills rent for $25 per day, or you could buy an angle attachment for your own drill for just a bit more.

## Drill straight, aligned holes

Keep the holes straight and at the same height. Pulling cable through several consecutive holes drilled at different angles or heights is difficult because the cable will snag on the sharp edges and fight you the whole time! Straight, aligned holes make pulling cable a breeze.

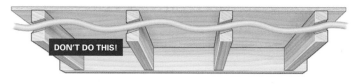
DON'T DO THIS!

## Ceiling fans need special boxes

A regular round electrical box isn't sturdy enough to support the weight and absorb the vibration of a ceiling fan. Special ceiling fan electrical boxes usually have an additional brace to stabilize the spinning fan. These types of boxes are a heck of a lot easier to install before the drywall is up, so even if there's a small chance that you'll replace the light with a fan sometime down the road, avoid headaches and spend a couple extra bucks on a fan box.

FAN BOX

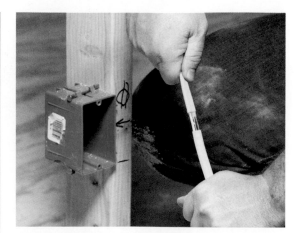

## Strip off the sheathing

It's easier to strip the sheathing from the cables out in the open before they get shoved into the box. Remember to leave at least 1/4 in. of sheathing visible inside the box. If there's only one cable entering a box, install it through the knockout farthest from the stud.

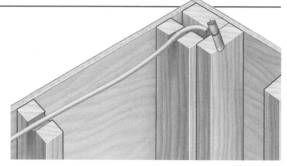

## Angle into corners

There's often not enough room to drill straight into an inside corner from both sides. This is one time when you'll have to drill into the stud at an angle. Fishing the cable through will be easier if you keep the holes at the same height. Sometimes it's not possible to fish a cable through a corner. In those cases, drill up through the double top plate of the wall, and route the cable up over the corner and down the other side.

DON'T DO THIS!
GARAGE WALL

## Avoid exposed open spaces

The electrical code doesn't allow exposed wires in open spaces. When cable is installed in exposed areas such as a garage or an unfinished basement, it needs to closely follow the framing members. Cables that span stud spaces or ceiling joists are in constant jeopardy of nicks and cuts, and it's too tempting to use the cables for tucking, hanging or trapping all kinds of toys and tools.

## Straighten before pulling

Pulling cable through holes in framing is a lot easier if you straighten out the cable first. Walk along the length of the cable, straightening it between your thumb and forefinger as you go.

Once you've pulled the cable through the holes, push it back a bit to leave a small amount of slack. This is handy insurance in case you cut the cable a little short and need extra length, and it also allows other tradespeople a little slack to push your cable out of the way of plumbing pipes or ductwork.

## Don't overbend the cable

Sharp bends in cable can damage the sheathing and the conductors, which could lead to a fire hazard. Cable should not be bent at more than a 2-1/2-in. radius (about the same as a soda can). Avoid overbending it by drilling holes 8 to 12 in. above (or below) the boxes so the cable can sweep down or up into the boxes. And never pull hard on cable that has a staple on the other end.

DON'T DO THIS!

## Install plates before pulling wire

CABLE PROTECTION PLATE

Electrical cables need to be set back 1-1/4 in. or more from the edge of a stud or wood-framing member to protect cables from wayward nails and screws. Install steel cable-protection plates over holes drilled closer to the edge. Keep several plates in your pouch while you're drilling and install them right away so you don't forget.

## Pull cable from the middle

Don't rip open the plastic wrapper on your spool of cable. Instead, lift a handful of coils from the center of the roll and lay them on the floor. Four loops equals about 12 ft. Following this method helps reduce tangles and keeps the cable contained for easier transporting and storage. If you plan to use all of the cable, just neatly unroll the entire spool across the floor (as if it were a garden hose) to avoid kinks, curls or twists in the cable.

BOTTOM OF BOX

## Mark box locations first

Before you drill any holes, go around the room and mark the locations for all the outlet, light and switch boxes. Install the switches 42 in. up from the floor (to the bottom of the box), and the outlets up 12 to 16 in. These are typical heights used by pros. But actually, there's no height requirement. The important thing is to make all box heights consistent. Many pros use the length of their hammer as a guide to mark the location for the bottom of outlets.

The National Electrical Code requires outlets to be spaced within 12 ft. of each other. The idea is that every appliance, lamp or device is always within 6 ft. of an outlet.

**SPECIAL SECTION**

# What Every Homeowner Must Know

## (but most don't!)

by **Gary Wentz, Senior Editor**

For more than 60 years, *The Family Handyman*'s mission has been to help homeowners do things. But smart homeowners don't just do things. They also know things. So we spent the last year compiling those things. We consulted scores of professionals—from plumbers to architects, real estate agents to insurance experts—and heard from hundreds of experienced homeowners.

The result is *100 Things Every Homeowner Must Know*, a book for new homeowners and veterans, devoted DIYers and people who have never picked up a tool. The following pages offer a small sample of the money-saving, problem-solving tips that fill the book.

**Disclaimer:** The "100 Things" in the title isn't quite true. The book actually contains nearly a thousand things homeowners should know, plus dozens of hints, tips, goofs and easy fixes.

**Get your copy today**
Visit rdstore.com/Homeowner and enter the promo code 100TEHMK for free shipping. *100 Things Every Homeowner Must Know* is also available wherever books are sold.

THE FAMILY
**Handyman**
**100 THINGS EVERY HOMEOWNER MUST KNOW**
*How to Save Money, Solve Problems, and Improve Your Home*

**Check for leaks**
Close windows and turn off fans and the furnace. Light an incense stick and hold it near the cover plate. If air is flowing in or out, the smoke will show you.

## Seal switches and outlets to save money

In most homes, especially older ones, sealing air leaks is the easiest, most effective way to cut heating and cooling bills. And the easiest place to start is with switches and outlets on exterior walls. A few packs of foam gaskets (available at home centers) will cost you about $5, and you can install a dozen in less than a half hour.

**Stop leaks**
Unscrew the cover plate, place the foam gasket and put the cover back on. There are live wires inside the junction box— keep fingers and tools out!

## No water? Flush with a bucket

Before shutting off the water supply to tackle a plumbing project, fill some buckets with water. That way you'll be able to flush the toilet, even with the water off. Dump a few gallons into the bowl or fill the toilet tank. It works just as well as the usual flush but won't refill the bowl. This trick will also help your family cope if the city water supply stops because of a power outage or storm.

## Pet accidents: Act fast

If your pet does a dirty deed on the carpet, clean it up immediately. Urine can damage carpet fibers and even change their color. The longer you wait, the greater the risk. If your pet is a frequent offender, consider buying a small, handheld carpet cleaner designed to extract liquids. Some models cost less than $50.

## Eraser sponges work

When nothing else works, one of these pads probably will. The material they're made from was originally used for insulation. But it also provides very aggressive, very fine abrasion; that means it scours away surface stains without damaging most surfaces. Mr. Clean Magic Eraser and 3M Scotch-Brite Easy Erasing Pad are two common brands.

# What Every Homeowner Must Know

## How to fix a dead doorbell

A wireless doorbell is an easy, inexpensive solution: Just mount the button by the front door and the chime anywhere indoors. But before you do that, check your existing doorbell button. The button is the most likely culprit and it's connected to low-voltage wiring, so you don't have to worry about getting shocked. Here's how to do it:

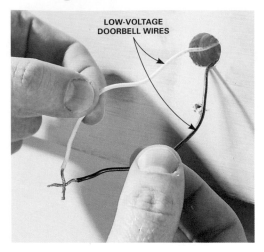

LOW-VOLTAGE DOORBELL WIRES

**1 Test the doorbell.** Unscrew the doorbell button to remove it from the wall. Loosen the screws on the back of the button and disconnect the wires. Then touch the two wires together. If the chime rings, the button is bad. If not, the chime, transformer or wiring is bad.

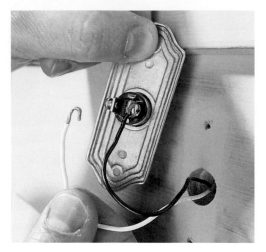

**2 Replace the button.** Connect the wires to the new button just as they were connected to the old one. Screw the button to the wall and you're done.

**Insulate ducts**
In attics and crawl spaces, wrap ducts with foil-faced fiberglass batts.

**Seal leaky ducts**
Cover seams in ductwork with aluminum foil tape. Where round ducts meet square ducts, use silicone caulk.

## Ducts can waste money

Ductwork that's full of air leaks can waste 40 percent of your heating and cooling dollars. Uninsulated ducts that run through attics or crawl spaces can waste 30 percent. The solutions are simple enough for any beginning DIYer, but there are complications: Sealing ducts is possible only in unfinished spaces. And working in an attic or crawl space is just plain miserable. So before you go through that ordeal, hire an HVAC pro to inspect and test your ducts. If your home was built within the past 15 years, your ducts are probably well insulated and sealed.

## Steam-clean grout

Professionals often use steam to clean grout, and so can you. A household steam cleaner doesn't have the power or speed of a pro model, but with a little extra patience, you can deep-clean grout effectively. In most cases, steam cleaning is much faster and easier than scrubbing—though working with steam in a small space is a hot, sweaty job. Switch on the bath fan! Small, handheld steam cleaners start at less than $30. Larger models like the one shown here cost $100 or more.

## Squeeze tubes are trouble

Squeeze tubes are convenient. But if you need to lay a neat, even bead of caulk, use a caulk gun instead. With a squeeze tube, it's difficult to produce a steady flow. And that means a lumpy bead.

## Our favorite floor protector

Canvas or plastic drop cloths are slippery on hard flooring like wood or tile. For protection that stays put, you can't beat rosin paper. Just tape sheets together and tape the perimeter to the floor. Be sure to vacuum before you lay the paper; grit trapped under the paper can lead to floor scratches. A single layer will protect against paint drips, but wipe up larger spills before they can soak through. For remodeling projects, tape down two or more layers. A big roll of rosin paper costs less than $15 at home centers.

## Clean your vacuum filter—or else

Bagless vacuum filters are convenient and efficient. But if you don't clean them regularly, the strain of pulling air through a dirty filter can burn out the vacuum's motor. The typical way to clean the filter of a bagless vacuum is to tap it against the inside of a trash can until most of the dust falls off. But that raises a cloud of dust and doesn't get the filter completely clean. For faster, neater, more effective filter cleaning, use a shop vacuum. Clean prefilter screens and post-filters the same way. Just remember to be gentle with the shop vacuum's nozzle. Some filters have a coating that you can scrape off if you press too hard.

# What Every Homeowner Must Know

### Before you build: Find your property lines

Before you build anything in your yard (a deck, fence, even a doghouse), you have to know where your property lines are. If you build over the line or too close to it, local authorities can make you demolish your project.

Iron stakes mark property lines in most communities. They're usually located at corners and jogs where lines meet. Start by requesting a plot plan from city hall. You may be able to locate stakes by dragging a rake over the suspected locations. But more likely, the stakes will be several inches underground. In that case, rent or buy a metal detector (some cost less than $40). When you've found the target, dig to make sure it's really a stake and not just a lost quarter.

### Synthetic soap = Less scum

Minimize scum with "synthetic" soap. Synthetic soaps make cleaning your shower or bath easier because they don't contain the ingredients that create tough soap scum. Any liquid or gel soap is synthetic. Most bar soaps are ordinary soaps. But a few, including Zest and Ivory, are synthetic.

### Hearing protection: Which one should I use?

Sure, the risk of hearing damage is highest for those who use loud equipment every day. But if you use a shop vacuum, leaf blower or circular saw without hearing protection, you're doing permanent damage every time. And that's just dumb because protecting your ears is so easy. The goal is to reduce noise levels to 90 decibels. All forms of hearing protection—earmuffs, disposable foam earplugs, reusable plugs—are adequate for most noise. With super-loud equipment like framing nailers and chain saws, it's smart to use both plugs and earmuffs.

Of the carpenters we talked to, some preferred earmuffs, others liked plugs, but they all said the same thing: "I hated them at first—uncomfortable, inconvenient, a #&%* nuisance. But after a day or two, I got used to them. Now I actually like them. Can't stand the noise without them." Give hearing protection a try, and you'll like it too.

## Shut off the water before vacation

Every insurance adjuster has a hundred stories like this one: The homeowners left town Friday and returned Sunday to find thousands of dollars in water damage. The moral of the story: Before going on vacation, turn off the main valve. In less than a minute, you can eliminate the most common cause of home damage. In most cases, you'll find two valves—one before the water meter and one after. Closing either of them will do the trick. If you have a well instead of city water, simply turn off the well-pump switch.

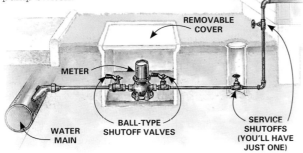

**In warm climates ...**
The main shutoff is often outside, attached to a wall or underground.

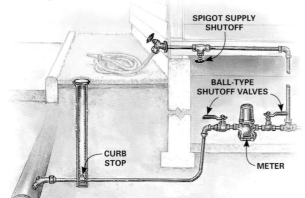

**In colder climates ...**
The main shutoff is typically in the basement. There is also a "curb stop" shutoff that requires a special tool to operate.

## Avoid disasters!

You'll find 83 disaster prevention tips in *100 Things Every Homeowner Must Know.* Buy your copy today at rdstore.com/Homeowner and enter the promo code 100TEHMK for **free shipping**. Also available wherever books are sold.

## A leaking water heater is a time bomb

Water heaters sometimes leak from the drain valve or relief valve. Those valves are easy to replace. But if a leak is coming from the tank, you've got serious trouble. The tank is lined with a thin coat of glass. Over years, that glass begins to crack, the steel begins to rust away and a puddle appears on the floor. Left alone, the tank will eventually rupture, causing an instant flood. It may take months for a leak to become a flood, or it may take days. But it will happen. Don't gamble. Replace that time bomb now.

## Don't fall off the roof

Personal fall arrest systems used to be for pros only. But prices have fallen—and you can afford them too. A complete kit costs about $100 (search online for "roof harness"). Whether you have a major roofing job planned or just need to clean the gutters, it's a smart, safe move.

# What Every Homeowner Must Know

### Buy better dust masks

Dust isn't just a sneeze-inducing nuisance—heavy repeated exposure can lead to severe allergic reactions and even harm your lungs. You can buy a dust mask for as little as 50¢, but don't. Instead, spend a few bucks on one with an "N95" certification. You'll get a mask that's more comfortable and truly effective at keeping dust out of your lungs.

LOOK FOR N95 CERTIFICATION

### Don't trust breaker panel labels

Inside your main electrical panel, you'll see labels or lists indicating which breaker controls which circuit. These labels are a reasonably good guide, but they're not completely reliable, especially in older homes that have been through remodeling projects.

For example, you might find that there's one outlet in a room that's not on the same circuit as all the others in that room, yet it's not listed elsewhere at the panel. That orphan outlet could be connected to almost any other circuit in your home. In some cases, you might even find wires from different circuits in the same junction box. The bottom line: Always use a voltage detector to make sure the power is off before you do electrical work.

### Daytime is crime time

Most of us think of burglary as a nocturnal activity. That used to be true. But these days, most burglaries occur between 10 a.m. and 5 p.m. In many cases, the crooks get in through unlocked doors or windows.

### Keep cash for blackouts

In a blackout, cash is king. Some stores may stay open, but they probably won't be able to process credit card purchases. And all the cash machines will be on strike. So keep an emergency cash stash on hand.

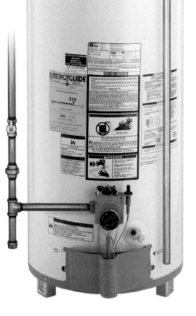

## White works now ... and later

Neutral colors—shades of white, gray or beige—are a wise choice for fixtures like toilets, tile, tubs and countertops that are not easy to change. They don't provide much drama, but you can add pizzazz with paint or simple, inexpensive accents like rugs or pottery. And as fashions change, you can update the look without costly remodeling.

## Water heater breakdown: Fix or replace?

A water heater's life expectancy is typically 10 to 15 years. So if your unit is 10 years old or more, replacing it is usually smarter than hiring a pro to repair it. Even if it's just eight years old, consider buying a new one.

But if you're willing to fix it yourself, the equation changes drastically. In most cases, replacement parts will cost you just $10 to $40. And that's a good deal, even if you get just a few more years out of the heater. To see how to make the most common repairs, go to familyhandyman.com and search for "water heater."

## What's R-value?

R-value is a measure of the resistance to heat flow, a way of indicating insulation's ability to stop heat from moving through it. The higher the number, the better. Insulation is labeled by total R-value. Two factors determine that number: the thickness of the insulation and the insulating ability of the material. The fiberglass batts shown here, for example, are all the same thickness but differ in R-value because of their different densities.

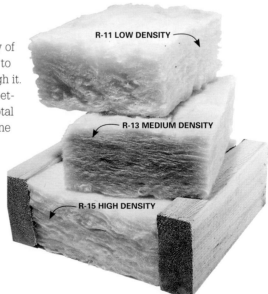

R-11 LOW DENSITY

R-13 MEDIUM DENSITY

R-15 HIGH DENSITY

# What Every Homeowner Must Know

## Plan your landscape

Planning a pond or patio? A retaining wall or planting bed? Don't just grab a shovel and start digging. Instead, lay down a rope or garden hose to map out the footprint. Stand back, survey the shape and make adjustments. Also check the layout from your kitchen window or a second-floor room. When you're happy with the shape, mark it with spray paint and get to work.

MARKING PAINT WORKS UPSIDE-DOWN

## Use a GFCI outdoors

House chores—especially outdoors—often bring water and electricity together. The best way to make those situations safer is to use a GFCI (ground-fault circuit interrupter). Newer homes have GFCI protection in bathroom, kitchen, garage and exterior outlets, but those GFCIs may no longer offer protection after 10 years or so. To be safe, plug your tools into a GFCI extension cord before you venture into the wet grass.

## Fight closet mildew

Because they're dark and lack air circulation, closet walls are especially prone to mildew. Here are a few proven solutions:

■ Add mildewcide to paint or use paint that already contains mildewcide (check the label).

■ Run a dehumidifier in damp rooms.

■ Cut closet humidity. Chemical dehumidifiers are nontoxic products that absorb moisture from the air.

■ Leave closet doors open or replace solid doors with louvered doors to increase airflow.

CHEMICAL DEHUMIDIFIER

PAINT WITH MILDEWCIDE

MILDEWCIDE ADDITIVE

## Preview a fence

Will a privacy fence really deliver privacy—or hide your neighbor's junk collection? Finding out is easy with a big sheet of cardboard. Along with a helper, you can determine the best location and height.

## Galvanized pipes get plugged

If you have galvanized steel pipes in your home and low water flow at faucets, chances are the pipes are to blame. Galvanized pipe is prone to mineral buildup, which eventually chokes off the water flow. The example shown here isn't unusual; any veteran plumber has seen much worse cases. Complete replacement of the water supply pipes is the best cure, but you can often improve flow a lot just by replacing exposed horizontal sections.

MINERAL BUILDUP

## Don't squish ants

To fight an ant invasion, place ant bait in areas where you've seen them, like under the sink and along walls. You'll probably see more ants after you set out the bait. That's a good thing. It means the ants have found the toxic bait and are working hard, carrying the bait back to the colony, where they'll share it with the rest of the ants, including the queen. Resist the temptation to step on them. Remember that they're working for you now—serving a deadly lunch to the whole colony.

## Dirty filters wreck furnaces

Any heating and cooling technician will tell you the same thing: Dirty furnace filters are the No. 1 cause of breakdowns. Plus, a dirty filter reduces the system's efficiency and raises your energy bills. Replacing filters on schedule is easy to do—and also easy to forget. So try this: Buy several filters and label them with the month they should be installed. Depending on your system and the filters, that may be every month or every few months.

## Solve problems!

Get 133 simple solutions for common problems in *100 Things Every Homeowner Must Know*. Buy your copy today at rdstore.com/Homeowner and enter the promo code 100TEHMK for **free shipping**. Also available wherever books are sold.

# What Every Homeowner Must Know

## How to water a new tree

For the first few weeks, you may have to water a new tree every few days depending on the weather. After that, longer (deeper), less frequent watering is much better than shorter (quicker), frequent watering. To help the tree create deep roots to resist drought and wind, encircle it with a soaker hose a few feet out from the trunk and run it at a trickle for an hour. Push a popsicle stick (or your finger) 2 to 3 in. into the ground. If the soil is damp down 3 in., you're giving it enough water. If not, water until the soil is damp but not saturated around the root-ball. Allow the soil's surface to begin to dry out between waterings.

## Before you buy a toilet ...

Here's a story we've heard a hundred times: Homeowners go toilet shopping and decide that an "elongated bowl" would be an improvement over the old "round" bowl. Only later—usually after installation—they discover that the bathroom door can't be closed, and laughing, crying or swearing follows. So if you want a longer bowl, measure first. A typical elongated toilet protrudes 2 in. more than a standard model. Also check the clearance for any nearby cabinet doors.

## Save a sinking sidewalk

Sinking concrete that's in otherwise good condition can be raised back to its original level by any contractor who has mudjacking equipment. The contractor first drills holes in the concrete, then injects a watery mix of sand and other components called "slurry" or "grout." The components in the slurry vary. The slurry is pumped in under enormous pressure—enough to lift sidewalks, driveways and even sinking steps. To find a contractor, just search online for "mudjacking" and the name of your city. Costs vary a lot, but most jobs are $300 to $700.

LIMESTONE
SLURRY

# 3 Plumbing, Heating & Appliances

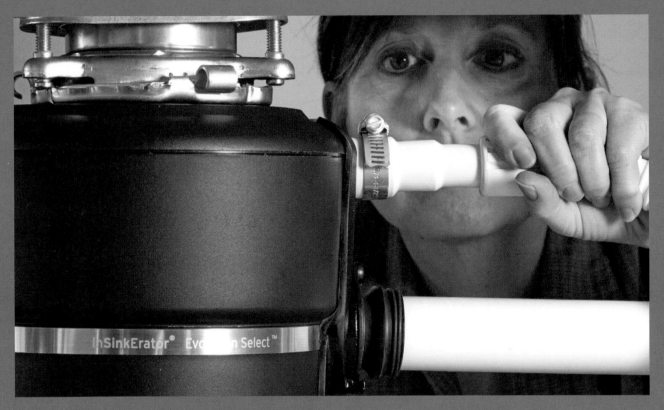

InSinkErator® Evolution Select™

## IN THIS CHAPTER

GETTY

## REPLACE THE BROKEN MOTOR ON A DRYER

When a dryer motor goes bad, the loud grinding, rumbling from the worn-out bearings makes it seem like the dryer's going to blow up any second. It won't, but fairly soon after the noise starts it will stop dead in its tracks when the bearings seize. If you think the repair cost compares favorably with the cost of a new dryer, you might be right to hire a pro. But if you have basic mechanical skills and aren't afraid to dig in, buck up and deal with it yourself. You can replace a dryer motor in a morning and be back in business cheap. Depending on the make and model, you can usually get a genuine factory motor for about $150; aftermarket motors cost about half as much.

Since you have to remove the drum to get to the motor, you may as well replace the belt, idler and drum rollers at the same time. That'll add about $35 to the cost. But in the end, your dryer could last more years than you spent raising your kids.

The motor and blower wheel on our dryer were located at the back of the machine. But they may be near the front on other models. However, the motor replacement procedure is similar for both. You'll need nut drivers or sockets, screwdrivers, a shop vacuum, slip-joint pliers and two large adjustable wrenches.

Our appliance expert, Costas Stavrou, showed us how to replace a motor on a typical Whirlpool electric dryer. He showed us how to avoid damaging the blower wheel and how to remove the motor without special tools.

### Pop the top and remove the front panel and drum

Unplug the dryer (and shut off the gas valve if you have a gas model). Then slide a putty knife between the front and the top panels to depress the latches located near the corners. Lift the top panel up and support it in the open position. Then disconnect the electrical connector to the door switch. Remove the screws that hold the front panel and pop it off. Disconnect the drive belt from the motor and lift out the drum (**Photo 1**). For more info on removing the top and front panels and the drum, search "clothes dryer repair guide" at familyhandyman.com.

**1** **Remove the drum.** Pop the lid and remove the front panel. Then disconnect the drive belt from the motor and lift the drum out the front of the machine.

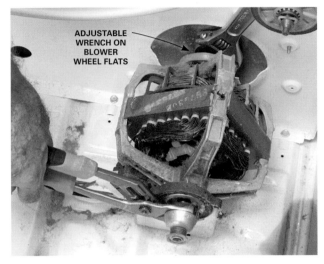

ADJUSTABLE WRENCH ON BLOWER WHEEL FLATS

**2** **Clamp the blower wheel.** Rotate the adjustable wrench clockwise until it wedges against a drum roller or the side of the cabinet. Grab the flats on the other end of the motor shaft and turn it clockwise too. Don't grab the belt pulley—it'll break.

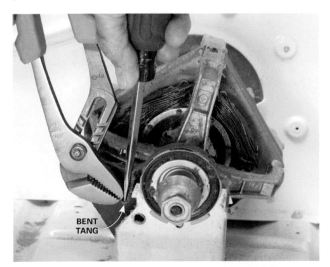

BENT TANG

**3** **Release the motor clamps.** Securely grab the bent tang on the motor clamp with slip-joint pliers. Then jam a flat-blade screwdriver between the clamp and the plier jaws and pry the clamp outward until it pops off. Repeat on the opposite end.

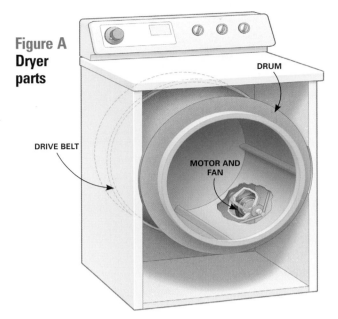

**Figure A**
**Dryer parts**

DRUM

DRIVE BELT

MOTOR AND FAN

## Remove the blower wheel and swap in the new motor

Pay attention here: The blower wheel is screwed to the motor shaft with left-hand threads. To remove it, hold the wheel while you turn the motor clockwise—the opposite of what you'd normally do. Hold the blower wheel by sliding an adjustable wrench over the flats on the neck where it meets the motor shaft. Tighten the wrench jaws so they fit snugly. Then grab the other end of the shaft with pump pliers and turn it to break it loose (**Photo 2**). Once you break it loose, spin the motor shaft clockwise with your hand until the blower wheel is loose. Then remove the motor clamps using the technique shown in **Photo 3**. Disconnect the electrical connector and lift out the old motor.

Slide the new motor into place and screw on the blower wheel (**Photo 4**). Then set the motor into the motor mount and install the clamps. Hook one end of the clamp to the base and force the other end over the catch using a flat-blade screwdriver.

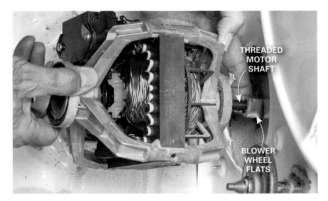

THREADED MOTOR SHAFT

BLOWER WHEEL FLATS

**4** **Connect the blower wheel.** Tilt the threaded portion of the motor shaft down to mate it to the blower wheel. Then spin the shaft counterclockwise until it's snug. Hold the blower wheel with the adjustable wrench and tighten by turning the opposite end with pump pliers.

# HomeCare&Repair

## REPAIR OR REPLACE A CONDENSATE PUMP

In the summer, central air conditioning units remove moisture from the air. And in the winter, condensing gas furnaces generate an enormous amount of wastewater. Plus, if your furnace has a humidifier, it also drains off extra water. All that water has to go somewhere. In newer homes, it goes right into a nearby floor drain.

But many older homes don't have a floor drain next to the furnace. So furnace installers mount a condensate pump right on the furnace and route the drain line to a far-off sink or floor drain. If that pump fails, the water overflows the pump and spills onto the floor. That doesn't necessarily mean the pump is bad; the problem could be just algae buildup in the pump's check valve.

So start your diagnosis by unplugging the pump. Disconnect the drain line and empty the water into a bucket. Then remove the check valve and plug in the pump (**Photo 1**). If the pump doesn't work, buy a new one from a home center or online HVAC store and swap out the old one. However, if the pump works, you've got a stuck check valve.

Try cleaning the valve by soaking it in warm, soapy water. Then flush it. Clean out any remaining crud with compressed air and test it (**Photo 2**). If you can't remove all the crud or the valve is still stuck, replace it with a new valve (about $10 from the pump manufacturer's parts department). The furnace or A/C will continue to drain while you're waiting for the new part to arrive, so jury-rig a bucket system (**Photo 3**). Clean any algae buildup from inside the pump with soapy water and a brush before installing the new valve. Then install the new valve and test. To prevent algae clogs, place algae reduction tablets (Pan Tablets is a brand that is commonly available at home centers) in the pump reservoir.

**1 Test the pump.** Hold a bowl over the pump outlet to direct water into a bucket. Then slowly pour water into the pump reservoir until the pump kicks in. If water shoots from the outlet, the pump is good.

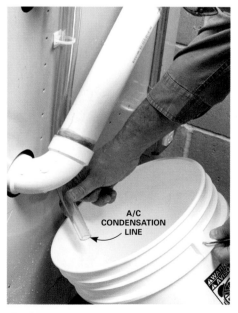

**3 Catch the water while you wait for parts.** Remove the pump and aim the drain tubes into a bucket. Empty often to prevent overflowing. Then reinstall the pump with the new check valve when it arrives.

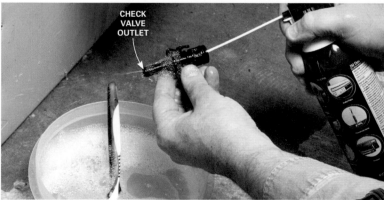

**2 Clean the check valve.** Soak the check valve in warm, soapy water. Then scrub with an old toothbrush. Rinse. Then blow it out with compressed air before testing.

CHECK VALVE

# PUT IN A DUCT BOOSTER FAN TO IMPROVE HEATING AND COOLING

If you have a room that's too cold in the winter and too hot in the summer, a duct booster fan can make the room more comfortable. There are three types of duct boosters. The simplest is a surface-mounted fan unit (available at home centers) that sits on top of the register; however, these are bulky and highly visible. Another option is an in-line fan that you can install directly in the duct line (see "Boost the airflow" on p. 57). The third type, shown here, is a recessed fan that fits into the duct and is flush with the floor.

Recessed duct fans are sized to fit either a 4 x 10-in. or 4 x 12-in. floor duct. If you have either of these sizes, order the fan and install it in place of the register. Then plug it in and you're done (see "Standard installation" below). However, if your floor duct is smaller (like 2 x 10 in. or 2 x 12 in.) you'll have to cut out a section of the floor and install a larger boot (see "Install a larger boot" below). If the ceiling below the duct is open, you could do most of the work from below. If you have a hardwood, tile or other finished floor surface with a finished ceiling below, it may

be easier to open the ceiling below the duct and patch it when you're done.

## Replace undersize boots

Buy a larger 4 x 10-in. or 4 x 12-in. right-angle boot (about $5 at home centers) and a matching recessed booster fan (one choice is the Tjernlund RB12; search online for sources). Pull up the carpet and padding around the duct to find and mark the joists on each side of the duct. Set the cutting depth to cut through the subflooring and any underlayment. Then cut and remove the flooring and the old duct boot. You may have to cut the old boot apart with tin snips to get access to the old sheet metal screws.

Next, swap in the larger boot. Enlarge the duct opening in the cut flooring pieces to fit the new boot. Reinstall the flooring with screws and staple the padding back in place. Lay the carpet over the duct and cut the opening to match. Then tuck the carpeting back onto the tack strip. Insert the fan into the duct. Install the register and cord. Connect to a receptacle or an optional fan speed controller.

PLUMBING, HEATING & APPLIANCES

## Standard installation

**1 Install the fan.** If the duct is a standard size, remove the register and drop the fan into the boot. Secure it to the floor on each side with screws. (If the duct is smaller than standard, see "Install a larger boot," below.)

**2 Connect to power.** Plug the power cord into the fan and route to the nearest receptacle. Add an optional fan speed controller to adjust the fan speed to your liking.

## Install a larger boot

EXISTING UNDERSIZE 2" x 12" DUCT

**1 Cut an access panel.** Pull out any nails on the cutting line. Plunge-cut down the centerline of the two joists next to the duct. Then make the bottom crosscut about 1 ft. from the wall. Cut out the corners with a reciprocating saw.

NEW 4" x 12" DUCT BOOT

**2 Install the larger duct boot.** Slide the new right-angle boot onto the round duct and secure it with sheet metal screws and aluminum duct tape. Attach the rectangular opening to the flooring with screws.

# TIPS FOR
# WEEKEND PLUMBERS

## Simple tips to make plumbing chores go more smoothly

by **Gary Wentz, Senior Editor**

**M**ore than any other type of home improvement job, plumbing can drive a DIYer crazy. Problems arise, projects grow, frustrations multiply. Even pros are not immune. But one way to manage the frustrations and achieve a successful plumbing project is to allow plenty of time—at least twice as much time as you think the project should take. Another smart step is to learn some tricks of the trade. Here are a few of our favorites.

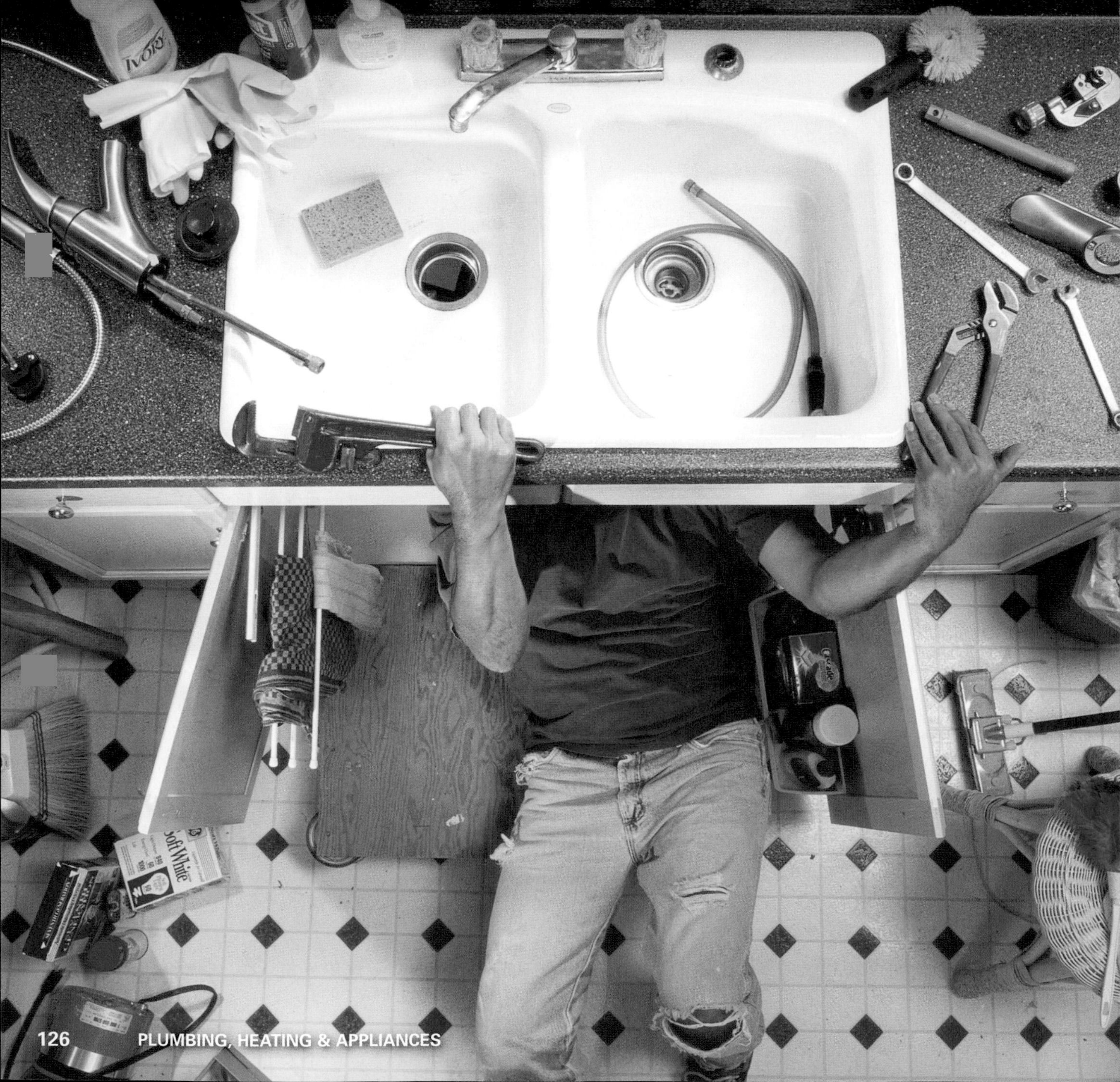

## 'Un-solder' connections—but only when you have to

The best way to disconnect a soldered pipe is to cut it. But sometimes you can't—either because you can't get a cutting tool into the space or because cutting would leave the pipe too short to make a new connection. The solution is to heat the joint and pull off the fitting as the solder melts.

Have a wet rag handy and immediately wipe away the molten solder before it hardens. (Wear gloves to prevent burning your fingers!) Sometimes a quick wipe will leave the pipe ready for a new fitting. More likely, you'll have to scour off some excess solder with sandpaper or emery cloth before you can slip on a new fitting.

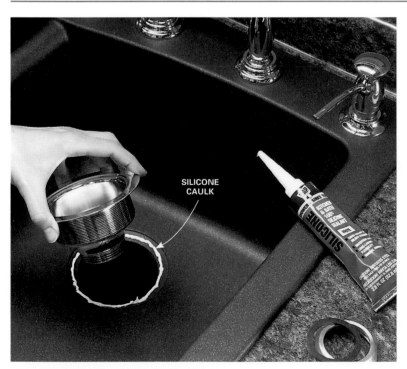

SILICONE CAULK

## Choose caulk, not putty

Despite the name, lots of plumbers never use plumber's putty. It damages some types of plastic and stains surfaces such as natural stone. Plus, it tends to dry out, crack and allow leaks. Silicone caulk is a safer, longer-lasting sealant in most areas where you might use plumber's putty.

## Don't fight with metal drain lines

Metal drain lines under sinks look a lot more reliable than plastic. But plastic is better in almost every way. It's cheaper, easier to install, and easier to adjust or tighten if a leak develops. And unlike metal, plastic won't corrode. So when a metal drain leaks, often the smartest move is to replace the entire assembly with plastic. To see how, go to family handyman.com and search for "stop leaks under sink."

## Buy more stuff!

Weekend plumbers often spend more time driving back and forth to the home center than actually working on the project. So before you go shopping, think through each step and try to anticipate problems. Make a list of everything you might need and buy it all. One trip to the return counter is better than three trips back to the store (while your family waits for you to turn the water back on).

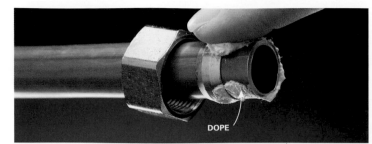

FLAME PROTECTOR CLOTH

## Dope everything

Thread sealant (aka "pipe dope") is formulated to seal threads. But it's great for almost any connection, even if the threads don't form the seal. Use it on compression fittings, ground fittings and rubber seals. Because it's slippery, it allows connections to slide together correctly for a good seal. And, if you use a type that doesn't harden, disassembly and repair will be easier years later. Some types of dope harm plastic parts, so check the label.

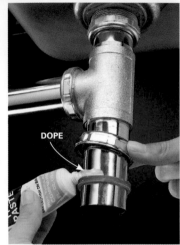
DOPE

## Loosen stuck pipes with heat

When a threaded connection won't budge, heat sometimes does the trick, especially on ancient connections that were sealed with pipe dope that hardened over time. Be patient. Getting the metal hot enough can take a couple of minutes. Protect nearby surfaces with a flame-resistant cloth (about $10 at home centers). This method is for water and waste pipes only, **never** for gas or fuel lines.

PICK-UP TOOL

PIGGYBACK VALVE

OLD SHUTOFF VALVE

## Fix a clog in seconds

Before you run a drain snake into a clogged pipe or disassemble the trap, there are a few other tricks worth trying: Often, you can yank out a clog with a flexible-shaft pickup tool (shown above) or a Zip-It (below; a few bucks at home centers). Likewise, a wet/dry vacuum just might suck out the clog.

WET/DRY SHOP VAC

## Piggyback stubborn shutoffs

Shutoff valves under sinks and toilets have a rotten reliability record. Sometimes they won't close completely; sometimes they won't close at all. In either case, there's an alternative to replacing the shutoff. Most home centers carry inexpensive "piggyback" shutoff valves that connect to existing shutoffs. Just disconnect the supply line and install the new valve (a new supply line is a good idea, too). If the old shutoff closes most of the way, you won't even have to turn off the main water valve; just set a container under the valve to catch the trickle while you work.

## Tips for using thread tape

Tape and dope are equally reliable for sealing pipe threads. The main advantage of tape is that it won't smear onto your hands or tools and end up on the carpet. Here are some tips for tape:

- Cheap tape works fine, but the thicker stuff (often pink for water, yellow for gas) is easier to handle and tears more neatly.
- Unlike dope, tape is for pipe threads only. Don't use it on compression or other connections.
- How many times should you wrap around the pipe? There are no rules, but the most common answer we got from pro plumbers was three.
- Always wrap the tape clockwise around the threads. Otherwise, the tape will unwrap as you screw the joint together.

PLUMBER'S TAPE

## Don't overtighten supply lines

It's tempting to crank supply lines on tight, just to be safe. But overtightening supply lines is actually riskier than undertightening. A loose connection that leaks is easy to tighten, but overtightening can wreck rubber seals and crack the threaded nuts. So get into this habit: Make the connections at both ends of the supply line finger-tight, then give them another one-eighth to one-quarter turn with pliers. If they leak, snug them up a little more.

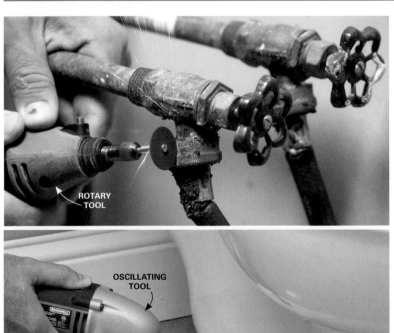

ROTARY TOOL

OSCILLATING TOOL

## Don't reuse supply lines

When you're replacing a toilet or a faucet, you can save 10 bucks by reusing the old flexible supply lines. But don't. Plastic degrades over time, and even a small leak can lead to catastrophic water damage. It's a small risk, but not one worth taking. Buy new lines that are encased in braided stainless steel; they're much less likely to burst. But even if you already have braided lines that are several years old, replace them.

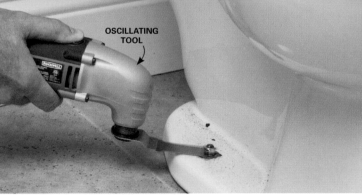

BRAIDED STAINLESS STEEL SUPPLY LINE

## Cut stubborn parts

Corrosion and mineral deposits have an amazing power to lock parts together, making them almost impossible to disconnect. Often, the best solution is to cut the stubborn part. Either slice it off or cut kerfs in the part so you can break it off. A hacksaw blade works well. Oscillating or rotary tools work even better.

### PERFECT PIPE INSULATION

To make fast and accurate cuts in pipe insulation, use a hand miter box and a bread knife. You can get precise 45- and 90-degree cuts for a tight fit and a professional look.

–Henry Haskell

### DISPOSER LIFT

To replace a garbage disposer, I used the scissor jack from the trunk of my car. That not only saved me some heavy lifting but also allowed me to precisely adjust the height of the disposer. Scissor jacks can help out with other heavy lifting too. I used one to position a heavy shower door.

–Mike McCleish

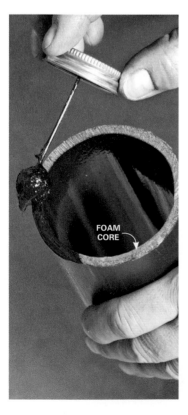

FOAM CORE

### SEAL ABS ENDS!

Most ABS pipes have either a cellular or a foam core that air will actually pass right through. If you don't believe it, wrap your lips around the pipe wall and blow through it. If you don't seal pipe ends with cement, air will escape into the porous center core and find its way out of the plumbing system and you'll fail a pressure test every time. Can you even imagine that disaster? You'd have to replumb everything!

–Ken Collier, Editor in Chief

### DIVERTER LUBE

Over time, the hard water in our area leaves deposits in the moving parts of the plumbing. When our tub spout diverter clogs, I use WD-40 with its spray nozzle curved up the spout to the diverter valve. A couple of sprays gets things loosened up and working again.

–Jackson Tutt

# SEPTIC SMARTS

Save big money by understanding how a septic system works—and what can go wrong

by **Jim vonMeier, Contributing Editor**

A well-designed, properly installed septic system can last for decades—or fail in just a few years. It's up to you.

Maintaining a healthy septic system isn't all that expensive, but you could easily spend tens of thousands to dig up and replace a septic system that has totally failed. As the old saying goes, an ounce of prevention is worth a pound of cure.

Good maintenance starts with understanding how a septic system works and how it can fail. Let's take a look underground and see what's supposed to happen in a well-functioning septic system. After that, I'll show you why things go wrong and give you some pointers for keeping your system in top shape.

## MEET AN EXPERT

**Jim vonMeier believes septic systems are the answer to America's water shortage because they deliver purified water to depleted aquifers. He travels the country advocating, lecturing and testifying on septic systems. If you have a septic system question, you can drop him an e-mail at jvonmeier@septicprotector.com.**

**Regular "pumping" removes sludge and scum from the tank.**

# HOW IT WORKS

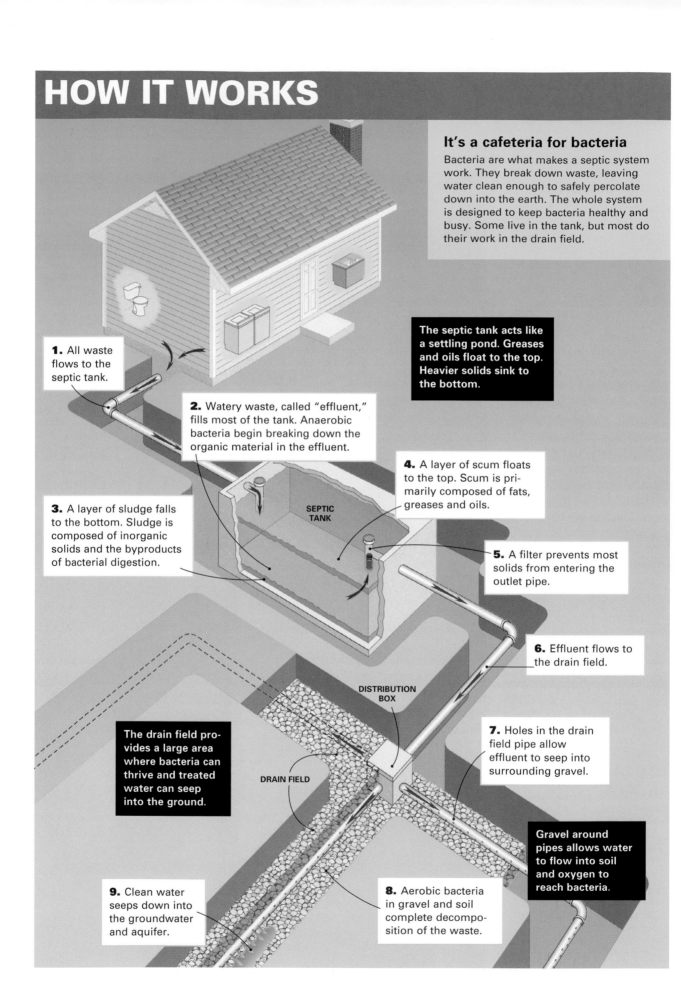

### It's a cafeteria for bacteria

Bacteria are what makes a septic system work. They break down waste, leaving water clean enough to safely percolate down into the earth. The whole system is designed to keep bacteria healthy and busy. Some live in the tank, but most do their work in the drain field.

**1.** All waste flows to the septic tank.

**The septic tank acts like a settling pond. Greases and oils float to the top. Heavier solids sink to the bottom.**

**2.** Watery waste, called "effluent," fills most of the tank. Anaerobic bacteria begin breaking down the organic material in the effluent.

**4.** A layer of scum floats to the top. Scum is primarily composed of fats, greases and oils.

**3.** A layer of sludge falls to the bottom. Sludge is composed of inorganic solids and the byproducts of bacterial digestion.

SEPTIC TANK

**5.** A filter prevents most solids from entering the outlet pipe.

**6.** Effluent flows to the drain field.

DISTRIBUTION BOX

**The drain field provides a large area where bacteria can thrive and treated water can seep into the ground.**

DRAIN FIELD

**7.** Holes in the drain field pipe allow effluent to seep into surrounding gravel.

**Gravel around pipes allows water to flow into soil and oxygen to reach bacteria.**

**9.** Clean water seeps down into the groundwater and aquifer.

**8.** Aerobic bacteria in gravel and soil complete decomposition of the waste.

# WHAT GOES WRONG

## Don't abuse the system

A septic system that was properly designed and installed needs only occasional "pumping" to remove the sludge and scum from the tank. But without knowing it, you can do things that harm—or destroy— the system.

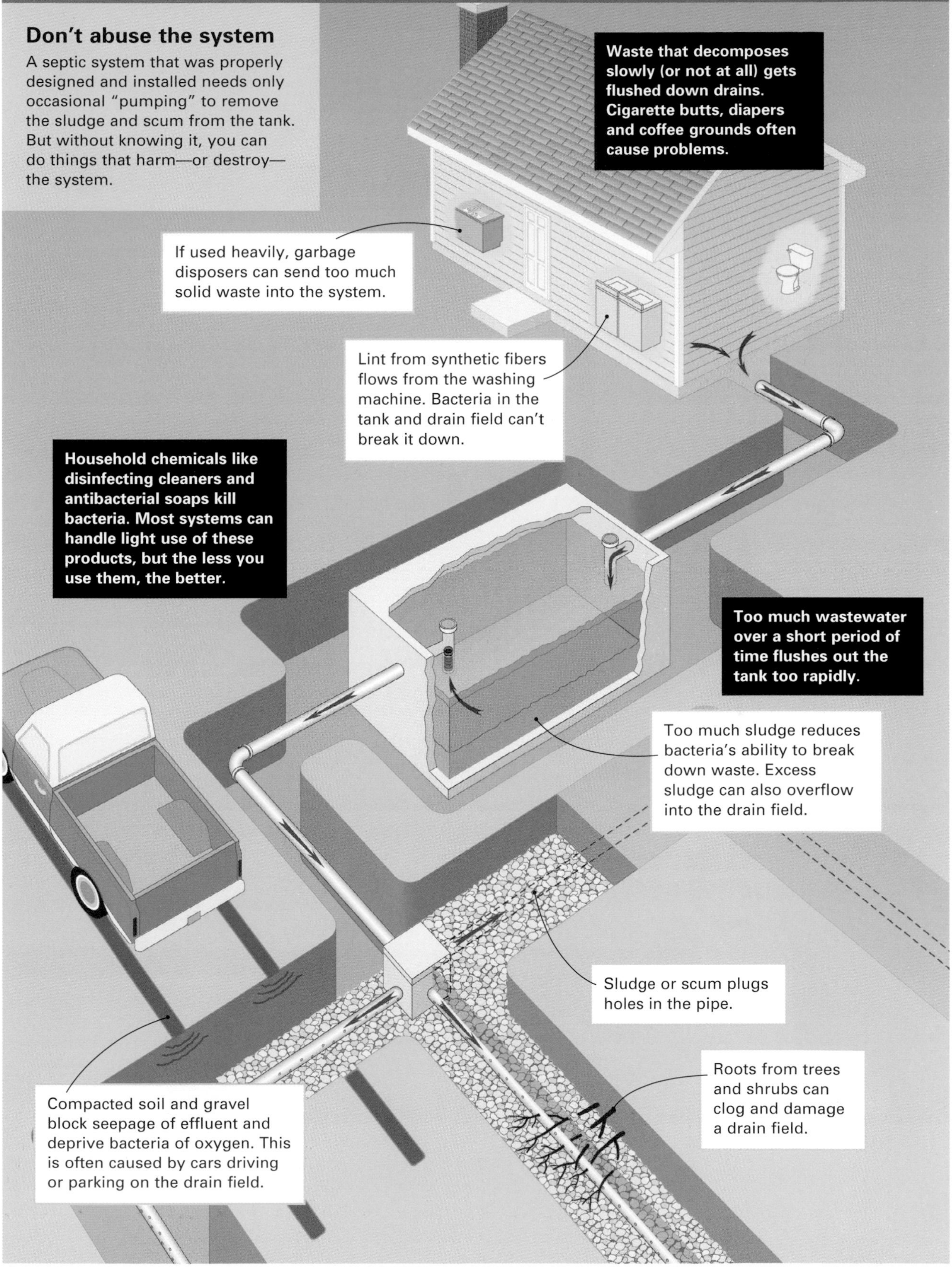

Waste that decomposes slowly (or not at all) gets flushed down drains. Cigarette butts, diapers and coffee grounds often cause problems.

If used heavily, garbage disposers can send too much solid waste into the system.

Lint from synthetic fibers flows from the washing machine. Bacteria in the tank and drain field can't break it down.

Household chemicals like disinfecting cleaners and antibacterial soaps kill bacteria. Most systems can handle light use of these products, but the less you use them, the better.

Too much wastewater over a short period of time flushes out the tank too rapidly.

Too much sludge reduces bacteria's ability to break down waste. Excess sludge can also overflow into the drain field.

Sludge or scum plugs holes in the pipe.

Roots from trees and shrubs can clog and damage a drain field.

Compacted soil and gravel block seepage of effluent and deprive bacteria of oxygen. This is often caused by cars driving or parking on the drain field.

# SEPTIC SOLUTIONS

## Get your tank pumped...

Your tank must be pumped out regularly by a pro. Pumping removes the buildup of sludge and scum, which slows down bacterial action in the tank. Your tank may need pumping each year, but it's possible to go two or three years between pumpings, depending on the size of your tank and the amount of waste you run through the system. Ask your inspector to make a rough recommendation for how often your tank should be pumped.

## ...but don't hire a pumper until you need it

Regular inspections and pumping are critical. But if you're not squeamish, you can check the sludge level yourself with a device called The Sludge Judge. It costs $100 to $125 and is widely available online. Once you've determined that your tank is one-third full of sludge, call a contractor to come pump it out.

"THE SLUDGE JUDGE"

SLUDGE

## Install an effluent filter

Ask your contractor to install an effluent filter on the outflow pipe on your tank. (It will probably cost $50 to $100, plus labor.) This device helps prevent solids from entering the drain field and will need to be cleaned out on occasion by a contractor.

EFFLUENT FILTER

## Get an inspection

A thorough initial inspection by a pro will cost $300 to $500; after that, regular inspections cost less than $100 each. Your pro will be able to tell you how often your system should be inspected.

Simple as a septic system may seem, evaluating its health really requires an expert. There are plenty of contractors who will gladly pump the sludge out of your tank, but in my experience many don't fully understand how a septic system works or how it should be maintained. I highly recommend looking for a contractor who has received some formal training in the science of septic systems. Some states have adopted certification programs for septic contractors—check with your Secretary of State's office to see if yours is among them.

A complete inspection will determine whether your system is up to code (many are not) and the condition of the tank and drain field. A good inspector will also be able to tell you whether your tank is large enough for your household, and the maximum volume of water you can pass through it in a day.

You may be able to improve the performance of your system by adding bacteria with a product such as RID-X. Your pro should be able to tell you if your system will benefit from this treatment.

## Alternatives to a new drain field

If an inspection or sewage backup reveals that your drain field is in trouble, the ultimate solution is to replace it. The cost can be huge, however, so it's worth discussing other options with a contractor.

■ **Clean the pipes.** A contractor can clear out the drain field pipes with a rotary pressure washer. "Jetting" the pipes usually costs about $200.

■ **Treat the system with chemicals.** Ask your contractor about treating your system with a commercial product (not a homemade one) that increases the amount of oxygen in the drain field. I recommend Septic-Scrub (arcan.com). A typical treatment costs $500 to $1,000.

■ **Loosen the soil.** In states where it's legal, some contractors can fracture compacted soil around the pipes by injecting high-pressure air in numerous locations around the drain field, a process called "terra-lifting." Depending on the situation, this can cost less than $1,000 or more than $4,000.

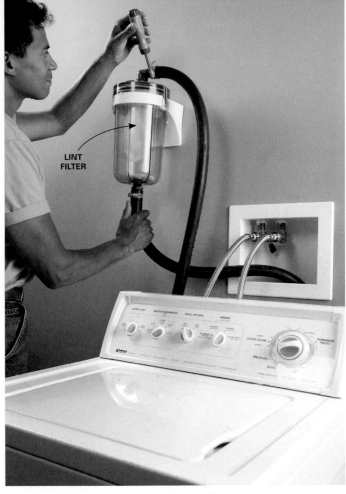

LINT FILTER

## Protect your drain field from lint

Install a filter on your washing machine's drain. This device prevents lint from entering the system, particularly the synthetic fibers that bacteria can't digest. I've developed one of these filters myself and named it the Septic Protector (septicprotector.com). It costs about $150, plus shipping, and includes a replacement filter.

## Don't overload the system

Limit your water use. Reducing the amount of water that runs into your tank, particularly over a short period of time, will prevent the flushing of untreated waste into your drain field. You can replace old toilets with low-flow models, install reduced-flow showerheads, and simplest of all, wash laundry throughout the week rather than just on Saturday morning.

# CHECKING FOR
# LEAKS

A plumbing project isn't over until the leak inspection is done

by *The Family Handyman* Editors

**At** the end of a plumbing project, most people turn on the water supply, take a quick look at their work and consider the job done. That's not good enough. You will detect major leaks that way, but you won't notice slow, small leaks. And those tiny leaks are the most serious. They can go on for months and do significant damage before anyone notices. So here are some tips to help you get them before they can get you.

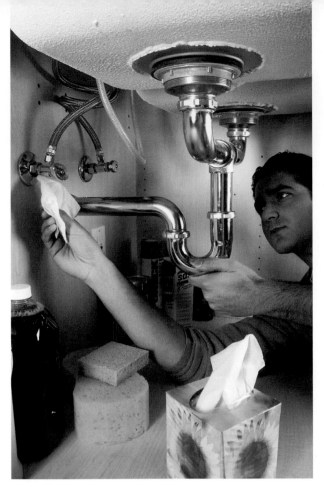

## The tissue test

Don't search for leaks by just looking at or touching pipes. Instead, wipe each connection with a dry tissue. Any moisture on the tissue will be easy to see. If you want to be super certain you don't have any leaks, spread newspaper under the plumbing and check for wet spots later.

## Sink rim leaks

Leaky seals around faucets or sink rims lead to slow-but-severe damage. (They can destroy a countertop, for example.) So after installing a new sink or faucet, dribble water around the area and wait a few minutes. Then get under the sink and look for leaks.

## Wait a few minutes

Of course you're anxious to declare the job done. But tiny leaks may not be detectable right away. Give the droplets at least 15 minutes to form before you do the tissue test.

## Check shutoff valves

Shutoff valves go unused and stay leak-free for years. Then, when you finally use them during a plumbing project, they often leak around the valve stem. The solution is simple and almost always works: Just tighten the packing nut, which seals around the stem. A slight turn is all it takes.

## Check drain lines

Unlike water supply lines, drain lines leak only when waste is running through them. So you'll have to flush toilets, run the dishwasher and turn on faucets to check for leaks.

To check the drain assembly under a sink, don't just run the faucet. Instead, fill the sink with lukewarm water. Then open the drain to release a strong, worst-case-scenario flow and do the tissue test.

## Don't get fooled by condensation

Cold water inside pipes makes condensation droplets form on the outside. And that can make finding leaks impossible. When checking drain lines, you can prevent condensation by running lukewarm water down drains. With cold water supply lines, all you can do is wait for the water in the pipes to warm up, wipe off the condensation and then check for leaks.

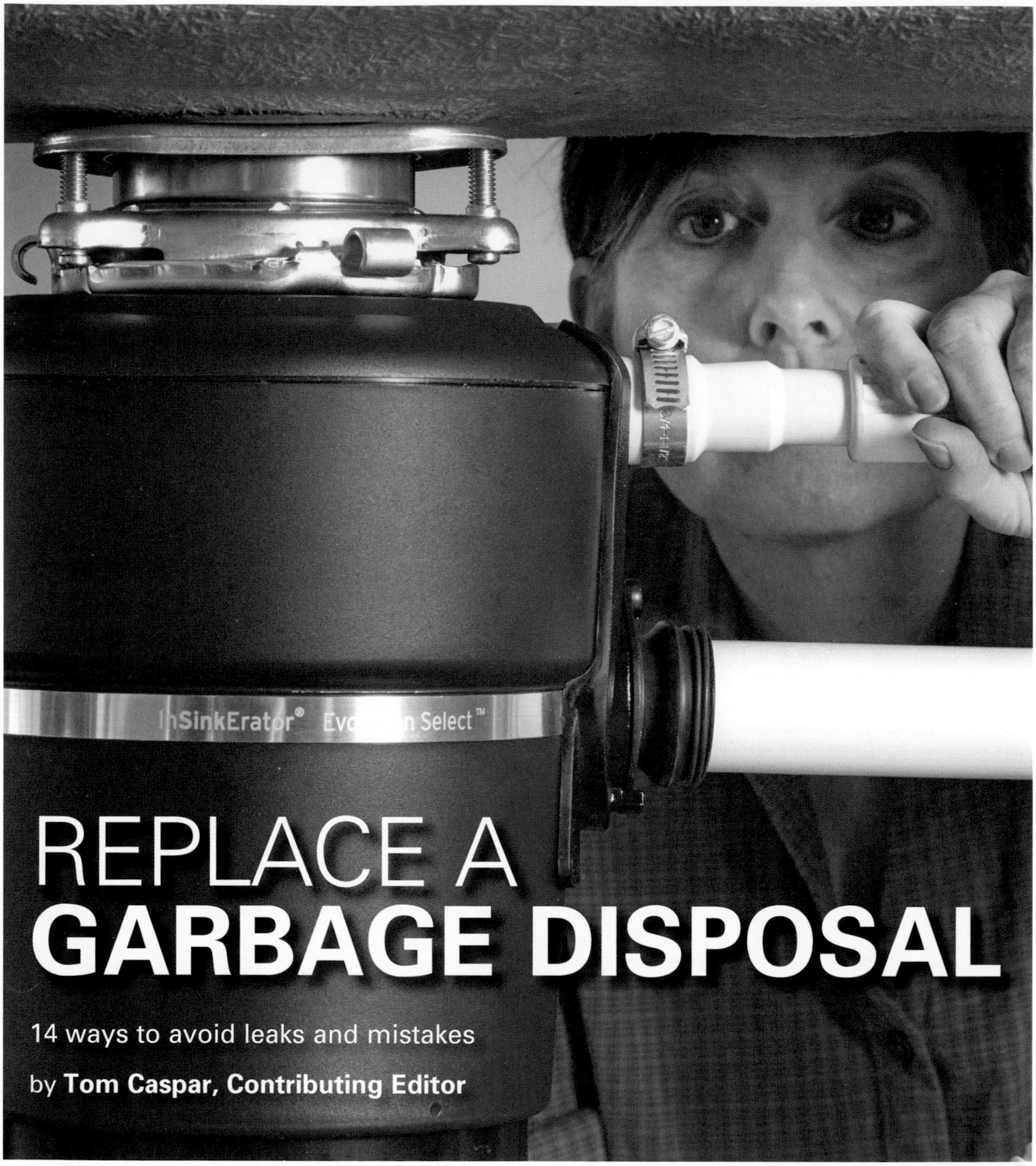

# REPLACE A
# GARBAGE DISPOSAL

14 ways to avoid leaks and mistakes

by **Tom Caspar, Contributing Editor**

InSinkErator® Evolution Select™

**W**hen you flip the switch to turn on the garbage disposal and all you get is a hum—or a loud, metal-on-metal grinding noise—you know something's wrong. Maybe it's just trash stuck in the disposal, but there's also a chance that the unit is dead, kaput, never to dispose again.

Fortunately, replacing a disposal isn't hard, even if you haven't done much plumbing. Manufacturers provide clear instructions that tell you most of the things you need to know—but not everything. We talked to veteran plumbers and collected their best tips for a smooth, trouble-free installation.

## What it takes

**TIME: 2 to 3 hours**

**COST: $80 to $300**

**SKILL: Beginner**

**TOOLS: Screwdriver, putty knife, tongue-and-groove pliers, hacksaw**

RESET BUTTON

HEX WRENCH

## Make sure it's really broken

A disposal that seems to be dead might be revived with a simple fix. Here are three things to try:

■ **Look for a jam.** Something too tough to grind, such as a piece of glass, could be jamming the motor. Turn off the power and water, then unplug the disposal. (If it's hardwired, turn off the breaker.) Remove the rubber baffle inside the drain—most just lift out—and shine a flashlight into the hole. Fish out the obstruction with a pair of tongs or needle-nose pliers.

■ **Turn the motor manually.** You'll need a hex wrench. Some disposals come with one bent at a convenient angle, but if you don't have it, you can buy one at a hardware store or use a standard Allen wrench. Rotate the wrench back and forth as shown above until the motor turns a full revolution, then remove the wrench and switch on the motor.

■ **Press the reset button.** If your motor has overheated by working too long, wait five minutes for it to cool down, then push the reset button. (It's usually located on the underside of the disposal.) The motor may also have overheated because of a jam. If the motor doesn't start after manually turning it, try pushing the reset button.

### Figure A
### Disposal mounting assembly

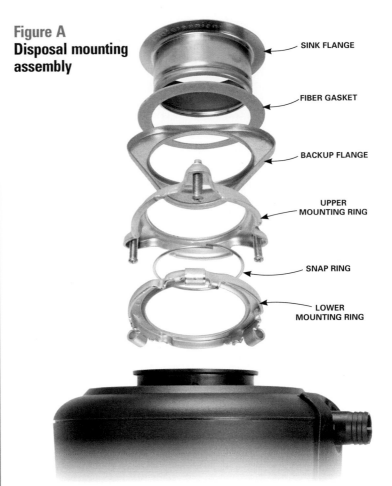

SINK FLANGE

FIBER GASKET

BACKUP FLANGE

UPPER MOUNTING RING

SNAP RING

LOWER MOUNTING RING

## Figure it out first

When you buy a new disposal, the box will contain all the parts you need to install it. Before you jump into removing the old unit, take a few moments to familiarize yourself with all these parts. Put them together in the correct order and try out the locking mechanism. Understanding how everything fits together ahead of time will make the job a cinch.

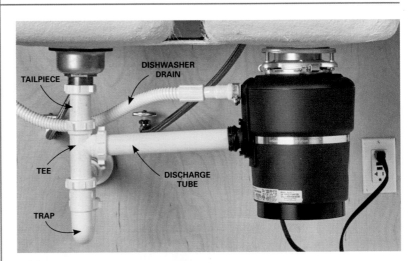

TAILPIECE

DISHWASHER DRAIN

TEE

DISCHARGE TUBE

TRAP

### Disposal system anatomy

If you have a double sink, the best way to plumb a disposal is to run its discharge tube directly to a tee below the opposite sink. The tube must drop about 1/4 in. in order to drain properly.

## Inspect the plumbing first

Look over all the pipes under your sink for any sign of leakage before heading to the store to buy a new garbage disposal. You might want to replace more than just the disposal itself, so you may as well make a list and be prepared!

## Spend a little more

You can buy a 1/3-hp disposal for $80 or less, but our experts suggest that a more expensive unit with at least 3/4 hp would be a better choice. The more powerful the motor, the less chance it will jam. In addition, higher-priced disposals are generally quieter and have longer warranties.

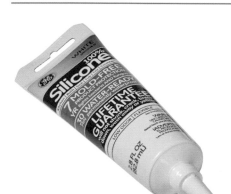

## Silicone seals best

Plumber's putty is typically recommended for sealing the sink flange to the sink itself, but silicone will provide a more reliable seal. With silicone, there's almost no chance—now or later—that the flange will leak.

However, when it's time to replace the disposal and the sink flange again, you should know that old silicone is much harder to remove than old plumber's putty. But that's why it works better!

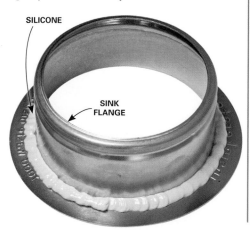

SILICONE

SINK FLANGE

## Compare outlet heights

A disposal's discharge tube must slant about 1/4 in. downhill in order for it to drain properly (see **Figure A**, p. 139). Creating that drop may be a small problem if the outlet on your new disposal (left) is lower than the outlet on your old one, as shown above.

To be prepared, measure the distance from the outlet to the top of each disposal before you remove the old unit. If the new unit's outlet is lower, you must also lower the tee that the discharge pipe connects to. Loosen the two nuts that connect the tee to the tailpiece above and the trap below. Try lowering the tee to see if the tailpiece is long enough. If it's not, you'll have to replace it with one that's slightly longer.

## Tighten with pliers

When you hang the new disposal, rotating the lower mounting ring tightens the seal between the disposal and the sink flange. The lower ring rides up a set of ramps on the upper ring—pretty neat! But the final inch or so of rotation requires a fair amount of force.

The easiest way to apply that force is to squeeze them together using tongue-and-groove pliers, such as Channellocks. You'll need medium or large pliers to do this. Unlike prying on the lower ring with a screwdriver or hex wrench—the method recommended in most instruction sheets—squeezing can't disturb the position of the sink flange and cause it to leak. Plus, it's easier on the wrists.

## Knock out the knockout!

Everyone who's installed a few disposals is aware of this mistake: Forgetting to remove the dishwasher knockout before hanging the unit.

If you have a dishwasher, the first thing you should do after removing the disposal from the box is to punch out the knockout with a hammer and a screwdriver. Fish out the knockout by reaching down inside the disposal. You don't want this plastic disc to be the first thing that the disposal tries to grind up!

This is also the best time to add the cord and plug to your disposal. It's really awkward to add these after the disposal is installed.

## Support the weight

Garbage disposals can weigh 15 lbs. or more. That's a lot of weight to suddenly catch with one hand while you're turning the lower mounting bracket with the other hand.

Before you unhook anything, assemble a support under the unit using a paint can and scraps of wood (or, see "Disposer lift" on p. 130 for another idea). Leave a 1/4-in. to 1/2-in. gap under the unit so it can drop a bit. Use the same support to help you install the new disposal.

## Don't forget the cord

Surprise! Most new disposals don't come with a cord and plug. If your old unit has a cord and plug, you can remove the whole assembly and reinstall it on the new unit. (Instructions are included with the new disposal.) Or you can simply buy a new cord and plug when you buy the disposal. They're usually located together in the store.

If you're not comfortable making electrical connections, you can buy a disposal that already has a cord attached. Ask at your home center or appliance store, or search online for "garbage disposal with cord attached."

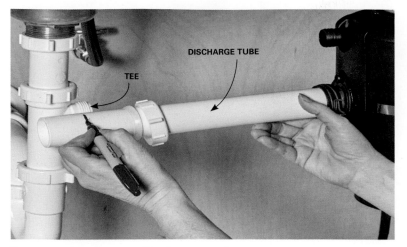

TEE

DISCHARGE TUBE

## Prepare for a new discharge tube

Your old discharge tube probably won't be the right length for your new disposal. If it's too long, simply connect it to the disposal, mark it and cut it with a hacksaw. (Loosen the other pipe connections, if necessary, to insert the tube back into the tee.) If the old discharge tube is too short, you may have to make a time-wasting trip to the store. To avoid this, make sure the new disposal includes a tube, or buy one separately at the same time for a few bucks.

UPPER MOUNTING BRACKET

FLANGE

SNAP RING

## Don't struggle with the snap ring

The snap ring fits into a groove on the lower end of the sink flange. When you're working under the sink, it prevents the upper mounting bracket from falling off. Removing an old snap ring can be frustrating—unless you know this trick: Starting at the break in the ring, insert a thin-blade screwdriver between the ring and the flange. Pull down on the ring with the screwdriver's blade and walk the blade around the ring. The ring will pop right off.

## Shortcut: Keep the flange

If your old sink flange is undamaged and tight, with no signs of leakage, you can probably leave it in place. Chances are good that the mounting brackets on the new unit will fit just fine. To find out, remove the old disposal and install the new flange on it. If it fits, you can install the new disposal using the old flange.

## Weight down the sink flange

After you install the new sink flange, you don't want it shifting around when you're assembling the parts underneath. Movement of the flange could break the seal between the flange and the sink, inviting a leak.

Your best bet is to ask a helper to press down on the sink flange, or if you're working alone, find something to weight it down, such as the old disposal. Place an old towel under the weight so you don't scratch the sink. If the bottom of your sink is quite concave, the old disposal might not contact the flange. In that case, place a can on the flange, then weight down the can.

# GET OUT OF PLUMBING JAMS

## 10 stress-relieving tips

by **Mark Petersen, Associate Editor**

S ometimes the best-laid plumbing plans go awry. Your project can come to a screeching halt when a vital piece breaks off, gets stuck or is too rotten to work with. Then what? Sure, cursing makes you feel better, but you need a real solution. We tapped our plumbing guru, Les Zell, to show us cool tools and tips to get you out of your next plumbing jam.

### MEET A PRO

Les Zell has been a plumber for almost 30 years and an invaluable resource to *The Family Handyman* for the past decade. He's the owner/operator of Zell Plumbing & Heating.

### Drop in a replacement closet flange

If the old toilet flange is broken beyond all hope of repair (like the old cast-iron closet flange in the photo above), drop in a replacement flange. Our expert prefers replacement flanges with a rubber compression gasket that expands. There are several styles, but the gasket on this one expands as you twist it into place. It's available for both 3-in. and 4-in. waste pipes at home centers and plumbing supply stores for $15 to $25.

REPLACEMENT FLANGE

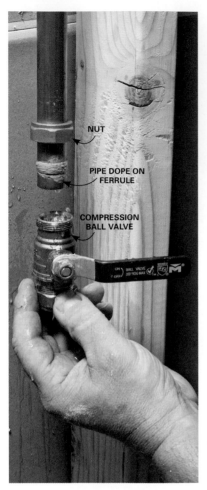

## Sweat-free shutoff fitting for easier soldering

You know that it's nearly impossible to sweat (solder) joints when there's the least bit of water inside the lines. So don't sweat it (plumbers' humor). Install a compression fitting or a push fitting instead. Neither requires any heat, solder or flux. Compression fittings just tighten with a wrench; push fittings simply slide on and seal themselves. Neither is affected by a little water. When you're installing compression fittings, lubricate the ferrule with a bit of pipe dope so it slides in and seats straight into the nut. Mechanical (shutoff) fittings like this need to be accessible, so don't bury them behind drywall.

*Labels in image 1:* NUT · PIPE DOPE ON FERRULE · COMPRESSION BALL VALVE

*Label in image 2:* SOCKET SAVER

## Ream out broken hubs

You can reuse an existing hub by reaming out the old pipe that's glued inside it. This PVC fitting saver will do the trick. It has a guide that rides inside the pipe you're removing so the hub won't get wrecked.

*Labels in image 4:* CUTTING BLADES · GUIDE

Since replacing a hub can mean having to open up a finished wall—or worse, busting up concrete—this $15 tool can save you a lot of time and money. The Socket Saver by Jones Stephens is available at home centers and online.

*Labels in image 3:* ABS · SHIELDED COUPLING · PVC

## Join incompatible pipes with a shielded coupling

If you need to tie into a white PVC pipe but the closest plumbing supplier carries only black ABS, you don't have to run all over town. Install a shielded rubber coupling between the two pipes. Shielded couplings are often referred to as "mission couplings," and they work great to connect other dissimilar pipes: galvanized steel to plastic, cast iron to plastic, ABS to PVC. Make sure you use a "fully banded" coupling because the couplings with just the two individual hose clamps may not be allowed in some situations.

## Use a cartridge puller for stuck cartridges

Some shower cartridges pull right out, but some need a little convincing with a cartridge puller (about $40), and there are others that need a puller and some heat to persuade them to break free. Heat expands the valve body, decreasing the pressure on the cartridge. Heat also softens the rubber seals. Hook up the cartridge puller and put the flame on the valve body of the cartridge. Add pressure to the puller as you apply the heat. Set a heat shield on the back of the cartridge so you don't burn down the house. And have a fire extinguisher at hand just in case. (Check out the Great Goof on p. 150!)

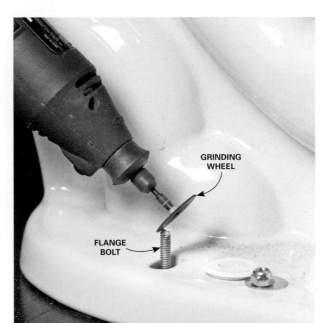

## Smooth bolts with a rotary tool

Sometimes a toilet can be reset using the existing flange bolts, but often the ends of the soft brass bolts are damaged, making it difficult to get the nut started. Clean up the ends of the bolts with a rotary tool fitted with a grinding wheel. You can use the same tool to cut off new flange bolts to the proper height if they're too long. Clean up the ends of the bolts to ease future repairs.

## Flange support bracket for rotted floors

If the floor is too spongy to screw down a toilet flange, attach a flange support bracket to the floor and then secure the toilet flange to that. This fix will work only if the majority of the floor under the toilet is solid. Probe the floor by poking it with a screwdriver. If more than an inch or so around the flange is rotten, you'll need to repair the floor itself.

The bracket shown here is part of the QUIK-FIX Wobbly Toilet Repair Kit. You can find the kit at some home centers, plumbing suppliers or online for about $15. It will also work over holes in the floor that have been cut a bit too large.

## Use double wax rings

The new bathroom floor looks great, but now the closet/toilet flange is 3/8 in. lower than the floor. Avoid leaks by installing two wax rings when you reset the toilet. Flange extenders are available, but some models are hard to seal properly. Our expert sets the wax rings on the floor instead of on the toilet. He installs a standard ring first, then sets a wax ring with a plastic gasket on top of that. If the new floor will be more than 1/2 in. higher than the flange, you'll need to remove the old flange, install the floor, then fasten the new flange on top of the flooring.

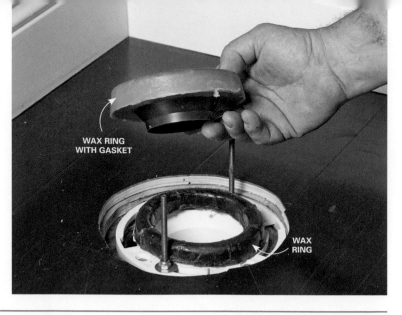

WAX RING WITH GASKET

WAX RING

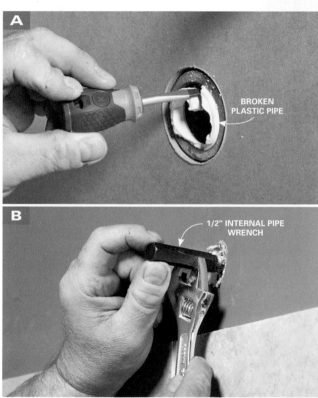

A

BROKEN PLASTIC PIPE

B

1/2" INTERNAL PIPE WRENCH

## Cut and pry broken threads

Pipes sometimes break off when you're trying to separate them, leaving the threads stuck inside the other pipe. When removing threads from steel pipes, carefully make two cuts with a hacksaw and then pry the piece loose with a screwdriver (**Photo A**). The top side of the pipe is subjected to much less water and is less likely to leak, so always make cuts on the top side of the pipe in case the steel threads get nicked a little. And make sure to use pipe dope or tape on the new pipe.

## ... or remove them with an internal pipe wrench

You can use an internal pipe wrench (about $10 at home centers) to remove small supply-line pipe threads (**Photo B**). A knurled cam slides out when the wrench is twisted, grabbing hold of the old threads from the inside. Another trick that sometimes works is to grab hold of the end of the thread with needle-nose pliers. Twist the pliers clockwise and the thread will wind out like a spring.

CAM

1/2" MALE PIPE THREAD

## Super-fast water heater connection

Most folks "can't live" without hot water, and when a water heater conks out, getting the new one installed is a high priority. There's no faster or easier way to install water heater supply lines than by using specially designed braided stainless steel water lines with a push-fitting shutoff valve on one end. All you need to do is apply a little pipe dope or plumbing tape to the water heater nipples, fasten the female ends to the water heater, and then just push the push fitting onto the water supply lines. But this convenience doesn't come without a price. The 3/4-in. x 18-in. ones shown here cost about $30 each at a home center.

# REPLACING
# SHUTOFF VALVES

Save future headaches by replacing your old valves with new, trouble-free versions

## by **Rick Muscoplat, Contributing Editor**

**If** you're servicing or replacing a toilet or sink faucet, the first step is to shut off the water supply valve that feeds the fixture. But the simple task of shutting off the valve can be the start of a whole set of unexpected headaches.

Unless your house is fairly new, chances are you have multi-turn shutoff valves at every toilet and faucet. Shutoff valves perform flawlessly for years. But when they aren't opened or closed for a long time, you may find that the valve handle either won't turn or will turn but won't stop the water flow completely. And even if the valve does shut off the water, it may leak when you reopen it—the last thing you need after a plumbing repair!

You can spend time rebuilding the old valve, but the problems will just reappear years from now. The best way to deal with bad valves is to replace them with modern quarter-turn ball valves. They rarely lock up, leak or wear out and cost about $10. Best of all, they'll take just an hour or so to install. Here's how to put them in.

### Identify the valve connection style

Most shutoff valves connect to copper plumbing pipes in one of two ways: compression fitting or sweat fitting (for another option, see "Can You Use a Push-Fit Valve?" on p. 150). Identify the connection type used in your home by referring to the photos on p. 148. If you have an older home with galvanized pipes, we suggest hiring a plumber to do the switchout. Unscrewing the old valve and screwing on a new one may seem easy enough. But if the pipe is rusted internally or the threads are rotted, this "simple" plumbing job can turn into a plumbing nightmare. If your home is plumbed with PEX or plastic pipe, these instructions don't apply.

Once you identify the connection type, buy a quarter-turn shutoff ball valve to match the size of the incoming copper pipe and the size of the supply tube connection. If you're replacing a sweat valve, you'll need a torch, solder, flux, emery cloth, wire brushes and a flame protection cloth to shield the wall. This is also a good time to replace an old supply tube and a corroded escutcheon (wall trim plate).

### Prepare for valve replacement

Shut off the water at the main shutoff valve. If you have a gas water heater, turn the knob to the "pilot" position. Shut off the circuit breakers to an electric water heater. Then open a faucet on the lowest level of your house and another faucet on an upper level to drain the pipes. Then disconnect the supply tube from the shutoff valve. Replace the valve.

### After replacement

Close the new valve. Then open the water-main shutoff valve and let the water run until all the air is out of the pipes. Then shut off the upper and lower faucets. Check the new valves for leaks. Turn the water heater gas valve back to "on" or flip on the circuit breakers to the electric water heater.

## Valve types

### Sweat valve:
A sweat shutoff valve doesn't have any hex flats where the copper tubing enters from the wall. Replace a sweat valve with another sweat valve or a compression valve.

**COMPRESSION NUT**

### Compression valve:
Examine the portion of the valve closest to the wall. Look for a hexagonal compression nut and matching hex flats on the body of the valve next to the compression nut. If the valve has a compression nut but no hex flats, look for two flats on the sides of the valve body.

**HEX FLATS**

### Threaded valve:
Look for threads and hex flats where the steel pipe enters the valve.

## Replace a sweat valve

Hold the valve with pliers, loosen the packing nut and unscrew the entire valve stem. Peek inside and remove the old washer if it's stuck on the seat. Removing the valve stem allows any remaining water to drain out, making the unsweating process easier. Before you do any torch work, make sure there's a fire extinguisher nearby and safeguard the wall with a flame protection cloth. Then remove the old valve (**Photo 1**) and the remaining solder (**Photo 2**).

Clean the tubing with emery cloth. If you're replacing a sweat valve with a compression valve, sand off all traces of solder before adding the new escutcheon, nut and sleeve. Otherwise, remove enough old solder to allow the new sweat valve to slide onto the tubing. Remove the stem and wire-brush the opening in the new quarter-turn valve and apply flux to the valve and the copper tubing. With the flame protection cloth in place, heat the valve just enough to draw in the solder.

**NEW SWEAT VALVE**

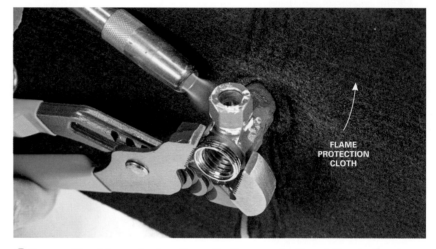

**FLAME PROTECTION CLOTH**

**1** **Remove the old sweat valve.** Drape the flame protection cloth over the copper tubing and tape it to the wall. Adjust the torch to a small flame and aim it toward the body of the valve. As soon as the solder melts, twist and pull the valve off the copper tubing with pliers.

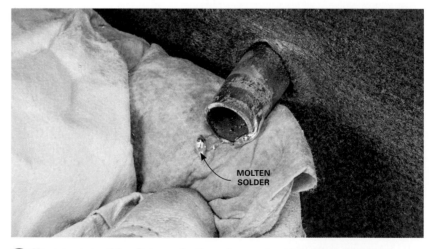

**MOLTEN SOLDER**

**2** **Clean excess solder.** Put on a leather glove and grab a damp cotton rag (microfiber cloth will melt). Heat the remaining solder with the torch until it's molten. As soon as the solder melts, wipe away the excess solder with a damp rag. Be sure to wear leather gloves to prevent steam burns.

## Remove and replace a compression shutoff valve

To remove a compression-style valve, hold the valve body with an adjustable or open-end wrench, or slip-joint pliers. Grab the compression nut with another wrench and turn it clockwise to loosen it. Then pull the valve off the copper tubing.

Next, remove the old compression sleeve and nut. Grab the old sleeve with pliers, using minimal pressure to avoid distorting the copper tubing. Then rotate and pull it off the tubing. If the sleeve is stuck, saw it (**Photo 1**) and break it (**Photo 2**).

Slide the new escutcheon and compression nut onto the copper tubing. Then add the new compression sleeve (**Photo 3**). Insert the new valve and apply a very light coating of pipe dope to the compression sleeve. Next, screw the compression nut onto the valve until snug. Hold the valve with a wrench or pliers and tighten the nut a one-half to three-quarters turn (follow the manufacturer's tightening instructions). Connect the supply tube and test for leaks.

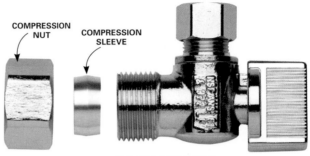

COMPRESSION NUT
COMPRESSION SLEEVE
**NEW COMPRESSION VALVE**

METAL-CUTTING BLADE
BRASS SLEEVE

**1** **Saw partially through the sleeve.** Use a hacksaw to cut partially through the sleeve at an angle. Use short strokes to avoid cutting into the copper tubing. Check your progress and stop cutting before you reach the copper.

PREVIOUS SLEEVE DEPRESSION

**2** **Twist and break the sleeve.** Insert a flat-blade screwdriver into the cut and twist the screwdriver to break the sleeve. Slide off the old sleeve, old compression nut and the escutcheon (if you're going to replace it).

**3** **Position the new compression sleeve.** Slide the new compression sleeve onto the copper tubing. If the old sleeve left depression marks, locate the new sleeve slightly forward of the marks.

## Can you use a push-fit valve?

Several companies make quarter-turn push-fit ball-style shutoff valves that install without tools. They're a good alternative to sweat and compression fittings if you have enough tubing projecting out from the wall and if that tubing is in good shape. They make the job even simpler. If your stub-out tubing is perfectly symmetrical, long enough and has a square-cut end, you might be able to use a push-fit valve to replace your old compression or sweat valve.

Most push-fit valves require at least 1 in. of stub-out tubing. So measure the length of the stub-out and refer to the valve manufacturer's length requirements before buying. If your tubing will work, shop for a valve that meets your configuration needs (straight or angled). Push-fit valves are available with and without a permanently mounted supply tube.

AT LEAST 1" STUB-OUT

We don't recommend the permanently installed supply tube version because you have to shut off the water and replace the entire unit if the supply tube ever needs replacement.

Before installing a push-fit valve, remove any burrs from the open end. If you're replacing a sweat valve, remove all traces of solder and ensure the tubing is perfectly round. Then mark the installed length on the tubing and push the valve onto the tubing until it reaches the mark.

# GreatGoofs®

### Smoldering soldering

Growing up in a historical home was both a privilege and a challenge. My father, an avid DIYer, decided to take on a project installing new vertical bead board on the walls in the hallway and in the bathroom. The last step in the project was to install a new toilet, which involved sweating a new shutoff fitting for the supply line.

Well, as luck would have it, he started a fire inside the wall, meaning we couldn't douse it with water. We called the fire department and within minutes they arrived. To get at the fire, the firefighters hacked away at the new bead board and then sprayed water inside the wall. Finally, it was extinguished, and we stepped back to look at what had become a much larger project. A soldering shield was a nice addition to the old toolbox!

–Robert R. Chapin

*You're welcome!*

### Levitating shower

As a new homeowner, I decided to put my do-it-yourself skills to the test by installing a new shower stall. The floor wasn't level, so I shimmed under the base and generously squirted in foam insulation to add support. When I returned to inspect the job several hours later, the base had risen about an inch, lifted by a big blob of foam. Too flustered to think straight, I called my father-in-law, who calmly spent several hours slicing away foam until the base settled back into place. After carefully adjusting the door hardware, it worked fine.

–Gregory Knight

# 4 Woodworking & Workshop Projects & Tips

## IN THIS CHAPTER

# RIDICULOUSLY SIMPLE
# STOOLS

Three stools inspired by the concept "simpler is better"

by **Spike Carlsen, Contributing Editor**

**FLIP-FLOP STEP STOOL**

I love projects that allow me to walk into my workshop with a few boards under one arm and then walk out a few hours later with something sturdy, useful and attractive. In other words, I like simple projects. Even more, I like ridiculously simple projects. I like them so much that a few years ago I wrote a book called *Ridiculously Simple Furniture Projects.*

Here are three stools inspired by that "simpler is better" concept.

**WORKSHOP STOOL**

**JIGSAW STOOL**

### Glue-and-screw furniture can look awesome

The three projects in this article have a few things in common: They're all stools, they're all made with dimensional lumber or plywood, and they're all better looking because they've been "dressed up" with a round-over router bit.

How often do I use that bit? So often that I have it in a dedicated router so that it's always ready to go. Round-over bits have a way of making jigsaw cuts look smoother, straight cuts look straighter, cheap wood look classier and paint jobs look better. Round-over bits also make wood furniture more comfortable to sit on and touch.

**1** **Mark the two side pieces.** Use a tape measure to swing arcs for the edges as shown in Figure A, then mark the holes for the pivot screws and the back dowel stop.

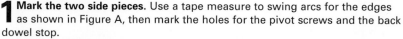

TEMPORARY
2x4 PROP
BLOCKS

**2** **Assemble the stool with 2-in. screws.** First screw the back brace to the bottom shelf, then secure this L-shape assembly to the sides. Drill the holes for the pivot screw and the back dowel stop.

1x6 BACK

BACK
STOP
DOWEL

1x4 BACK
BRACE

WASHERS

2" BOLTS WITH
LOCKNUTS

**3** **Install the back.** Screw the back to the pivot arms to create a U-shape. Drill the holes in the pivot arms, then secure the back using 2-in. bolts, washers and nuts. Don't permanently fasten the top until you've "test swiveled" the back to make sure you have enough clearance.

# FLIP-FLOP STEP STOOL

You'll find plenty of uses for a flip-flop stool. With the back swung up, it's the perfect chair for little kids to plunk down on. With the back swung down, it's the perfect step stool for reaching slightly-out-of-reach faucets, shelves and cabinets—for kids of all ages.

Begin by cutting the two sides to length and laying out the boards (**Photo 1** and **Figure A**). Note that the sides will be mirror images. To mark the curved sides, hook your tape over the lower corners then swing 15-in.- radius curves on each side. Use a pint can to create the rounded inner edges of the legs. The positions of the pivot and dowel holes are critical, so measure carefully. The pivot hole goes all the way through the board, but the dowel holes are only 1/2 in. deep. Drill the holes, then use a jigsaw to cut out the parts. Use a 1/4-in. round-over bit or sandpaper to soften all the edges.

Connect the 1x10 bottom shelf and 1x4 back brace to create an "L." Secure this assembly to the sides so the top edge of the 1x4 is flush with the upper back corner of the sides. Use 2x4 blocks to ensure the right spacing (**Photo 2**).

Cut the three parts for the back assembly (**Figure A**). To create the curved back, drive a pair of finish nails 3-1/2 in. from the edge of a 1x6, and flex a thin piece of wood upward between the nails to create an arc. Mark the arc with a pencil, then cut it out with a jigsaw. Secure the back to the two 1x4 sides to create a U-shape. Use 2-in. bolts (**Photo 3**) to secure the back assembly to the sides of the stool. (Tip: To install the washer between the back assembly and the stool, tape it over the hole in the side before installing the assembly.) Finally, position the top far back enough—about 1/2 in. from the front of the sides—so the back doesn't hit the front lip as it pivots.

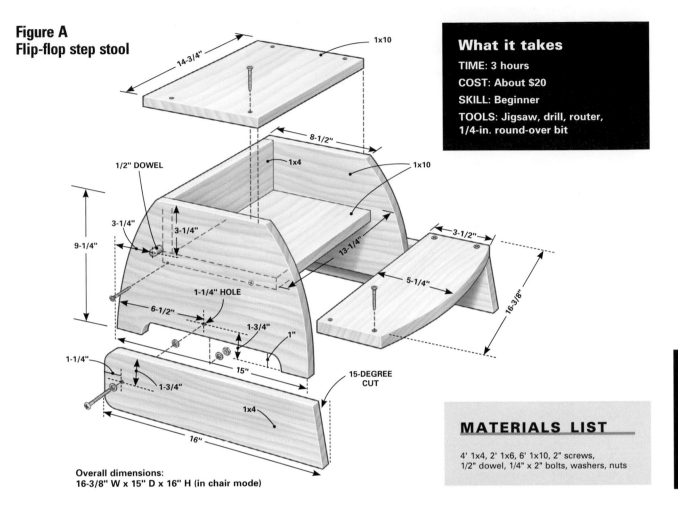

**Figure A**
**Flip-flop step stool**

1x10

14-3/4"

8-1/2"

1x4

1x10

1/2" DOWEL

3-1/4"

3-1/4"

9-1/4"

3-1/2"

13-1/4"

5-1/4"

16-3/8"

1-1/4" HOLE

6-1/2"

1-3/4"

1"

1-1/4"

15"

1-3/4"

15-DEGREE
CUT

1x4

16"

Overall dimensions:
16-3/8" W x 15" D x 16" H (in chair mode)

**What it takes**

TIME: **3 hours**
COST: **About $20**
SKILL: **Beginner**
TOOLS: **Jigsaw, drill, router,
1/4-in. round-over bit**

**MATERIALS LIST**

4' 1x4, 2' 1x6, 6' 1x10, 2" screws,
1/2" dowel, 1/4" x 2" bolts, washers, nuts

WOODWORKING & WORKSHOP
PROJECTS & TIPS

---

# GreatGoofs®

### Screen repair again....

Recently I was working in my garage making some molding for my screen windows. The garage just happens to be where I store my screens in the winter—right behind my table saw. As I was ripping some strips of wood, a small

piece jammed and the saw kicked it back fast and furious. Luckily I was out of harm's way, but my stack of screen windows wasn't so lucky. The chunk of wood made it through six screens before coming to a stop. Now I really have a repair project!

–Joe Magee

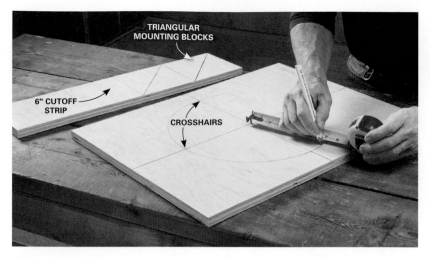

TRIANGULAR MOUNTING BLOCKS

6" CUTOFF STRIP

CROSSHAIRS

**1** **Lay out the legs and top.** Rip the plywood into 18-in. and 6-in. strips. Draw "crosshairs" on the larger piece, drive a screw in the center, hook your tape over it, then with a pencil snugged against the 7-in. mark, draw the circle. Cut four support blocks from the narrow piece.

LEG WITH TOP NOTCH

TOP

ROUTER WITH ROUND-OVER BIT

**2** **Cut out the parts and rout the edges.** Use a jigsaw to cut out the parts (see Figure A), then use a router with a 1/4-in. round-over bit to ease the edges as shown.

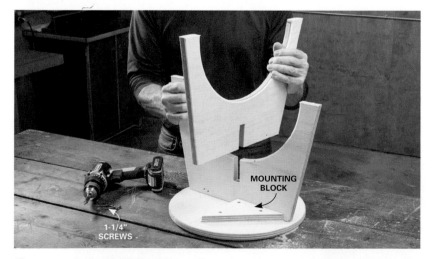

MOUNTING BLOCK

1-1/4" SCREWS

**3** **Assemble the stool.** Screw two triangular blocks where the top layout marks intersect (kitty corner from each other), then secure the legs using 2-in. screws. Install the other two blocks, then apply a finish.

You want simplicity and economy? These stools are designed so you can create eight of the short ones or four of the tall ones (or combinations thereof) from a single sheet of plywood. Here we'll show you how to build the short version; the taller stool is a couple inches wider, but employs the same concept to build.

Rip a 24 x 24-in. piece of plywood into 18-in. and 6-in. strips, then draw "crosshairs" (**Photo 1**) to locate the center of the larger board. Drive a drywall screw in the center and use that as a pivot point for swinging a 7-in.-radius circle. Draw lines 3/8 in. away from the crosshairs on each side (**Figure A**) to create 3/4-in.-thick layout marks for cutting the interlocking notches and installing the leg brace blocks later on.

Drill a 1/2-in. pilot hole in the lower notch as shown in **Figure A**, then insert a fine-tooth jigsaw blade and cut out the round top. Use your jigsaw to cut out the legs and the 3/4-in. x 2-1/2-in. notches for interlocking the legs. Use a router with a 1/4-in. round-over bit to soften both sides of the top and legs except for those edges along the tops of the two legs (**Photo 2**). If you don't have a router, ease the sharp edges with sandpaper. Cut the triangular blocks from the 6-in.-wide cutoff (**Photo 1**) and secure two of them to the underside of the top disc with glue and 1-1/4-in. all-purpose screws. Slip the legs into place as shown in **Photo 3**, then secure them to the blocks using 2-in. screws. Add the other two triangular blocks and apply a finish of your choice. We applied sanding sealer, a dark stain and then a coat of polyurethane.

## Figure A
## Jigsaw stool plywood layout
## (short version)

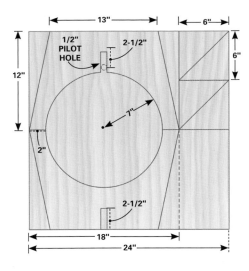

13"
6"
1/2" PILOT HOLE
2-1/2"
12"
6"
7"
2"
2-1/2"
18"
24"

## Figure B
## Jigsaw stool plywood layout
## (tall version)

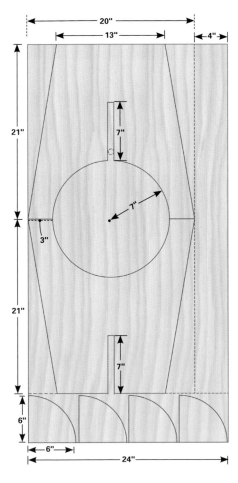

20"
13"
4"
21"
7"
7"
3"
21"
7"
6"
6"
24"

## Figure C
## Jigsaw stool assembly
## (tall version)

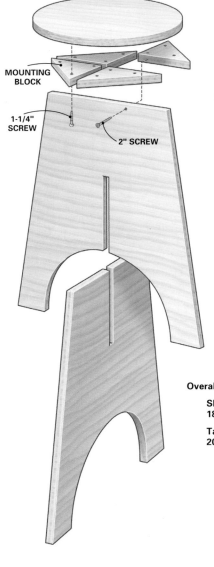

MOUNTING BLOCK
1-1/4" SCREW
2" SCREW

### What it takes

**TIME:** 2 hours

**COST:** About $8

**SKILL:** Beginner

**TOOLS:** Jigsaw, drill, router, 1/4-in. round-over bit

Overall dimensions

Short version:
18" W x 18" D x 12-3/4" H

Tall version:
20" W x 20" D x 21-3/4" H

## MATERIALS LIST

Short stool: 3/4" x 24" x 24" plywood

Tall stool: 3/4" x 24" x 48" plywood

Either stool: 1-1/4" screws, 2" screws, wood glue

## MEET THE BUILDER

Spike Carlsen is a Contributing Editor to *The Family Handyman* magazine and the author of five books including "Ridiculously Simple Furniture Projects" (Linden Publishing).

## WORKSHOP STOOL

Flip the top down and you have a stool for sitting or working; flip it up and you have a small stepladder for reaching. Build two of them and you have sawhorses for supporting sheets of plywood or long boards when working.

Begin by building the two side ladders using the spacing shown in **Figure A**. Use a square to ensure each "rung" is square to the leg, then secure each using glue and 1-1/4-in. screws (**Photo 1**). Use a 1/4-in. round-over bit to soften the outer edges of each leg. Stand the two ladder sides facing each other and install the two steps and the back brace. Predrill the holes to prevent splitting.

Cut the two top boards to length and round over the top edges. Secure the two top edges to each other using 2-1/2-in. no-mortise hinges; regular hinges will also work but will leave a slightly wider gap. Position the hinged-together top boards so they overhang the sides of the legs by about 3/4 in. and the front and back by about 3/8 in. Attach one of the top boards to the top "rungs" of the ladder using 2-in. screws.

**Figure A
Workshop stool**

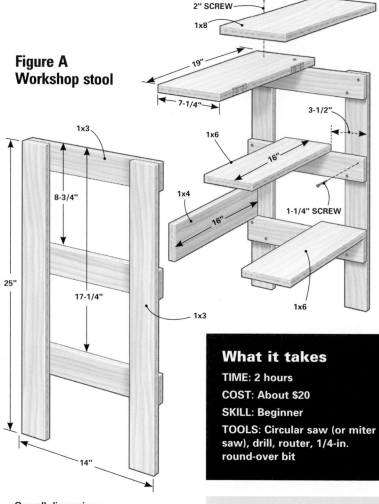

Overall dimensions:
19" W x 14" D x 25-3/4" H

### What it takes

**TIME:** 2 hours

**COST:** About $20

**SKILL:** Beginner

**TOOLS:** Circular saw (or miter saw), drill, router, 1/4-in. round-over bit

### MATERIALS LIST

16' 1x3, 2' 1x4, 3' 1x6, 4' 1x8, hinges, 1-1/4" screws, 2" screws, wood glue

**1** **Build the two side ladders.** Cut the pieces to length, then glue and screw the crosspieces to the legs. Use a square to ensure the assemblies are square.

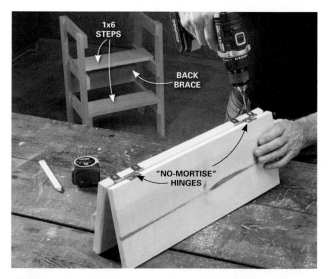

**2** **Put it all together.** Attach the two steps and the back brace to the ladder sides. Use hinges to join the two top pieces, then secure one of the boards to the top "rungs."

# MITER SAW TRICKS

## Simple details make your miter saw work harder for you

### by **Mark Petersen, Associate Editor**

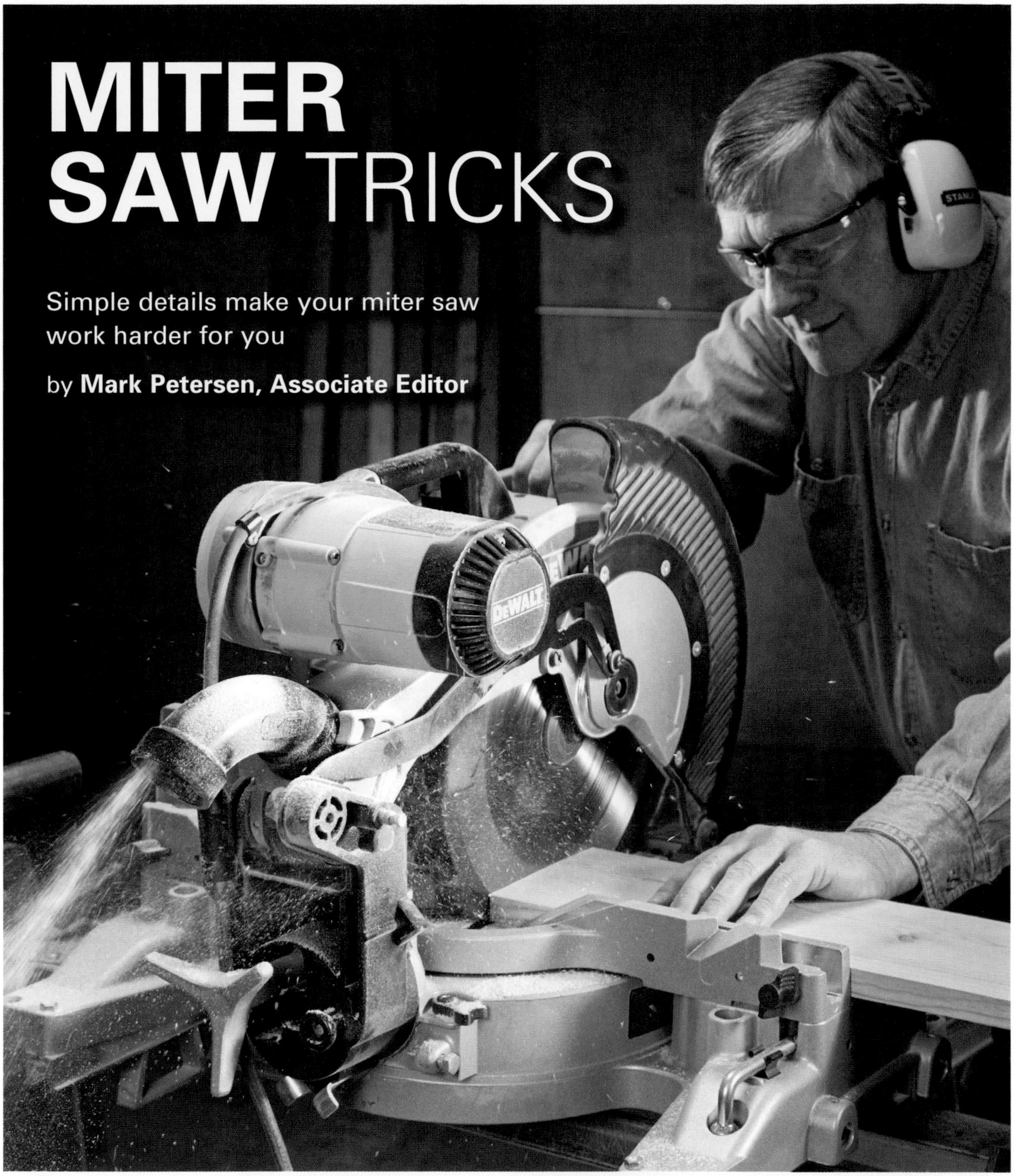

**Y**ou already know how to use a miter saw, and maybe even some slick tricks, but you probably haven't been using this tool all day, every day for 30 years. So we talked to a guy who has. He showed us how to get the most out of a miter saw and shared great tips on how to cut small pieces, reduce tear-outs and, most important, how to do it all safely.

## MEET AN EXPERT

Jerome Worm has worked as a trim carpenter for more than 30 years and has logged a few hundred thousand cuts on a miter saw. In addition to his experience and expertise, we love the fact that he still has all 10 fingers!

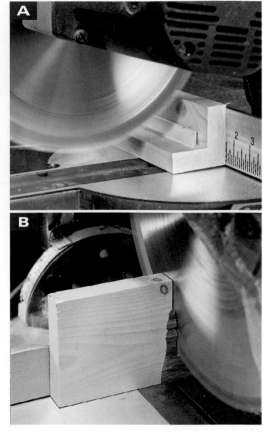

## Cut small parts with a sacrificial fence

To avoid launching small pieces across the room, use a sacrificial fence. Build a two-piece fence for tiny material like this cove molding (**Photo A**). Or just use a scrap board to back up small cutoffs (**Photo B**). Hold the saw down at the end of the cut and let the blade come to a complete stop.

## Patience makes clean, safe cuts

Dropping the blade into the workpiece too fast is dangerous and will likely result in a rough cut or splintered wood. This is especially true when you're cutting thin, narrow pieces. Give the motor a few extra milliseconds to reach full speed, then lower the blade slowly as you cut.

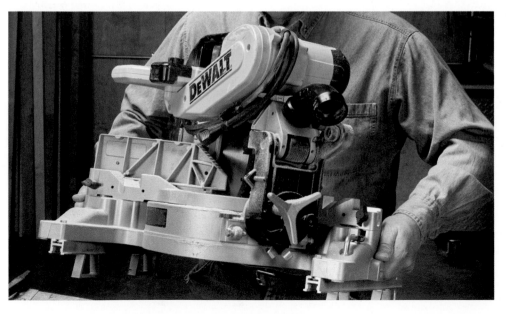

## Carry the saw by the base

Miter saws are heavy and awkward to carry. Some saws have handles near the top so you can lug them like a suitcase, but get into the habit of carrying them by the base instead. It's easier on your back and won't beat up the side of your leg. It's also easier to get through door openings without banging up the trim.

## Send the dust down

Controlling dust created by a miter saw is notoriously difficult. The collection bags do little, and even if you hook up a vacuum, dust is still going to fly. Our expert replaced his bag with an ABS plumbing elbow that fit snugly onto the dust chute. It doesn't control all the dust, but it sends a good portion of it to the floor instead of all over. Dust chutes vary in size, so measure yours before heading to the hardware store. The only surefire way to completely avoid dust indoors is to do your cutting outside.

## Mark a guideline on the base

Here's a fast way to cut a bunch of parts to the same length: Position the first one and then mark the location of the end on the saw base with a pencil. Now you have a guideline for the rest of your parts. This method may not be as accurate as a stop block, but sometimes perfection is unnecessary. The pencil mark easily rubs off when you're done.

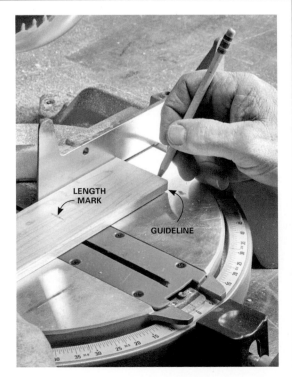

## Wear hearing protection

If you asked Jerome why he never wore hearing protection when he was younger, he would probably give you a blank stare unless he's wearing his hearing aids. Miter saws are loud and will damage your ears unless you protect them. Jerome would be the first to tell you that hearing loss is no joke!

## Shave off just a little

Here's a tip when you need to shave off just a tiny bit: Lower the blade while it's not spinning, and push the material tight up against the body of the blade. Get a firm grip on the material and raise the blade. Next, fire up the saw and lower the blade again. Because the teeth of the blade are slightly wider than the body, you'll end up shaving off just a hair.

## Cut wide boards with the best side down

Splinters and tear-outs occur where the blade breaks through the wood. That's the bottom side when plunge-cutting narrow boards, so it's best to cut narrow boards with the "show" side face up. But when you're cutting wider material on a sliding saw, you'll pull the blade toward you, lower the blade and then push it forward as you cut. In that process, splintering will occur on the top of the board, so cut with the board face down.

## Screw down guides

Clamping down a temporary guide makes cutting crown molding a lot easier, but sometimes the clamps are difficult to install because of the irregular shape of most miter saw bases. Clamps can also get in the way when you're changing the angle of a cut.

Don't be afraid to screw down a guide right into the base of your saw. A small hole is not going to affect the way the saw performs. Self-tapping screws work great in bases made of aluminum: Just make sure you position the stop so it doesn't interfere when you're changing angles. Install a couple screws on each side if the guide will get cut in half, and save your guides so you can use the same screw holes next time.

SELF-TAPPING SCREWS

CROWN MOLDING GUIDE

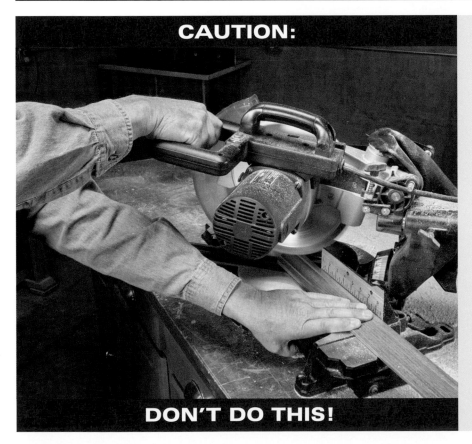

CAUTION:

DON'T DO THIS!

## Never cross your arms

Sorry, lefties, but most miter saws are designed for right-handed users, meaning the saw is operated with the right hand and the material held down with the left. But sometimes the material will have to be held down on the right side of the blade. On those occasions, it's tempting to still use your right hand to operate the saw, but doing so will cause your left hand to cross in front of the path of the blade—that's bad. It will feel weird, but in this situation, use your left hand to operate the saw and your right to secure the material. Our expert knows carpenters who have ignored this advice and have the scars on their arms to prove it.

# SIMPLE KITCHEN SHELF

Easy for anyone to build—and fun to customize!

by **Ken Collier, Editor in Chief**

## MEET AN EXPERT

**Ken Collier, a former cabinetmaker and custom woodworker, has been working wood for 40 years. He's built everything from coat hooks to kitchens, and dozens of different shelves. He's also the Editor in Chief of *The Family Handyman.***

Lots of kitchens have a little wall space that would be perfect for a storage or display shelf. Plenty of bathrooms do too. When I was a cabinetmaker, I built shelves like this for customers, and I liked them so much that I built a fleet of them for my own home. However, those shelves were made with an arsenal of high-powered woodworking tools. This time, I wanted to design a shelf that anyone with basic tools could build. This shelf is a great project for a beginning woodworker, and since it's so easy to adapt to different uses, a more advanced DIYer can have a lot of fun customizing it.

## Tools and wood

You'll need a jigsaw, a drill and two accessories for the drill. The first is a No. 8 combination drill bit and countersink (shown with "Low-Tech Woodworking" on p. 165), which you can pick up inexpensively anywhere drill bits are sold. The second accessory is a small sanding drum (**Photo 3**), which you can find at home centers or online for about $12. The one I used is made by Vermont American. The only other tool you might need is a nail set, for setting the heads of finish nails below the surface. Obviously, if you have a band saw and a miter saw, they will make this project a piece of cake.

You can build this shelf from just about any type of wood. Resist the urge to use the least expensive knotty pine, unless that's the look you're after. Knotty pine will be harder to work with and to paint well. Instead, get clear pine, poplar or any other knot-free board. If you're planning to paint the shelf, avoid oak. I used alder from a local home center.

## Cut out the shelf and brackets

Begin by cutting the shelf to length with a jigsaw (**Photo 1**). Then cut a piece 6 in. long from which you can cut the two brackets (**Photo 2**). Jigsaws often make a rougher cut on the top surface, so label that "top." The roughness will be hidden by the edging, even if the top of the shelf is visible after hanging it. But use a fine-tooth blade and set your oscillating feature (if your saw has it) to zero.

You can trace the curve for the brackets from the full-size pattern on p. 166, or even easier, use the bottom of a coffee can or a small plate. The exact curve isn't important. After the brackets are cut, smooth the sawn edges with a file, sanding block and the sanding drum in your drill (**Photo 3**) until the wood is smooth. You can stop sanding at about 150 or 180 grit.

## Install edging strips on the shelf

Start edging the shelf by cutting the end strips to length. Instead of measuring, just hold the molding to the end of the shelf and mark it for cutting. It won't hurt if it's a hair too long. Mark one edge of the shelf as the front edge, then nail on the side strips (**Photo 4**), keeping the front edge flush. Make sure the rounded edge faces out. Put a thin bead of glue on the shelf edge before nailing, and keep the bottom edge as flush as you can. If the strips are a little long in back, you can easily sand or file off the

### Low-tech woodworking

This is a low-tech project. A jigsaw and a cordless drill are the only power tools you need, though there are more accurate and faster options. You'll also need some basic hand tools and two specialized accessories for the drill: a sanding drum and a combination drill/countersink bit. (See the text for more info.)

COMBO DRILL/ COUNTER- SINK

SANDING DRUM

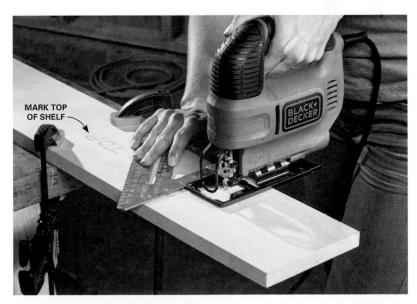

MARK TOP OF SHELF

**1** **Cut the shelf to length.** Use a fresh blade and a square to guide your cut. A miter saw is the best tool for the job, but if you don't have access to one, you can substitute almost any other saw.

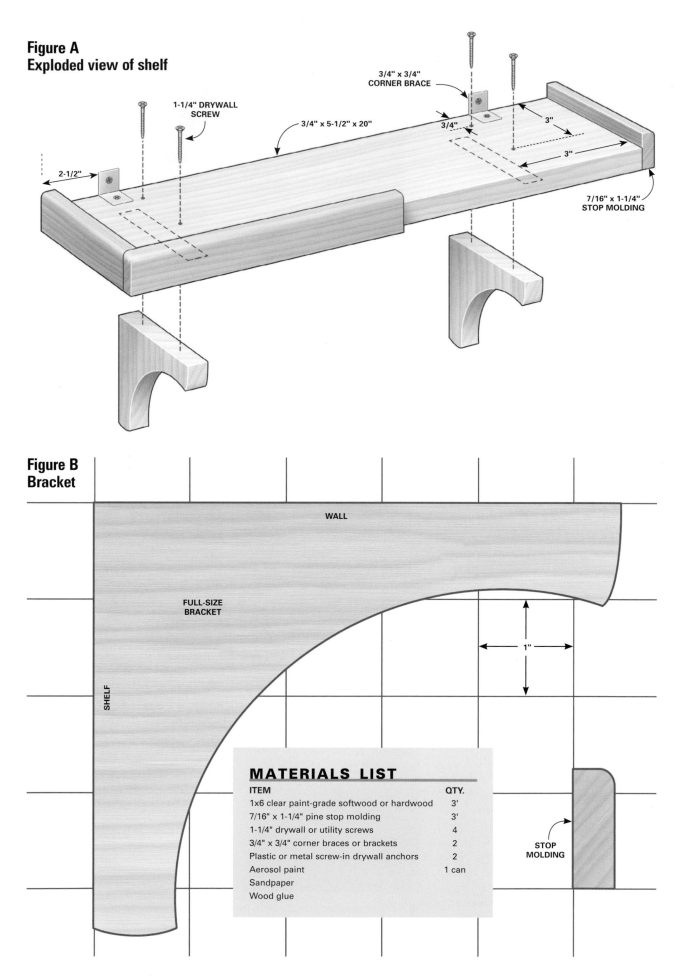

**Figure A**
**Exploded view of shelf**

3/4" x 3/4"
CORNER BRACE

1-1/4" DRYWALL
SCREW

3/4" x 5-1/2" x 20"

3/4"

3"

3"

2-1/2"

7/16" x 1-1/4"
STOP MOLDING

**Figure B**
**Bracket**

WALL

FULL-SIZE
BRACKET

1"

SHELF

STOP
MOLDING

## MATERIALS LIST

| ITEM | QTY. |
|---|---|
| 1x6 clear paint-grade softwood or hardwood | 3' |
| 7/16" x 1-1/4" pine stop molding | 3' |
| 1-1/4" drywall or utility screws | 4 |
| 3/4" x 3/4" corner braces or brackets | 2 |
| Plastic or metal screw-in drywall anchors | 2 |
| Aerosol paint | 1 can |
| Sandpaper | |
| Wood glue | |

excess, and if they stick out a little on the bottom edge, that can be sanded off too. Finally, nail on the edging strip in front.

Now set the nails and put a little painter's putty on them. When the putty is dry, sand the edging so the corners are smooth and the bottom edge is flush with the shelf. The bottom of the shelf will have a seam between the shelf and the edging. It's pretty much impossible to eliminate that seam permanently. Expansion and contraction of the wood will open it up even if you caulk or putty it, so don't be too much of a perfectionist. However, if your cut on the 1x6 is particularly rough, some putty there will help clean things up.

## Screw the brackets to the shelf

The next step is to drill some screw holes in the shelf for attaching the brackets. The idea is simple: two screw holes on each side of the shelf so you can screw down into the brackets. Here's what to do. First, hold a bracket where you want it to be, but on the top of the shelf. Trace around the bracket, then do the same thing for the other bracket. Mark the screw locations and drill screw holes in the shelf from the top, using your combination drill/countersink bit.

Now hold a bracket in position on the bottom of the shelf, make sure the back edge is flush with the back edge of the shelf and that the screw holes are centered on the bracket. You can do it by eye, but if that's hard, put the two screws in their holes and use the points of the screws to guide you. Drive the screws by hand into the bracket (**Photo 5**), then repeat with the other bracket. Now is a good time to step back and admire your work, because you're almost done. But if for some reason you messed this part up, just drill new holes and fill the old ones with putty. You can shift the position of the brackets if you want.

## Paint your shelf

Begin this part of the project by unscrewing the brackets. It's always easier to paint a project well if you can

**2** **Cut the curved brackets.** For a curve like this, a smooth continuous cut is more important than following the line exactly. Any bumps or blips will be hard to sand out.

**3** **Sand the curves with a sanding drum.** The trick is to go against the direction of rotation of the drill, with the drill going fast. If you make a gouge, angle the drum slightly to remove it.

**4** **Nail on the edging.** The edging is a stock molding from home centers. It keeps stuff from falling off the shelf and covers the rough ends of the shelf.

**5** **Screw the brackets to the shelf.** Notice that we've traced the shape of the bracket on the top of the shelf to help position the screw holes. We used a combination countersink/drill bit for the holes.

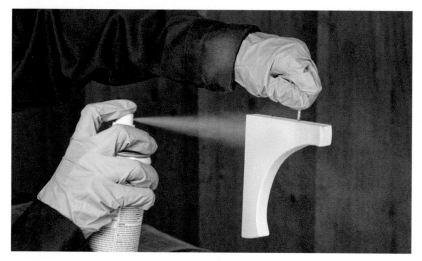

**6** **Spray-paint the shelf parts.** You'll get better results by unscrewing the brackets and painting everything separately. A screw in the top of the bracket is a handy handle.

**7** **Hang your shelf with small angle brackets.** For a light-duty shelf like this, you don't need to screw it to the studs. Just make sure the shelf is level and use drywall anchors in the wall.

do the parts separately. Sand the pieces thoroughly to about 150 to 180 grit, removing sharp edges and corners, but not rounding them over too much. Wipe the sanding dust off with a rag and vacuum the parts thoroughly. Set up your painting area. I highly recommend using spray paint for this project because it'll get you the smoothest finish.

Cover your work surface with paper or plastic, and set your shelf on strips or blocks to get it up off the surface. The shelf is pretty easy to paint, but go light on the edges to avoid drips. After the first coat of paint is thoroughly dry, sand it lightly with fine sandpaper, just enough to take off any roughness. Wipe and vacuum, then apply two final coats.

There's a trick to painting the brackets: Drive a long screw in one of the holes and use it as a little handle. That way you can spray the whole piece evenly in one shot (**Photo 6**). Then carefully set it down on a couple strips of wood to dry. When the paint is dry on all the parts, reassemble your shelf.

## Hang your shelf

We recommend using small angle brackets to hang your shelf (**Photo 7**). Normally the top of a shelf is above eye level and the brackets are hidden, especially with items on the shelf. If your brackets are more exposed, give them a little spray paint to match the shelf, and paint the part that goes on your wall to match your wall. They'll be barely noticeable. Generally, though, this step isn't necessary.

To hang the shelf, use drywall anchors. Don't worry about hitting studs; there shouldn't be enough weight on this shelf to require it. Just put the shelf where you want it to go, make sure it's level, mark through the brackets where the anchors will go, and install the anchors. If it seems like you need a third hand to manage everything, you could draw a level line on the wall where the shelf will go. With the anchors in place, use the screws that came with the anchors to attach the shelf. Your shelf is complete! When you're ready to build more, check out the variations on p. 169.

## Customize your shelf

Go ahead—play with this project! It's easy to make your shelf as long as you want it to be. Just put more brackets underneath it, maybe one every 2 ft. or so. You could also scale it up by using 1x8 lumber, or even wider stock, as long as you also scale up the brackets. Some of my other favorite variations are shown below. However, I have one strong recommendation: If you're doing anything more than changing the size or color, first make a prototype out of inexpensive pine. Your plates, pot lids, cooking tools or whatever will be different from ours, so make sure they fit.

### POTHOOKS AND LIDS

This shelf has hooks screwed underneath to hold frying pans. We gave the hooks a dark finish by heating them with a torch as shown below. On our shelf, we cut off some of the threaded part of each hook with a bolt cutter because they were too long. The pot lids are held in place with two rows of 5/16-in. dowels. For heavier lids, use 3/8-in. dowels.

**Blacken screw hooks with oil**
Working outside, burn off the plating with a torch. Dip the hook into cooking oil and heat it until the oil burns off. You may need to repeat a couple times. This makes a hard, baked-on coating that resists wear. It's like seasoning a cast iron pan.

### PLATES AND SPOONS

This shelf has a strip of molding (any kind will work) nailed on the top a couple inches from the back edge. This will keep plates from sliding off. The rod is 5/16-in.-diameter steel available at hardware stores. Cut it with a hacksaw and file the ends smooth. The trick is to drill the brackets before assembly, both at the same time, so the rod is perfectly aligned. The hooks are simple S-hooks, also a hardware item, opened up with a pair of pliers.

**A wood strip makes it a plate rack**
Tack a piece of molding to the top of the shelf to keep plates from sliding. Experiment with your plates to find the best location for the molding.

# MACKINTOSH TABLE

Build this Arts & Crafts table with
inexpensive wood and two basic power tools

by **Tom Caspar, Contributing Editor**

For a while now, I've been on the lookout for a simple piece of furniture for my brother to make. He has a modest shop and some experience building, but he's ready to tackle a "real" project. This table is perfect. It's also a great design for a more experienced builder who appreciates a quick and easy project.

You can build the table from paint-grade yellow poplar. It's widely available at home centers in 1x3s, 1x4s and other standard sizes. You'll also need 1/2-in.-thick and 1/4-in.-thick material for the drawer. The total cost for the wood will be well under $100. Aside from a drill, all you'll need to build the table are two power tools: a table saw and a plate joiner. A drill press is helpful but not necessary.

This table was originally designed in 1904 by the Scottish architect Charles Rennie Mackintosh for a home in Glasgow. Like so many other things Scottish, it's economical in terms of time, materials and tools.

## First make the sides

When you buy your lumber (see Materials List, p. 173), select pieces that are straight and flat. To make finishing easier, stay away from pieces that are green or have black streaks. Most stores have large piles to pick through—and you won't need much wood—so be choosy.

Start by cutting the legs (A) from your 1x3 material. You won't have to rip the wood; just cut the pieces to final length. Mark the top end of each leg to indicate which sides face out (**Photo 1**). I always

### TWO POWER TOOLS
**A table saw and a plate joiner are all the muscle you'll need.**

### READY-TO-GO MATERIALS
**Make the whole project from paint-grade yellow poplar.**

### A WELL-CRAFTED DRAWER
**The joints are simple 1/4-in. oak pegs.**

mark each piece of a project like this. If you make your marks anywhere else, sanding will erase them. Ends usually don't get sanded.

Draw centerlines for the biscuits that will join the legs to the sides (B) and drawer guides (C)—see **Figure A**, p. 172. Draw these lines across the inside faces of the legs. Position each leg so that its outside edge faces up, then place a poplar offcut under the plate joiner and cut the slots (**Photo 2**).

Use 1x6s to make the sides and 1x4s to make the drawer guides. Again,

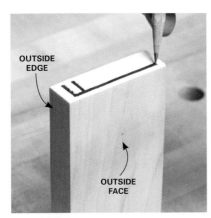

OUTSIDE EDGE
OUTSIDE FACE

**1 Cut the table legs.** Begin by cutting the table legs from poplar 1x3s. Mark the ends of all the parts to identify the sides that face out.

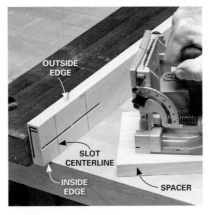

OUTSIDE EDGE
SLOT CENTERLINE
INSIDE EDGE
SPACER

**2 Make the biscuit slots.** Cut a pair of No. 20 biscuit slots in the top end of each leg. Place a 3/4-in. scrap under the plate joiner to space the slots.

DRAWER GUIDE
SIDE

**3 Glue sides and guides.** Glue together the table's sides and drawer guides, cut 1 in. extra long. After the glue dries, trim them to final length.

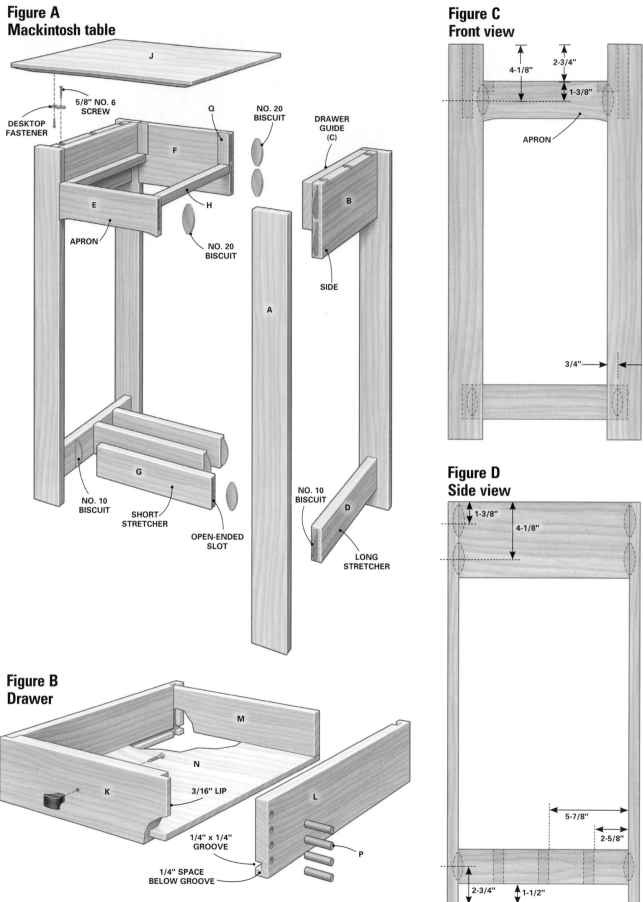

## Figure A
### Mackintosh table

J

5/8" NO. 6
SCREW

DESKTOP
FASTENER

Q

NO. 20
BISCUIT

DRAWER
GUIDE
(C)

F

B

E

H

SIDE

APRON

NO. 20
BISCUIT

A

G

NO. 10
BISCUIT

SHORT
STRETCHER

OPEN-ENDED
SLOT

NO. 10
BISCUIT

D

LONG
STRETCHER

## Figure C
### Front view

4-1/8"

2-3/4"

1-3/8"

APRON

3/4"

## Figure D
### Side view

1-3/8"

4-1/8"

5-7/8"

2-5/8"

2-3/4"

1-1/2"

## Figure B
### Drawer

M

N

K

3/16" LIP

1/4" x 1/4"
GROOVE

1/4" SPACE
BELOW GROOVE

L

P

## MATERIALS LIST

| ITEM | QTY. | ITEM | QTY. |
|---|---|---|---|
| 1x3 yellow poplar | 16 lin. ft. | 1/4" oak dowel | 1 ft. |
| 1x4 yellow poplar | 6 lin. ft. | No. 20 biscuits | 14 |
| 1x6 yellow poplar | 4 lin. ft. | No. 10 biscuits | 10 |
| 1x8 yellow poplar | 5 lin. ft. | Desktop fasteners | 6 |
| 1/2x4 yellow poplar | 3 lin. ft. | 5/8" No. 6 screws | 14 |
| 1/4x6 yellow poplar | 3 lin. ft. | Knob and glue | |

## CUTTING LIST

| KEY | QTY. | DIMENSIONS | NAME |
|---|---|---|---|
| A | 4 | 3/4" x 2-1/2" x 29-1/4" | Legs |
| B | 2 | 3/4" x 5-1/2" x 12-1/2" | Sides |
| C | 2 | 3/4" x 3-1/2" x 12-1/2" | Drawer guides |
| D | 2 | 3/4" x 2-1/2" x 12-1/2" | Long stretchers |
| E | 1 | 3/4" x 3" x 9-1/4" | Apron |
| F | 1 | 3/4" x 5-1/2" x 9-1/4" | Back |
| G | 3 | 3/4" x 2-1/2" x 10-3/4" | Short stretchers |
| H | 2 | 3/4" x 3/4" x 12-1/2" | Drawer runners |
| J | 1 | 3/4" x 16-3/4" x 17" | Top |
| K | 1 | 3/4" x 2-3/4" x 9-1/4" | Drawer front |
| L | 2 | 1/2" x 2-3/4" x 12-3/4" | Drawer sides |
| M | 1 | 1/2" x 2-1/8" x 8-3/4" | Drawer back |
| N | 1 | 1/4" x 12-1/4" x 8-11/16" | Drawer bottom |
| P | 8 | 1/4"-dia. x 1" | Drawer pegs |
| Q | 2 | 1/4" x 1" x 2-3/4" | Drawer stops |

you won't have to rip the wood, but this time cut each piece 1 in. extra long. Glue the pieces together, making sure their top edges are flush (**Photo 3**). Cut some more 1x3 material to make the long stretchers (D). Also make these pieces 1 in. extra long.

After the glue dries, cut the side/guides and long stretchers to the same final length. Draw biscuit-slot centerlines on the outside faces of the side/guides, then place the pieces face up on your bench and cut slots in them (**Photo 4**). Use the same offcut as a spacer under the plate joiner. This method ensures that the drawer guides will be flush with the inside edge of the legs. That's essential for the drawer to work right.

Next, adjust your plate joiner to make No. 10 slots. Mark and cut slots in the legs to receive the long stretchers. Place the spacer under the plate joiner this time too. Cut corresponding slots in the ends of the long stretchers (without using the spacer, of course).

Cut vertical slots on the inside faces of the long stretchers (**Photo 5**). Make a 2-5/8-in. spacer from a 1x3 for positioning the outside slots (**Figure D**). Make a 5-7/8-in. spacer for the middle slots.

### Figure E
### Top detail

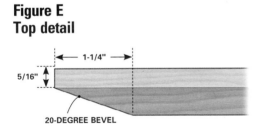

1-1/4"

5/16"

20-DEGREE BEVEL

### Figure F
### Apron detail

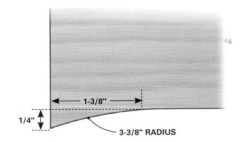

1-3/8"

1/4"

3-3/8" RADIUS

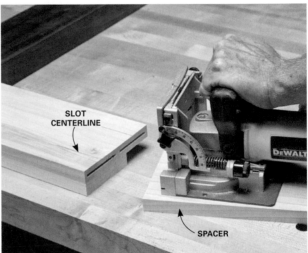

SLOT CENTERLINE

SPACER

**4** **Make slots in the guides.** Cut biscuit slots in the side/guides, using the spacer again. This puts the drawer guides flush with the inside edge of the legs.

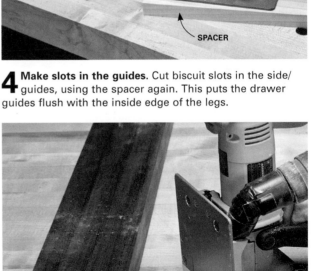

SPACER

SLOT CENTERLINE

**5** **Cut slots in stretchers.** Make vertical slots in the stretchers that go between the legs. Butt the plate joiner against a spacer to locate each slot.

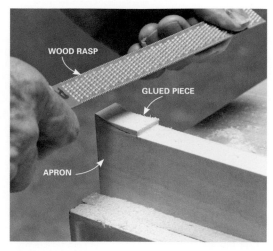

**6** **Glue table sides.** Glue the sides of the table. Use a combination square to make sure the stretcher is in the correct position.

**7** **Create arches.** Shape arches from small pieces glued to the table's apron. With so little wood to remove, just use a rasp and sandpaper.

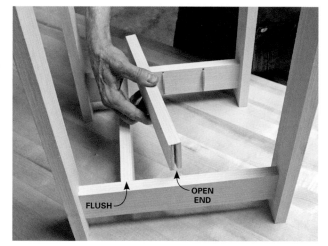

**8** **Glue the base.** Glue the table's base. Clamp spacers between the legs to make sure they're parallel. Be sure the table is square.

**9** **Cut slots in stretchers.** Cut open-ended slots in the short stretchers. Slide them in place, making sure their top edges are flush.

Smooth the inside faces of the legs with 150-grit sandpaper. In addition, sand the outside faces of the side/guides and both faces of the long stretchers. Glue all these pieces together (**Photo 6**).

## Join the sides

The curves on the table's front apron (E) are a beautiful detail—and easy to make. Start by cutting the apron 1 in. extra long from a piece of 1x4. Rip it 3-1/4 in. wide. Discard the waste, then rip it again to 2-3/4 in. wide. Cut 1-3/4-in.-long pieces from both ends of the narrow offcut and glue them back to the main piece. Once the glue dries, trim 1/2 in. from one end of this piece, then trim the piece to final length. Cut the table's back (F) from a piece of 1x6 and trim it to the same length. In addition, cut two 1x3 spacers to this length.

Using a 1-gallon paint can as a guide, draw the apron's arches on the small pieces you cut and glued to the apron

(**Figure F**, p. 173). Form the arches with a rasp and sandpaper (**Photo 7**). Adjust your plate joiner to make No. 20 slots, then mark and cut biscuit slots in the ends of the apron and back pieces. Mark and cut corresponding slots in the base (**Figure D**, p. 172).

Glue the base together, clamping the spacers between the legs (**Photo 8**). After the glue dries, cut short stretchers (G) to fit between the long stretchers. Cut biscuit slots in the short stretchers. The lower end of these slots must be open so you can slip the parts in place (**Photo 9**). That's easy to do—just make three overlapping cuts with the plate joiner to form each slot. Glue biscuits into the long stretchers, then apply glue to the short stretchers and slide them over the biscuits.

Cut the drawer runners (H) to size and glue them in place. Their front edges must be level with the top of the apron. Use a combination square to make sure the runners are parallel to the top edges of the drawer guides.

**10** **Saw bevel edges.** Saw bevels around the table's top. Use a tall sliding fence to support the top.

**11** **Fasten top to base.** Screw the top to the base using desktop fasteners. Positioned on the outside, they won't interfere with the drawer.

**12** **Cut rabbets.** Begin making the drawer by using a dado set to cut rabbets in the drawer's front.

DESKTOP FASTENER

DRAWER BOTTOM GROOVE

**13** **Drill holes in sides.** Drill 1/4-in. holes through the drawer's sides, then cut grooves in the front and sides to receive the drawer's bottom.

**14** **Glue the drawer.** Glue the drawer together. Position the back of the drawer so it sits just above the groove for the drawer's bottom.

## Make the top

Assemble the top (J) from three pieces of 1x8. Trim each piece to final length, then glue them together, making sure their ends are even. Rip the top to width after the glue dries. Sand the top to even the joints, starting with 60-grit paper. Continue with 100 grit, then finish with 150 grit. Cut bevels around the top by tilting your saw blade to 20 degrees (**Photo 10** and **Figure E**, p. 173).

Using a Forstner bit, drill holes for desktop fasteners in the top edges of the table's sides (**Figure A**, p. 172). Screw the fasteners in place, then turn over the table's base and center it on the top. Fasten the base to the top (**Photo 11**).

## Build a well-crafted drawer

Now build the drawer. Cut the drawer front (K) slightly undersize—it should be 1/32 in. narrower than the space above the table's apron and 1/32 in. shorter than the distance between the table's legs. Using 1/2-in. poplar, cut the drawer sides (L) the same width as the front. Trim them to final length. Using a 1/2-in.-wide dado set, cut rabbets in the ends of the drawer front to receive the sides (**Figure B**, p. 172 and **Photo 12**). (You could also make multiple cuts with a regular blade.)

Drill 1/4-in. holes in the sides (**Photo 13**). A drill press is best, but you can do this by hand—just make sure the holes are perpendicular. Using a 1/4-in. dado set (or by making two passes with a regular blade), cut grooves for the drawer bottom in the front and side pieces. In addition, cut 1/4-in.-wide dadoes in the side pieces to receive the drawer's back (M). Cut the back to width and length.

Glue the drawer together using clamps in both directions to make sure the front joints are tight (**Photo 14**). After the glue dries, drill through the holes in the drawer's sides, making them 1 in. deep. Note: Don't drill the holes directly opposite the drawer bottom grooves.

**15 Glue in pegs.** Drill through the 1/4-in. holes to make them deeper, then glue in short pegs. This makes a very strong joint.

**16 Glue up bottom.** Glue up the drawer's bottom from 1/4-in. poplar. Use opposing wedges to squeeze the pieces between two clamped boards.

**17 Fit drawer bottom.** Slide the bottom into the drawer. Don't use glue, because the bottom must be free to expand and contract.

**18 Seal and stain.** Seal the wood with two coats of poly, then use thin coats of gel stain. Plain poplar can look quite pretty!

Cut 1-in. pegs from 1/4-in. oak rods, then glue them in the holes you drilled (**Photo 15**). Glue 1/4-in.-long pegs in the other two holes (they're just for show).

Cut pieces for the drawer's bottom (N) from 1/4-in. poplar. Trim them to final length and glue them together (**Photo 16**). Clamping boards this thin is very difficult—I use wedges instead. Cut the bottom to final width.

Using 60-grit paper, sand the edges of the bottom until the bottom slides easily in the drawer's grooves (**Photo 17**). Fasten the bottom to the drawer's back with screws. Remove the table's top, then slide the drawer into the table. Position the drawer's front flush with the legs, then make stops (Q) to fill the small gap behind the drawer's sides. Glue the stops to the base.

## Finally, finish your table

Finish the top of the table separately. It should have equal coats of finish on both sides, so it doesn't warp.

The original Mackintosh table was painted white, and if you'd like to paint your table, we recommend aerosol paint. You can also let the wood darken naturally. I chose to stain my table instead. To avoid a blotchy look, I first sealed the table with two coats of water-base poly. Then I applied a coat of amber shellac, thinned 50 percent with denatured alcohol, to give the wood a golden color. I applied two coats of gel stain (General Finishes' "Candlelite") followed by two more coats of poly (**Photo 18**). Whatever stain approach you choose, be sure to test it thoroughly on pieces of scrap.

# RESAWING ON A BAND SAW

Resawing opens up a world of possibilities for your woodworking

by **Tim Johnson, Contributing Editor**

utting a board into thinner pieces of the same length and width is my favorite band-sawing operation because it opens a world of woodworking opportunities. Called "resawing," this process allows creating wide panels from narrow boards, cutting a board into thin pliable pieces for bent laminations, slicing thin sheets of veneer, and even turning logs into lumber. Like any woodworking skill, resawing takes time and practice to master. Here are a few of my best tips to help make resawing your favorite band-sawing operation too.

## Start with a board that's thick enough

Resawing consumes some of a board's thickness, so don't expect to get three 1/4-in.-thick boards from a 3/4-in. board. In addition to the material lost during the initial cut, you have to plane the resawn pieces to flatten them and remove the saw marks. When I resaw a 3/4-in.-thick board, I only expect to get two 1/4-in.-thick boards.

## Three must-dos for resawing success

**1. Use a resaw blade.** Specifically designed to make straight cuts in thick stock, resaw blades are wide and have only three to four teeth per inch (TPI). Don't scrimp on the price: Buy a high-quality blade such as the Timber Wolf 1/2-in. 3PC blade I'm using here (about $36 online). Resawing with a dull blade wastes both time and materials, so replace the blade at the first signs of dullness—when the feed rate slows or the cut starts to wander.

**2. Install a tall resaw fence** like the one shown at the bottom of "Set the Fence at the Correct Angle," p. 178. Just glue the face to the base at 90 degrees, using a pair of gussets for stability. For the best results, make the fence tall enough to completely support the board.

**3. Match the feed rate to the cutting action.** Simply feed the stock at a steady pace that efficiently advances the cut without significantly slowing the blade or bogging down the motor.

### MEET AN EXPERT

**Tim Johnson has worked with wood for more than 40 years as an antiques dealer, a professional furniture maker, and most recently as senior editor of** *American Woodworker* **and** *Woodwork* **magazines.**

## Set the fence at the correct angle

It sounds crazy, but on most band saws, you have to angle the stock to make a straight cut. Finding this "drift angle" and setting the fence to match it is crucial to successful resawing.

Start by marking a straight line on a scrap board, parallel to its edge. Then follow the line to make a straight cut, angling the board as necessary. When you've cut far enough to establish the drift angle, hold the board in position and transfer the angle to the saw's table (**top photo below**).

Use the line you've marked to position the fence at the same angle (**bottom photo below**). Then make test cuts and adjust the fence as necessary to fine-tune the setup until the stock stays flush against the fence, without binding against it or wandering away.

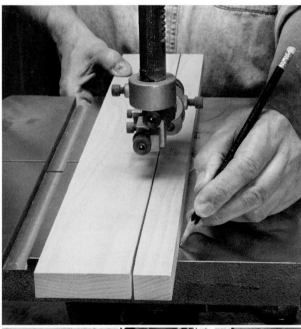

RESAW FENCE

ALIGN WITH
PENCIL MARK

## Square the blade and the board

Making sure the blade is perpendicular to the table is especially important when you're resawing a wide board. For the best results, raise the guidepost all the way and use a square with an arm that matches the saw's resaw capacity (**photo above left**). Adjust the table so no gaps appear between the blade and the arm. Next, make sure the board has a square corner (**photo above right**). That way it will ride flush against both the tall fence and the table during the cut.

## Box in long boards

Resawing long boards is a breeze with this setup, because it automatically holds the board against the fence so your hands are free to feed the board. Make the box about as tall as the board is wide, about as wide as the distance between the blade and the front of the table, and about as long as the distance between the blade and the table's right edge. Position the box in front of the blade and clamp it so the board fits snugly but slides between the box and the fence without binding or wobbling.

## Double your resaw capacity

Imagine creating a 24-in.-wide book-matched table-top or turning a 12-in.-diameter log into lumber. Installing a riser block on a typical 14-in. band saw increases its resaw capacity from 6 to 12 in. Check with the manufacturer to see if a riser block kit is available for your saw.

The kit includes the block and all the other parts you need to stretch your saw, such as a longer guidepost and blade guard. Of course, you'll also have to buy new, longer blades, and if your saw bogs down easily when resawing those super-wide boards, you may have to install a larger motor to handle the increased workload.

**12" RESAW CAPACITY**

**6" RISER BLOCK**

## Easy resawing

Partially resawing a board on your table saw makes resawing with your band saw easier, because the blade has less to cut and the saw kerfs keep it from wandering. It's a great method to use if your band saw bogs down during full-width resawing, and in many cases, it can save time by allowing you to resaw without installing a resaw blade. Even if you can completely resaw the board by raising the table saw's blade, I prefer this method, because it's safer to finish the cut on the band saw.

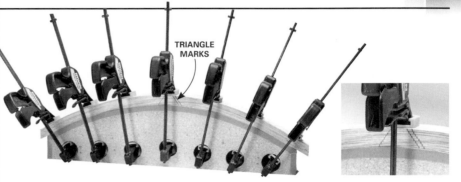

**TRIANGLE MARKS**

**CABINETMAKER'S TRIANGLE**

## Make it easy to stack resawn pieces

Resawing a board into thin, pliable pieces allows you to create curved shapes by bending and gluing the pieces around a form—a process called "bent lamination." Marking the board with the cabinetmaker's triangle (**photo at left**) allows you to reassemble the thin pieces as they came from the board, so the lamination closely resembles a single piece of bent wood (**photo above**).

## Create stunning grain patterns

Opening a pair of resawn pieces for the first time is my favorite part of resawing. That's because resawing transforms an ordinary —or even homely—board into something extraordinary. It also turns a narrow board into a panel that's twice as wide. Opening the pieces like a book —called book-matching— creates a mirror image. And that's just the start: By simply rearranging the two pieces, you can create other patterns that are completely different but just as spectacular.

# Tool&Shop Tips

SPECIAL SECTION

## HAND TOOL TIPS

### Drywall knife protector

I came up with a nifty solution to keep the fine edges of my drywall knives from getting dinged up. I buy 3/8-in. clear tubing at the hardware store and cut lengths to fit the blades. I then take a sharp utility knife and slit the tubing lengthwise and slip it over the blade. The tubing is somewhat clingy, so it stays put even in a tool-box tote.

–Richard Wisz

### Improvised T-bevel

Not long ago, I needed to make some angled wood parts to build a new soffit on my garage. I didn't have the customary tool for the job, but I had some steel joining plates. I screwed through one of the holes in the plate, set my angle, then added another screw to lock the angle. I could then use it as a template to mark all the pieces at the same angle and cut them with my circular saw.

–Ryan Bartsch

MAGNET

### Magnetize a screwdriver

This old trick could save you hundreds of dropped screws over your DIY lifetime. Grab a magnet and rub it along the shaft of a screwdriver a dozen times or so. Rub in one direction only, kind of like sharpening a knife. In about 10 seconds, you'll have a magnetic screwdriver. Repeat as needed.

## Hand screws to the rescue

When I started woodworking, I thought hand screw clamps were old-fashioned school-shop tools, not something any modern woodworker would use. Boy, was I wrong. Sure, fast-action metal clamps are better for most jobs, but for anything out of the ordinary, reach for a couple of hand screws. Why? First, the jaws can clamp tapered parts or parts that aren't parallel. And second, because they're made from wood, you can cut them, drill them and screw stuff to them.

Here's just one example: The oval stool seat above would be tough to clamp with standard clamps. But with hanger screws driven into a hand screw clamp, it's easy. Drill a couple of holes into the seat, insert the hanger screws and squeeze the split seat together.

**HANGER SCREWS**

–Ken Collier, Editor in Chief

## Is your level a liar?

Once upon a time, a man built a house using a lying level, so his floors were not level and his walls were not plumb. And all of the interior work, from installing cabinets to hanging doors, was a real nightmare.* If you want to live happily ever after, give your level a 60-second checkup. Set it on your workbench and slip a shim under the low end until the bubble is centered. Then flip the level around, positioning the other end on exactly the same point on the shim. If the bubble isn't centered, the level is a horizontal liar. To check vertical accuracy, follow the same steps against a wall.

*Yep, this is a true tale.

## Clamp a nail

When there's no room for a hammer, sink the nail with a C-clamp. This trick works for plumbing and electrical straps, junction boxes, and even joist hangers.

## Stand-at-attention screws

When I need to insert small screws and bolts and keep them positioned until they find their place, I use a rare earth magnet attached to the shaft of the screwdriver. It holds better than the usual magnetized tip. I just keep the magnet stuck inside my tool chest and use it with any size screwdriver. It's also great for picking up dropped nuts and screws in tight spaces.

–Robert Slunaker

# Tool & Shop Tips

## POWER TOOL TIPS

WOOD
SCRAP

### Curves with a circular saw

A circular saw will cut long, gradual curves in a fraction of the time a jigsaw will. Plus, you'll get a much smoother cut. If you're cutting plywood, set the saw to cut just deep enough to cut through the wood. The deeper the blade, the harder it'll be to make the cut because it'll get bound in the kerf. If you're cutting thicker material, cut halfway through on the first pass and then make a second, deeper final cut following the original cut.

–Ken Collier, Editor in Chief

### Miter saw stop

I use binder clips for a lot of things around the shop, and here's one that I thought I'd share. When I need to make multiple cuts all the same length, I just clamp my jumbo binder clip to my fence and use a 1/4-in.-thick wood scrap pinched in the clip as a stop. Works like a charm! When it's not in use, I clamp it to the cord so it's always nearby.

–John Muchow

### Belt sanders aren't just for wood

Any shop teacher will tell you: Use a tool only for its intended purpose. But I confess—I often use a belt sander for jobs other than sanding wood. It works great to scour dried gunk off putty knives and trowels, and I use it to sharpen chisels, scrapers and shovels too. In fact, I'm a double offender: I use my chisel for all kinds of rough jobs that it wasn't intended for, then I sharpen it with a belt sander. My belt sander actually gives my chisel a better edge than a grinder does.

–Jeff Gorton, Associate Editor

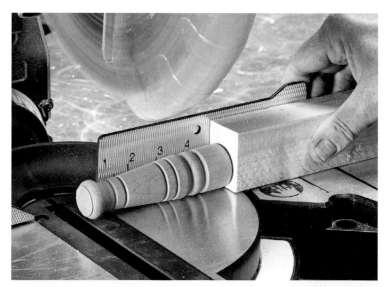

### Cut small parts safely

Recently I needed to cut some small furniture legs on my miter saw. With their irregular shape, they were impossible to hold safely, so I attached each leg to a scrap 2x2 with a dowel screw. These assemblies stayed straight and kept my hands far from the blade.

–David Alexander

DOWEL
SCREW

## Wood chip catcher

My planer blasts shavings all over the shop floor. I decided to make my own dust chute from 4-in. PVC sewer pipe (which has thinner walls than regular Schedule 40 pipe) and a couple caps. I cut a slit in the pipe and used a heat gun to soften the plastic. That allowed me to open the slit. (Heating PVC releases fumes; ventilation is critical.) I then drilled holes in the flap and screwed it to the planer housing. Finally, I cut a 2-1/2-in. hole in one of the end caps to accept my shop vacuum hose. Works great!

–Luis Arce

## Straight-up drill guide

To bore a perfectly perpendicular hole, you need either a drill press or a couple of scraps of wood screwed together. The corner created by the scraps will steer the bit straight in every time. But if you're looking for an excuse to buy a drill press, forget you ever saw this tip.

## Before a blade change ...

Crank the blade to 45 degrees or so. With the arbor tilted up, you have better access and you're less likely to drop the nut into some unreachable cranny.

–Jim Pease, TFH Field Editor

## Table saw mate

If you're building any kind of workbench or table for your shop, make it about 1/4 in. lower than your table saw. That way, you can use it as an outfeed or side-support table.

–Bob Rogers, TFH Field Editor

## Belt sander stop block

A belt sander is a great tool for sending boards flying across your shop. If you don't want that to happen, clamp a stop block to your workbench. A block of the same thickness as your board will also prevent the sander from tipping down and tapering the end of your workpiece.

# Tool & Shop Tips

## MISCELLANEOUS WORKSHOP TIPS

### Homemade nut loosener

Rusted bolts and nuts can be stubborn as all get out to loosen. I make my own rust penetrant by mixing half automatic transmission fluid and half acetone in a metal oilcan. The solution really penetrates—after a few minutes, even the toughest bolts and nuts spin loose (with a little elbow grease, that is). Best yet, it's stuff I already have on the garage shelf.

–Calvin Stevens

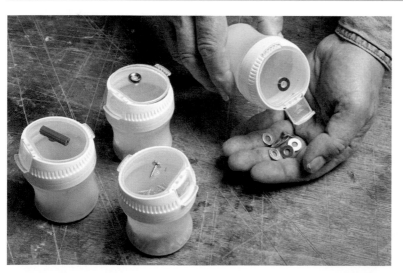

### Small-parts solution

We buy chewing gum in these nifty reusable plastic containers. The tops open completely and they have a smaller opening that works great for dispensing small hardware items. We just glue one of the parts to the top so we can quickly identify the contents.

–Jerry Bullock

### Wrench within reach

When I change blades on my band saw, I usually need to adjust the thrust bearings and guides with an Allen wrench. I was tired of hunting around for the wrench, so I decided to stick it to the steel housing with a rare earth magnet (neodymium) about the size of a jacket button. Now it's always handy!

–Bill Wells

## Customized tote

As a carpenter, I need to bring certain items with me every day. I bought a cheap plastic tote in the tool storage area at a home center and modified it for my needs. I made a small plywood deck, drilled a couple of 3-in. holes for coffee cups or glue bottles and then fastened it to the tote. Another piece of plywood has holes to keep pencils upright and organized. My tote sits nicely on my bench seat, but it could also be attached to the floor with hook-and-loop fasteners. You could easily customize these totes for plumbing, garden or painting tools, electrical supplies—what have you.

–Don Simms

## Saving hardwood scraps

Short scraps of hardwood are too good to throw away but hard to store neatly. So I bought a 4-ft. tube form made for concrete footings, cut it in half (the cardboard-like material cuts easily) and set the tubes on end. I tack the tubes to a wall or a bench leg so they don't fall over. With the wood scraps stored upright, it's easy to find a piece just the right length. Tube forms are available in various diameters for $5 and up at home centers.

–Bill Wells

## Upright for edge work

A woodworker's vise is the best way to hold boards on edge. But a pair of hand screws works almost as well. Depending on how you set it up, you may want to insert strips of cardboard under the board to protect it from the hand screws' sharp threads.

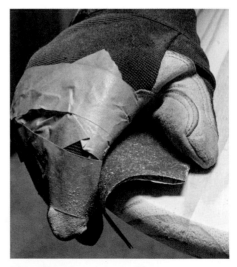

## No slipping, no splinters

To prevent friction burns and splinters while sanding a curved tabletop, I put on a leather glove and wrapped painter's tape around it, sticky side out. The tape kept the sandpaper from slipping, and the glove protected my hand.

–Eliot Sennett

# Tool & Shop Tips

## MISCELLANEOUS WORKSHOP TIPS continued

### Perfect worktable

An old hollow-core door isn't trash; it's the perfect portable worktable. Set it on a couple of sawhorses and you've got a surface that's flat and strong but lightweight and easy to store.

–Hank Huff, Field Editor

### Recharge station

Cordless tools are the greatest advance in human history. Well, at least for us. But they've also brought charger chaos. We recommend herding all your chargers into one place and plugging them into a power strip. You'll get organization, surge protection and an instant way to switch them all off after the batteries are charged.

### Blade storage tubes

My reciprocating saw gets used a lot, and the tool case becomes a mess. To keep my blades in order, I made storage tubes from 1-1/4-in. PVC waste pipe and end caps. I just cut the pipe to length, glue one end and then label and store my blades. The open end gets friction-fitted with the cap. Now I can find the right blade at a glance!

–Phil Streit

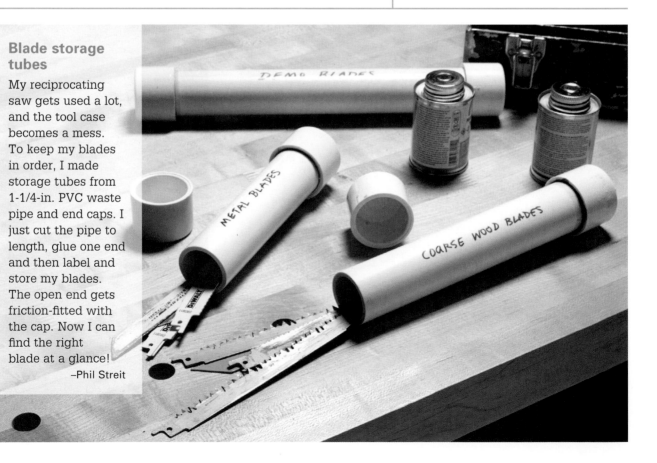

## Nonslip ladder

I use my multi-position ladder for repairs during Montana winters, and I used to have trouble getting good footing. My solution was to apply anti-slip tape to the rungs. Its heavy-duty grit really helps grip my boots. I cleaned the rungs and then just cut the tape to size with a utility knife and straightedge. No more slips for me!

–Henry Reuter

## Final paint-prep step

Prep is the key to a fine paint job, as I learned from a 35-year veteran painter. Here's how he taught me to do it: First, patch the walls, then sand down all the walls with 100-grit paper. (He used a drywall pole sander.) That leaves a bunch of dust and debris on the wall, so the next step is to vacuum with a wide floor brush. It's faster and more thorough than a damp rag, and it gets rid of any cobwebs at the same time. You'll still need a rag or small vacuum brush to reach into corners, but then it's on to taping off the woodwork.

–Travis Larson, Senior Editor

## Outlet strip protector

I do a lot of power sanding at my workbench, and all the sawdust kept getting into the outlet strip and interfering with the electrical contact. Now I put a strip of masking tape over outlets I'm not using and replace it as needed. The outlet strips last a lot longer!

–Helene Lesel

## Nonslip sandpaper

Whenever I use sandpaper sheets that are folded in half, the sandpaper slides on itself as I sand. To solve the problem, I just spray a light coat of contact adhesive on the back of the sheet. Once it has air-dried for a couple minutes, I fold the sheet in half for a permanent bond. Works like a charm.

–Brian Flynn

# Tool & Shop Tips

## MISCELLANEOUS WORKSHOP TIPS continued

### Pet collar cord hanger

A few weeks ago while I was at the pet outlet store getting food and treats, I noticed the display of collars for dogs and cats. They looked like the perfect strap to keep my electrical cords organized in the shop. I bought several, and now I use them for air hoses too. The leash ring is perfect for hanging the cords on the hooks, and the quick-release fastener makes for fast strapping and unstrapping.

–Chris Neely

### Half-pencil marks exact copies

While trying to trace an exact copy of the throat plate for my table saw, I came up with this nifty technique using an ordinary pencil. I just shaved my pencil into a half-pencil by carefully grinding it on my belt sander. The flat edge enables my modified pencil to ride straight up along the edge of the template. It also works great for marking and then shaping inlays for my woodworking projects.

–Tim Reese

### Stop a wandering bit

Even the sharpest bit tends to skate across hard materials like tile, metal or glass, leaving loopy scratches behind. To steady a wandering bit, give it a softer place to start. Thin cardboard (the stuff cereal boxes are made from), taped firmly in place, works perfectly.

### Smoother caulk

I used to cut caulk tube nozzles at an angle to get a nice bead in corners. The problem was, when I had to switch direction while caulking, the cut edge was in the wrong place to continue the bead. My solution is to cut the nozzle straight and then round it smooth on all sides with an abrasive pad or a nylon carpet scrap. Just rub the cut edge for a minute or so until it's smooth. Now you can caulk in any direction with a nice, continuous bead.

–Brian Flynn

## Simple shop helper with many uses

Simple T-blocks have endless uses. They support long boards, raise projects off your workbench so you can work more comfortably, prop up assemblies so you can slip clamps under them, make a drying rack for finishing projects—the list goes on and on. Build a few from scrap wood and you'll find uses we haven't even thought of.

## Extract a stuck plug from a hole saw

Struggling to pry the plug out of a hole saw might make you mutter, "Aw, screw it." And that is indeed the correct approach. Drive a long screw into the plug. When the screw hits the back of the hole saw, keep driving and the screw will magically pull out the plug. If the plug is really stub-

born, you might have to add a second screw on the other side of the drill bit. Then alternate between the screws, turning one and then the other until the plug is out.

## Tape measure markup

When a project requires lots of similar measurements—jobs like roofing and siding—I minimize mistakes by marking my tape measure. It's best to choose a permanent marker and use different colors for different lengths. When I no longer need the marks, I erase them with a rag and a little acetone.

–Steve Wilson

## Mustard bottle for glue

I no longer put up with the messy "overdesigned" carpenter's glue dispensers. Instead, I use old mustard bottles; they don't clog and they easily reseal between uses.

–Richard Painter

# Tool & Shop Tips

## GETTING CREATE

### Shine on....

Recently I needed to polish brass parts for a project. I didn't have a buffing disc, so I looked around the shop for an alternative. I saw several paint roller covers that I thought might work—but how to drive them? I found that they fit tightly on a

1-1/2-in. hole saw. I cut a 3-in. length of roller cover, inserted the hole saw and chucked it into my drill press. It worked great, and I've used this method often to buff and polish jewelry and all sorts of other items. You can buy buffing compound at a hobby store.

–Bill Wells

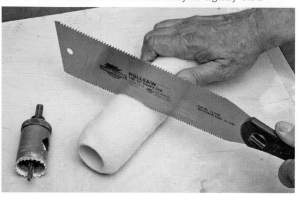

### Stretchy clamps

Old bicycle inner tubes work great for clamping odd-shaped projects. I used them recently to hold the rungs secure in a set of chairs I glued up. Just knot the tube to the right size and then stretch it over. Set the chair on a flat surface as the glue dries. The tubes can handle jobs that conventional clamps just can't.

–Allen J. Muldoon

### Homemade air cleaner

Here's my inexpensive alternative to factory-made air cleaners: After measuring my window fan, I went to the home center and found the perfect size filter to fit the fan (less than $5). I taped it to the "draw" side of the fan and paid attention to the filtration direction printed on the filter. I turned on the fan and found that it worked great. Now I can get the air clean enough to do my finish work in the shop.

–Thomas Wnorowski

### Assembly aid

I was assembling some plywood storage boxes and needed a third hand to hold the parts square while I screwed them together. I found an old 4-in. electrical box in the garage and decided to give it a try. The box was sturdy and perfectly square, and the clamps fit nicely inside to hold the assembly tight while I drilled pilot holes and drove screws.

–Steve Rodgers

# 5 Exterior Repairs & Improvements

## IN THIS CHAPTER

## FIX DRIVEWAY CRACKS

Over time, every asphalt driveway develops cracks. They're more than just an eyesore; they actually speed up the demise of your driveway if you ignore them. And in cold climates, water seeps in and destroys the asphalt when it expands during freezing. If you plan to topcoat your driveway, you'll need to fix the cracks first.

You can buy squeeze bottle and caulk tube–style crack filler products from any home center. They're quick and easy to apply, but they shrink and crack and don't last very long. However, there's another way to fill asphalt cracks: with melt-in filler that doesn't shrink—the same type used by highway crews.

It'll take almost a full day to repair several cracks if they're 20 ft. long or so, but the repairs will last much longer than other quick fixes. In addition to the melt-in and trowel mix products, you'll need a propane torch with an extension hose, and a leaf blower or compressed air gun. Use an angle grinder fitted with a diamond wheel to widen hairline cracks and to quickly remove previously applied crack fillers.

### Buy the supplies and tools

We used melt-in 1/2-in.-diameter Latex-ite Pli-Stix Crack and Joint Filler and Latex-ite Trowel Patch for this project. Our driveway had several 25-ft.-long cracks. So we bought four 30-ft. packages of the crack filler (about $15 each at home centers) and four 2-gallon pails of the trowel patch (about $17 each). We already had a propane torch. But we bought a 5-foot-long extension hose to eliminate the flame-outs that occur when you tip a propane cylinder upside down (Bernzomatic Universal Torch Extension Hose).

### Check the weather and prep the cracks

Choose a sunny day with no rain in the forecast for at least 24 hours. Start by rolling the crack filler rope onto a sunny section of the driveway so it warms and softens. While it's warming, remove all

the dirt, weeds and old crack filler from the cracks. Scrape out the old material with a flat-blade screwdriver or 5-in-1 paint tool. It's a painstaking process, but it's critical to getting a successful repair. So don't skip it or take shortcuts. Cleaning and filling hairline cracks are more time consuming, and the fix won't last. unless you widen them with an angle grinder and diamond wheel (**Photo 1**).

Once you finish digging out all the cracks, blow the dust and debris out of the cracks and off the driveway using a leaf blower or compressed air gun.

### Add the filler and melt it

Push the melt-in filler deep into the cracks (**Photo 2**). If any filler bulges above the surface of the driveway, cut off the excess with a knife or compress it so it sits below the surface (**Photo 3**).

Then screw the extension hose onto your propane tank and mount the torch to the other end and fire it up. The melt-in filler burns easily, so don't try to melt it in one fell swoop. Using just the tip of the flame, slowly

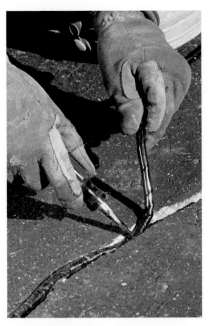

**1** **Widen hairline cracks.** Plunge the diamond wheel into one end of the crack and drag backward to dig out any old filler and widen the crack.

**2** **Stuff the crack with filler.** Jam the filler deep into the crack using a flat-blade screwdriver. Add a second layer to fill deeper or wider cracks.

**3** **Compress the filler.** Hammer the filler so it sits at least 1/16 in. below the surface of the driveway. Don't overfill.

*Image labels:* PREVIOUSLY FILLED HAIRLINE CRACK · WIDER CLEAN CRACK · 1/16" BELOW DRIVEWAY SURFACE

**4** **Melt the filler.** Sweep the torch flame side to side slowly over a 12-in. section until the filler begins to melt. Then move on to the next section. Return to the previous section and heat again until the filler levels out and seeps into the crack.

**5** **Add trowel mix and then smooth it.** After the filler has cooled, scoop up the trowel patch and tap it onto the crack filler to create a small mound. Smooth it with a trowel and let dry overnight. If a depression remains the next day, apply a second coat.

melt the filler (**Photo 4**). If the filler starts to burn, blow out the flames and use a faster sweeping motion or move the flame farther from the crack.

Allow the filler to cool to the touch (at least 20 minutes)

before covering it with the trowel patch material. Then lay down a bead of trowel patch and smooth it (**Photo 5**). Let the trowel patch dry overnight. Apply a second coat if you see a depression where the crack was filled.

# HomeCare&Repair

## PATCH PITTED ASPHALT

Asphalt driveways can develop pitted areas from motor oil and coolant contamination and repeated freeze/thaw cycles. If the pits are 1/2 in. or less, you can fill them with a spreadable filler product. (Latex-ite Trowel Patch is one choice that's available at home centers.)

Clean oil stains and prime with oil stain primer. Then coat the entire pitted area with patch material and let dry overnight (**Photo 1**). Apply a second coat to top off any partially filled pits (**Photo 2**) and smooth the surface. Let dry.

**1** **Fill the pits.** Force the filler material into the cracks and pits with a trowel. Then smooth the streaks with an old broom.

**2** **Enlarge the area and smooth.** Pour more filler material onto the pitted area and spread it with a floor squeegee to smooth the surface.

## HandyHints®
### FROM OUR READERS

### NO KINKS, NO DAMAGE

Several years ago, I noticed my neighbor pressure-washing her driveway. The hose was "dancing" all over the concrete from the pulses generated by the pump, and as a result, it was almost worn through in several

spots. To preserve the hose on my pressure washer, I went to the auto supply store and bought some inexpensive black split-wire loom. It slips over the high-pressure hose quite nicely, and it protects the hose from wear. Plus, it prevents kinking, the most common cause of hose damage.

–William R. Law

### WINDOW LABELS

Each year I wash all my screens and storm windows assembly line–style. It can be a hassle getting each one back in the right window. To avoid mix-ups, I labeled each screen and storm with a permanent marker in an inconspicuous spot on an outside edge. Problem solved.

–Linda Gum

# MAKE **EXTERIOR** **CAULK** LAST

10 tips for a long-lasting—and attractive—exterior caulk job

by **Gary Wentz, Senior Editor**

EXTERIOR REPAIRS
& IMPROVEMENTS

E xterior caulking is a lot like interior caulking: Your goal is a neat-looking seal over cracks and gaps. But outdoor caulking deserves some extra attention. It will have to withstand all the extremes that nature can dish out. And when an outdoor seal fails, water gets in and serious trouble follows. So here are some tips for caulking that lasts.

## Choose acrylic for most jobs

Acrylic caulk is easy to use, easy to smooth out and easy to clean up. And since it offers reasonably good flexibility and adhesion, it's a good choice for most exterior gaps narrower than 1/4 in. Some acrylics are labeled "acrylic latex." With others, you have to read the fine print to find "acrylic." Price is a good guide to quality; bypass the cheap stuff and spend $4 to $5 per tube. Saving a few bucks on the seals that protect your home from water damage is a bad bargain.

## Don't 'caulk' with paint

Paint will fill or bridge tiny gaps—but only temporarily. Paint simply doesn't have the flexibility of caulk. As gaps shrink and grow, the paint will eventually crack. That will allow moisture to get behind the paint and it will start to peel. So even if a gap is "paintable," caulk it.

## Consider polyurethane

In terms of performance, polyurethane is just plain better than acrylic caulk. It sticks better and retains its flexibility longer. The downside is that polyurethane is more difficult to apply neatly, harder to smooth out and tough to clean up. You have to mask off porous surfaces and keep mineral spirits handy. For some situations—concrete, roofing, gaps wider than 1/4 in.—polyurethane is definitely worth the hassle. But consider it for some standard jobs too. With all the time and effort a repair or redo would take, polyurethane might save you trouble in the long run.

### Start with a clean crack

Caulk won't stick well to dirty surfaces. On siding and trim, dig out any loose paint, caulk or other crud, then sweep them with a dry paintbrush or—better yet—blast them with a compressor and an air nozzle. You may not get cracks completely clean, but the cleaner the better. To clean out cracks in concrete or other masonry, all you need is your garden hose. Just be sure to allow plenty of drying time before you caulk.

**FOAM BACKER ROD**

### Use backer rod

Foam backer rod is cheap and easy to use, and it can add years to the life of a caulk joint. Just stuff it into a gap before caulking and you'll automatically get the ideal seal (thin in the middle, with thicker "adhesion zones" at edges). Always use it on joints wider than 1/4 in. You can also use it on narrower gaps, but you may have trouble finding backer rod that's thin enough for small gaps. Buy backer rod that's 1/8 to 1/4 in. larger than the gap, and expect to pay less than $5 for 20 ft. at home centers.

### Prime before you caulk

When it comes to wood (or wood-based materials like hardboard), primer sticks better than caulk and provides a great adhesion surface for caulk. So if caulking is part of a painting project, it's best to prime before you caulk. Work the primer into gaps, but don't try to fill them with primer.

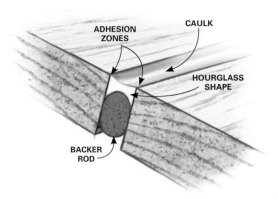

ADHESION ZONES

CAULK

HOURGLASS SHAPE

BACKER ROD

## Form an 'hourglass' bead

Gaps move. They constantly grow wider or narrower as the temperature and humidity change. A shrinking gap is the lesser problem; it just compresses the caulk. But when a gap widens, it puts a major strain on the seal. The caulk has to stretch without tearing in half or pulling away from the surrounding surface.

To prevent those failures, you want a bead that stretches easily in the middle and sticks stubbornly along the edges. An hourglass-shape bead accomplishes both of those goals. It stretches easily because it's thin in the middle and sticks well because it has wide "adhesion zones" along the edges. Backer rod makes a perfect hourglass bead easy (see the tip on p. 196). In situations where you're not using backer rod, a perfect bead may be easy, difficult or impossible. But use it whenever you can—you'll get a seal that will last much longer.

## 'Tool' the caulk

Smoothing a caulk bead with your finger doesn't just make it look neater. It also shapes the bead to withstand movement better (see the tip at left). With acrylic caulk, most of us simply moisten a finger and smooth the bead. With polyurethane, slip on a latex surgical-style glove and dip your finger in mineral spirits. If the gap is too wide to tool with your finger, try a plastic spoon.

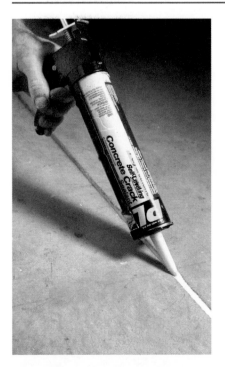

## Get a perfect bead on concrete

On horizontal concrete, you can skip the tooling mess and get a perfect bead by using a self-leveling polyurethane sealant. Just insert backer rod and inject the syrupy sealant. Resist the urge to tool the caulk; it will slowly level out and form a neat seal. Be sure the backer rod completely seals the crack. If the caulk seeps past the rod, you'll get an ugly sinkhole and a weaker seal, and you'll waste expensive caulk (this specialty caulk will cost you about $8 for a 10-oz. tube).

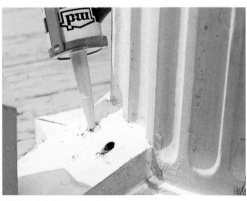

## Fill hidden holes

In some ways, caulk is a better filler for nail and screw holes than fillers that are formulated for that purpose. It goes on fast, and unlike fillers that harden, it won't crack or fall out. The trouble with caulk is that it doesn't look as good as filler. It can't be sanded smooth, and it shrinks as it cures, leaving a slight depression over the hole.

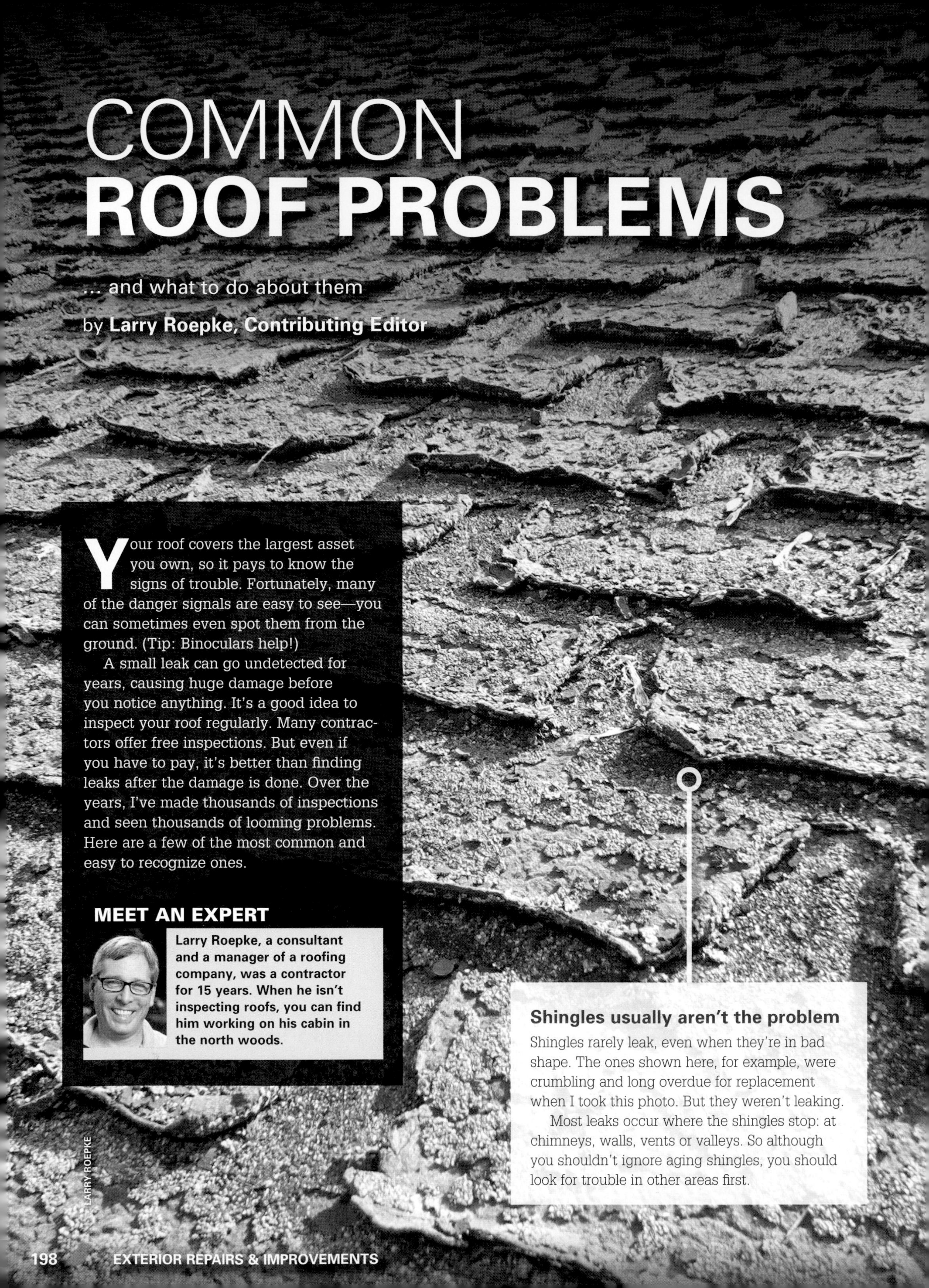

# COMMON ROOF PROBLEMS

... and what to do about them

by **Larry Roepke, Contributing Editor**

Your roof covers the largest asset you own, so it pays to know the signs of trouble. Fortunately, many of the danger signals are easy to see—you can sometimes even spot them from the ground. (Tip: Binoculars help!)

A small leak can go undetected for years, causing huge damage before you notice anything. It's a good idea to inspect your roof regularly. Many contractors offer free inspections. But even if you have to pay, it's better than finding leaks after the damage is done. Over the years, I've made thousands of inspections and seen thousands of looming problems. Here are a few of the most common and easy to recognize ones.

## MEET AN EXPERT

**Larry Roepke, a consultant and a manager of a roofing company, was a contractor for 15 years. When he isn't inspecting roofs, you can find him working on his cabin in the north woods.**

LARRY ROEPKE

### Shingles usually aren't the problem

Shingles rarely leak, even when they're in bad shape. The ones shown here, for example, were crumbling and long overdue for replacement when I took this photo. But they weren't leaking.

Most leaks occur where the shingles stop: at chimneys, walls, vents or valleys. So although you shouldn't ignore aging shingles, you should look for trouble in other areas first.

## Roof cement

Metal flashing prevents leaks where shingles meet other surfaces, like walls and chimneys. Proper flashing work takes time and know-how, so sloppy roofers sometimes slather on roof cement instead. It seals out water long enough for them to cash your check, but it soon hardens, cracks and leaks. In the end, all it does is make a proper repair more difficult. So if you see heavy "tar" patchwork on your roof, fix it right—before it leaks and leads to interior damage.

TAR

### TAR MEANS TROUBLE
Roofing cement may seal out water for a few months, even a few years. But "tar" is sure to fail eventually.

LARRY ROEPKE

## No chimney cricket

A wide chimney forms a dam on your roof. Debris builds up behind that dam and holds moisture, which leads to rusted flashing and wood rot. Any chimney wider than 30 in. needs a "cricket," or "saddle": Basically a small roof built behind the chimney. A properly installed chimney cricket will direct water and debris around the chimney and off the roof. If your chimney doesn't have one, watch for holes rusting through the flashing. If you're getting a new roof, be sure the contractor's bid includes a cricket.

### A DAM ON THE ROOF
A wide chimney traps debris, which stays wet and causes rust or rot.

CRICKET

### A CRICKET DIVERTS DEBRIS
A mini roof behind the chimney channels water flow and debris away from the chimney.

## Missing kick-out flashing

Kick-out flashing is critical where a roof edge meets a sidewall. Without it, roof runoff flows down the wall and possibly into the wall. This is worst when there is a door or a window below and water can seep behind the trim. You might not notice it for years, but eventually rot will destroy sheathing and framing. I've seen homes where the stucco was the only thing holding up the wall! Don't wait for that to happen to you. To see how to add kick-out flashing, go to familyhandyman.com and search for "kick out flashing."

### WATER GETS INTO WALLS
Without kick-out flashing, water flows down the wall and seeps behind siding and trim. Water may enter the walls close to the roof as shown here, or at any point downhill from the roof.

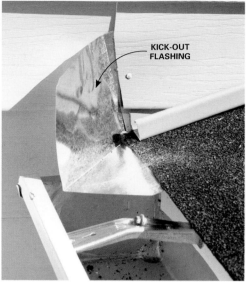

### KICK-OUT FLASHING IS SIMPLE
Kick-out flashing just consists of a bent section of step flashing that diverts water away from the wall.

## Bad chimney flashing

Good chimney flashing includes sections of "step flashing" that run up the sides of the chimney, and "counterflashing." Counterflashing fits into grooves cut into the chimney and covers the step flashing. Cutting, fitting and installing all those parts takes time, so sloppy roofers take shortcuts.

Improperly flashed chimneys cause lots of rotting roof sheathing and framing members. Chimneys need to be properly step-flashed and counterflashed so that water can't run down the face of the chimney and into the attic. I can't tell you how many times I've seen chimneys with no flashing, or bad flashing that relies on caulk or roof cement. If you suspect your flashing is shoddy, crawl into the attic after a heavy rain. Look for signs of water around the chimney and downhill from it.

### SHORTCUT FLASHING
Instead of several sections of flashing covered by counterflashing, the side of this chimney has just two pieces of flashing. Big, leaky gaps have opened at the ends of the flashing.

### GOOD FLASHING
Proper flashing includes many parts, including counterflashing to cover the step flashing. Counterflashing may be a single piece or several as shown here.

## Missing gutter apron

When water flows off the edge of your roof, some of it clings to the underside of the shingles and dribbles toward the fascia. If you have gutters but no gutter apron to stop the water, it will wick behind the gutter. Eventually the fascia, soffits and even the roof sheathing will rot. You may see water stains below the gutter on the fascia and soffit. This is a sure sign that the gutter apron is missing.

The best time to add gutter apron is when you're getting new shingles. But it is possible to slip gutter apron under existing shingles. A dab of roof cement every couple feet will "glue" it to the shingles and hold it in place. You'll have to remove gutter brackets or straps and then refasten them after the apron is in place. Gutter apron is cheap, and is available at home centers in 10-ft. lengths.

### GUTTER APRON RETROFIT
Adding gutter apron under existing shingles is easiest on a warm day, when shingles are more flexible. If you need a new roof, make sure the contractor's bid includes gutter apron.

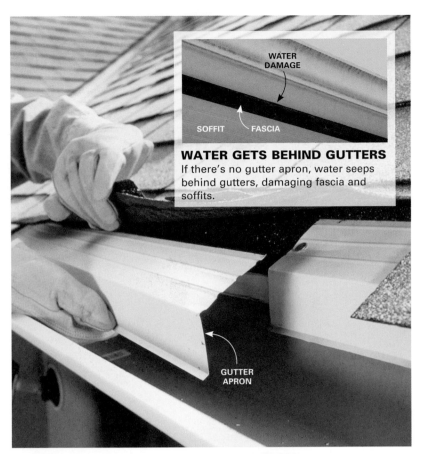

WATER DAMAGE

SOFFIT    FASCIA

**WATER GETS BEHIND GUTTERS**
If there's no gutter apron, water seeps behind gutters, damaging fascia and soffits.

GUTTER APRON

## Vent flashing failure

Your plumbing system includes "vent" pipes that pass through the roof. And like any other roof penetration, that sometimes means trouble. There are two kinds of flashing used to seal vents: a "boot" that relies on a snug rubber seal, and all-metal flashing with soft lead that can be bent over and into the pipe. Some versions are made completely from lead; others are galvanized steel with a lead collar. When any type of vent flashing fails, the solution is to replace it. To see how, go to family-handyman.com and search for "plumbing vent flashing."

TORN RUBBER

**RUBBER BOOTS CAN CRACK**
After years of sun and weather, the seal around this plumbing vent cracked and tore open.

LEAD COLLAR

**METAL FLASHING ISN'T BULLETPROOF**
The lead collar on metal vent flashing usually outlasts the shingles. But it can corrode, crack or even fall victim to gnawing squirrels.

## Hail damage

When a large hailstone hits an asphalt shingle, it can tear or even puncture the shingle. But usually, it just knocks granules off the surface. When a shingle loses its protective layer of granules, UV rays from the sun begin to destroy it. More granules fall off around the damaged spot and the bruise grows. The damage may not be obvious at first, so if you suspect hail damage, get an inspection from a roofing contractor. Most offer free hail damage inspections.

HAIL DAMAGE

HAIL DAMAGE

### IT DOESN'T LOOK THAT BAD
You may not even notice hail damage at first, but the spots where granules are missing will grow as sunlight degrades the shingles.

### DAMAGED METAL IS A CLUE
Any hailstorm that was harsh enough to dent metal probably damaged the shingles, too. Look for dents in metal vents, siding, gutters and flashing.

## GreatGoofs®

### Avalanche!!

Last winter we had such a huge snowfall that I became concerned about the weight of the snow on our fiberglass-paneled lean-to carport roof. To relieve the stress, I decided to thread my garage broom head to a telescoping painter's extension handle to pull off some of the snow. Just as I started pulling, the whole mass slid off at once, burying me in about 3 ft. of snow. The task was completed—just a little faster than I expected!

–Brian Westerhoff

# HOW TO
# SEAL A DRIVEWAY

It's a tedious job, but you can do it for about one-third of the cost of hiring a pro

by **Rick Muscoplat, Contributing Editor**

**An** asphalt driveway can last almost 30 years. But you can't achieve that long life span unless the driveway was installed properly and you perform regular maintenance, like annually filling cracks (see p. 192) and applying sealer when needed. Here you'll learn how to clean and prepare the driveway so you get the longest life and best protection from driveway sealer.

Preparation can take a full day (including drying time), and it's tedious. The application phase is much faster, taking only a few hours per coat for a typical driveway. Most sealer manufacturers recommend two coats with a minimum drying time of eight hours between coats, so this project will fill an entire weekend.

The materials for an average driveway cost about $100, but you'll save about $200 in labor over a professional job. A power washer speeds the cleaning process, but you can do the job without it. In addition to a squeegee or application brush, you'll need a broom, drill, mixing paddle, duct tape, dashing brush and poly sheeting to protect painted surfaces.

## Buying the right materials

Driveway sealer is available in various grades and price ranges, from as little as $15 per 5-gallon pail to about $35 per pail for a premium product. Some bargain products contain almost 50 percent water and have lower coverage rates and a correspondingly shorter guarantee, so they're not the most cost-effective solution over the long term. Use one of them if you're trying to spiff up the driveway before selling your home. Premium products, on the other hand, are made with higher-quality resins and UV stabilizers and contain filler and elastomeric material, so they last longer and carry a longer guarantee.

### Avoid these common driveway-sealing mistakes

■ Depending on the sealer to fill cracks. It won't. Fill them properly before applying sealer.
■ Failure to clean and prep the driveway before applying the sealer. If you don't want to spend time cleaning the driveway, you may as well skip the sealer too, because it won't stick to a dirty driveway.
■ Failure to stir properly. Don't depend on a stir stick. It simply won't blend the water and solids enough to get a consistent mixture.
■ Use of the wrong applicator. Using a brush when the manufacturer specifies a squeegee (or vice versa) will cause premature sealer failure.
■ Applying sealer too often. Too much sealer will flake off. Wait until you begin to see asphalt aggregate before you apply a new coat of sealer.

**1 Soap and scrub.** Use the soap nozzle on your power washer or a garden hose applicator to apply the driveway cleaner. Then scrub the entire driveway with a stiff-bristle push broom.

40-DEGREE NOZZLE SETTING

**2 Rinse with a strong stream.** Flush the soap and dirt residue with a 40-degree power washer nozzle or a strong stream of water from your garden hose.

**3 Pretreat the oil stains.** Pour the oil spot primer on the damaged areas and brush it into the pores with a disposable chip brush. Apply a second coat to heavier stains. Let the primer dry fully before applying the driveway sealer.

Manufacturers also make different formulas for different driveway conditions: one formula for newer driveways in good condition and another formula for older driveways that haven't been well maintained. The two formulas also vary in their coverage, so read the labels carefully and choose the correct sealer and quantity for your particular driveway. Follow the manufacturer's directions for the type of applicator to use (brush or squeegee). Using the wrong one can cause premature failure.

You'll also need liquid driveway cleaner/degreaser to remove oil and tree sap. If your driveway has visible oil stains, pick up a bottle of oil spot primer.

## Check the weather before you start

You'll need at least two days of dry weather to seal your driveway. Temperatures must be above 50 degrees F during application and throughout the night. And, it's best to avoid scorching-hot sunny days (the sealer may dry too quickly). If you ignore the weather forecast, you may see $100 worth of sealer wash away in a heavy rain, which is not only expensive but highly polluting.

## Start with cleaning and priming

Even if you think your driveway is clean, rest assured that it isn't. Exhaust gas contains combustion byproducts that deposit a light, sometimes oily film on your driveway. That film, along with dirt and tree sap, must come off if you want the sealer to stick. So clean the driveway first (**Photo 1**).

Next, rinse the driveway with clear water (**Photo 2**). Let the driveway dry completely before applying the sealer. Then perform a final sweep with a push broom. Treat any oil stains with an oil spot primer (**Photo 3**).

## Mask, stir, and trim

Driveway sealer will splash onto your garage door and sidewalks as you pour it. And it'll get all over your shoes and clothes. It's very difficult (often impossible) to remove later, so wear old work clothes and shoes. Mask the garage door with poly sheeting and apply strips of duct tape to concrete walks where it butts up to the asphalt.

Choose an area on the driveway for mixing and cover it with poly sheeting to protect against spills (dried spills will show through the sealer). Remove the pail lids and cut a small hole in the center of one lid. Use that lid to prevent splashing during mixing. Stir until the mixture is smooth (**Photo 4**).

Next, cut in all four edges of the driveway with a large dashing brush (**Photo 5**). Clean the brush with soap and water as soon as you're done cutting in the edges—you'll need it again the following day. Then stage the pails equally down the driveway (**Photo 6**).

## Pour and spread

Pour the sealer onto the driveway (**Photo 7**). Then spread the puddle with a squeegee or broom, depending on the manufacturer's directions (**Photo 8**). Pour enough sealer to maintain a puddle in front of the applicator tool.

When you reach the bottom of the driveway, cap the remaining pails and clean the squeegee or brush. Set the empty pails along the curb to prevent cars from ruining the job. Then let the sealer dry overnight.

Repeat the sealer application the next day. Let the sealer dry for 48 hours before driving on it (better safe than sorry).

**4 Mix the sealer.** Start the mixing paddle near the top of the pail and slowly lower it into the contents settled at the bottom. Cycle the mixing paddle up and down while it spins to combine the water and solids into a smooth consistency.

**5 Cut in the edges.** Dip the dashing brush into the sealer and apply a liberal coating to all four edges of the driveway. Don't spread it too thin; you want it to fill in all the pores.

POLY SHEETING TO MASK DOOR

STAGED PAILS

**6 Stage the pails.** Guesstimate the coverage of each pail and stage each additional pail along the driveway. That saves time and reduces the need to walk through wet sealer to get the next pail.

**7 Pour the sealer onto the driveway.** Start at the top left or right edge of the driveway and pour the sealer in an upside-down U-shape pattern.

**8 Spread the sealer.** Start at one leg of the upside-down "U" and apply even pressure to spread the puddle across the driveway and down along the opposite leg. Then pick up the excess sealer on the down leg and start the next row.

## Driveway sealers: Real protection or just black paint?

Some asphalt driveway companies tell their customers that driveway sealer is a waste of money, that it's cosmetic and doesn't do anything to extend the life of the asphalt.

It's true that driveway sealer can't replace the liquid asphalt (oil/tar) that oxidizes and bakes out of the mixture from heat and sun exposure. But a high-quality sealer can dramatically reduce future heat and UV damage. Plus, it seals the pores to prevent aggregate breakup damage caused by water penetration, freeze/thaw cycles and chemicals. So it really does extend the life of your driveway.

# PRESSURE WASHER
## USE & CARE

10 tips to help you get the best use out of this highly useful tool

by **Rick Muscoplat, Contributing Editor**

Once you've used a pressure washer, you'll wonder how you ever got along without one. In fact, you'll find new uses for it every time you fire it up! We talked to a few power washer fanatics and several manufacturers to learn the best tips for using and maintaining a pressure washer. And we learned how to avoid the most common mistakes DIYers make, like leaving water in the pump through winter, using the wrong nozzle for the job, and letting the engine idle for more than a few minutes.

## Three ways to keep from wrecking stuff

■ Don't park the unit too close to structures. Hot exhaust can melt vinyl siding and start fires. This damage was caused in less than two minutes.

■ Never run a gas-powered pressure washer in the garage while you clean the garage floor. Move it well away from the house (at least 5 ft.) to prevent carbon monoxide poisoning.

■ Never use a strong spray to remove caulk around windows. The stream can force water behind siding, causing extensive water damage.

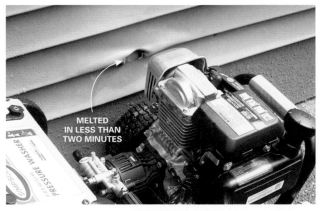

MELTED IN LESS THAN TWO MINUTES

## Make your pump last longer

Leaving water in the pump can result in mineral buildup and corrosion, which wear out the pump seals and pistons (a $200 repair). So it pays to flush the pump after every use—a quick job. Pick up a can of pump lube/antifreeze solution (such as Briggs & Stratton 6151 Pressure Washer Pump Saver; found at home centers). Screw the garden hose adapter onto the pump inlet and press the trigger until you see foamy liquid shoot out the other port. That means the pump is fully lubed and protected against freeze damage.

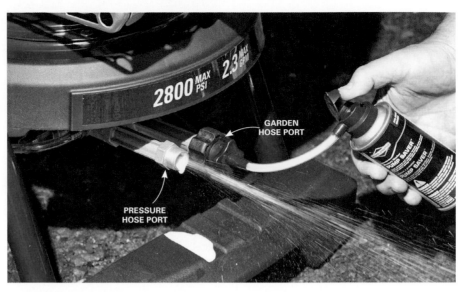

**Flush after every use** Attach the lubricant can to the garden hose port. Press the trigger for about two seconds, until water and lube shoot out the other port.

## Prep the engine for winter storage

The small engines on consumer pressure washers have a limited life span (sometimes less than 200 hours). But you can extend the life of the engine by following these simple pre-storage tips.

■ Even if you have only a few hours' use on the crankcase oil, drain the oil and refill with fresh oil (follow the manufacturer's recommendation for viscosity and type). Then run the engine for a few minutes to coat all the internal parts with clean oil and fresh anti-corrosion additives. That will provide the best protection during storage, and you'll be ready to rock and roll at the start of the next season.

■ Whether you run the engine dry or fill the tank to the brim, always run the engine with fresh gas treated with fresh fuel stabilizer first. Run the engine for a few minutes so the treated gas fills the carburetor. Then drain the tank and run it dry. Or fill the tank to the brim.

■ Be sure to flush out the pump (see tip above) before putting it away for the winter. If you leave the pump full of water and you live in a freezing climate, your pump will be destroyed.

## Buy an extra hose to save time

Most consumer pressure washers come with a 25-ft. hose. That means you have to lug the machine up stairs to wash your deck or constantly shut down the engine so you can move the machine as you work. Phooey on that! Just add a 50-ft. extension hose to your 25-ft. and leave the pressure washer in one spot. (You can buy a 50-ft. extension hose for about $50 and an inexpensive hose-to-hose coupler at any home center; both are also found through many online sources.) The extra hose will cause a slight pressure and volume drop, but you'll still have enough power to clean most surfaces.

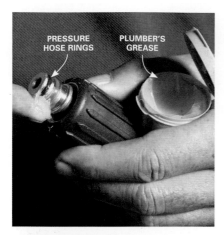

PRESSURE HOSE RINGS     PLUMBER'S GREASE

## Lube the hose connectors with silicone

Dry O-rings in the hose connector can twist slightly and tear as you make the connection, causing them to fail. Since regular oil washes off when it gets wet, buy a small container of silicone plumber's grease instead. It doesn't wash off and it's compatible with all types of O-ring materials. Tape the container to your machine so you'll always have it handy. Then apply a new coating every five uses or anytime the O-rings look dry.

## Use only cleaning fluids designed for pressure washers

Pressure washer soap dispensers are designed for dedicated pressure washer fluids only. General-purpose degreasers, heavy-duty cleaning liquids, bleach and acids can destroy the pump. Even if the soap is rated for pressure washer use, make sure it's the right soap for the job—the soaps aren't interchangeable. Vehicle wash soap, for example, won't clean concrete, and the chemicals in concrete soap can discolor alloy wheels and bright metal trim pieces if used to wash your car or truck. For the best results, let the soap set

for the recommended time and scrub heavily soiled surfaces with a brush before you rinse.

Finally, never leave soap in the dispenser when you store the machine—it can dry into crystals and cause pump damage. Flush the soap dispenser after each use and pull the gun trigger to run clear water through the pump before you shut it down.

## Use the right nozzle for the right job

Nozzle tips are color coded to denote their spray pattern (see chart). A zero-degree nozzle provides the most power for really stubborn stains. But that force can etch concrete and brick, blast holes in wood siding, break windows and even rip trim off your car. So test the area first and back the tip away from the surface if you notice any etching or damage. The soap nozzle (which is black) has a large opening to allow maximum water flow through the pump. The high water flow is needed to siphon soap out of the dispenser nozzle. The soaping function won't work with any other nozzle.

**Red 0°**

A zero-degree nozzle produces a pencil-point spray with no fan. Use it to blast mud or debris off surfaces from a distance or remove weeds from cracks in concrete.

**Yellow 15°**

A 15-degree nozzle produces a slight fan pattern. Hold the nozzle at a 45-degree angle to use it like a scraper when you're removing peeling paint or dislodging other coatings.

**Green 25°**

A 25-degree nozzle produces a wider fan pattern that's perfect for removing dirt and grime. This nozzle can also be used as a water broom to sweep debris off a driveway.

**White 40°**

A 40-degree nozzle produces the widest fan pattern. Use it to wash delicate surfaces like deck boards, glass and vehicle exteriors.

## Pull the trigger first

Before you yank the starter rope, pull the gun trigger (or have someone else do it). This will relieve pump pressure and lower engine resistance, making it easier to start (gasoline pressure washers only).

## Tarp the area before you remove paint

Lay down tarps before using your pressure washer to remove peeling paint. When you're done, just grab the corners and pour the chips into a container for disposal or recycling.

### Buy these accessories to get the most out of your pressure washer

■ **Replacement O-ring kit** with filtering screens (less than $10 at home centers)

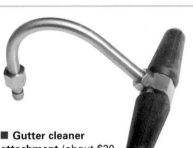

■ **Gutter cleaner attachment** (about $30 at home centers). Snap this attachment onto a telescoping extension wand (such as the General Pump 6-ft. to 24-ft. Telescoping Wand; about $150 online). You'll be able to blast the gunk out of your gutters without climbing a ladder.

■ **Quick-connect adapters and couplers** (about $30 per set at home centers). Convert your screw-on pressure washer hose to quick-connect fittings and you'll never have to worry about O-ring damage or cross-threading.

ADAPTER TO GUN

COUPLER ON EACH HOSE END

ADAPTER TO PUMP

■ **6-in-1 dial nozzle** (about $30 at home centers). Stop fiddling around with individual nozzles. If your hose uses quick-connect nozzles, just snap this on and you're done.

■ **Adjustable pressure regulator** (the Simpson Dial-N-Wash Pressure Regulator is shown; about $35 at home centers). Snap it onto your hose and connect the other end to your gun. Then adjust the pressure from max down to 1,000 psi to prevent damaging delicate items.

# SCAFFOLD SMARTS

Learn to work safely and efficiently with scaffolding

by **Mark Petersen, Associate Editor**

**W**hether you're changing sky-high warehouse lightbulbs or replacing windows on a two-story home, using scaffolds is a safe and easy way to get things done off the ground. We picked the brain of a scaffold expert, and he gave us great advice on how to work smart and stay safe on and around scaffolds.

## MEET AN EXPERT

**Joel Almquist started out working on scaffolds as a commercial mason. Every morning his boss would say, "Let's make sure everybody goes home tonight." Joel always took** safety seriously and now works at Scaffold Service Inc. in St. Paul, MN, where he teaches scaffold safety to pros in the trades.

## Haul the scaffold safely

Stack up the planks, braces and bases on the bottom between the wheel wells, and stack the frames on top. Avoid propping the frames up on the side of the bed. It's best to have everything as low as possible so parts don't get blown or bounced out. And frames that stick out past the side of the bed can be a conk hazard for someone walking by the truck. If you have a shorter bed, you may have to keep the tailgate open; just make sure to secure it all with a tie-down strap.

DIAGONAL GOOSER BRACE

## Plank the whole bay

Whenever possible, cover the whole width of the scaffold with planks. This creates a larger work area and reduces the risk of a fall. When it isn't possible, especially when you're working midway up ladder frames like these, install another plank higher up to create a sort of guardrail. See "Build a Handy Workbench" on p. 214. When you work on casters, install a diagonal "gooser" brace. It will keep the scaffold square and stable.

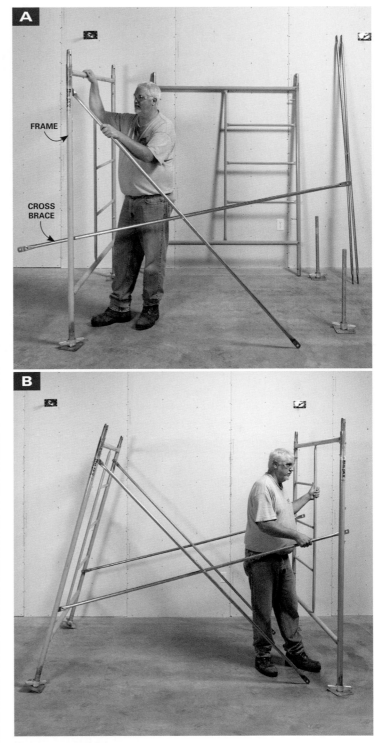

A

FRAME

CROSS BRACE

B

## Safe solo setup

Install the base jacks or casters first so you don't have to lift the entire scaffold to slide them in. Install both cross braces on one frame. It will stay upright with the support of the cross braces (**Photo A**). Move the second frame into position and attach the cross braces to that (**Photo B**). Slide the scaffold about 14 in. from the wall before installing the planks.

EXTERIOR REPAIRS & IMPROVEMENTS

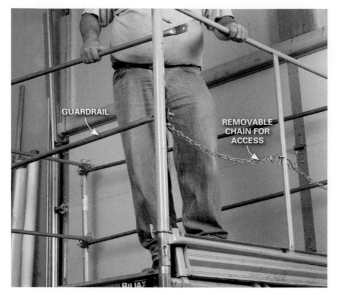

## Install a guardrail

Installing a guardrail is the best way to prevent accidentally stepping off the edge of the platform. Safety harnesses aren't necessary when you're working on this type of scaffold. In fact, if you fall while wearing a safety harness, you could pull the whole platform down with you, endangering everyone working in the area.

## Build a stable base

Scaffold frames are designed for use with either casters or base plates. If you skip them, the frame tubes can get damaged and structurally weakened. Set a 2x10 block of wood under each leg, even when using a base plate. This will help prevent sinking into soft soils or hot asphalt.

Setting the scaffold on blocks when working on concrete isn't necessary, but it's still a good idea. An uneven floor or a slightly cupped base plate could result in a small mating surface. The slight flex in wood ensures a nice, even distribution of weight. When you're working on an uneven surface, level and plumb the scaffold with an adjustable base jack. Never set the scaffold on masonry or stacks of wood.

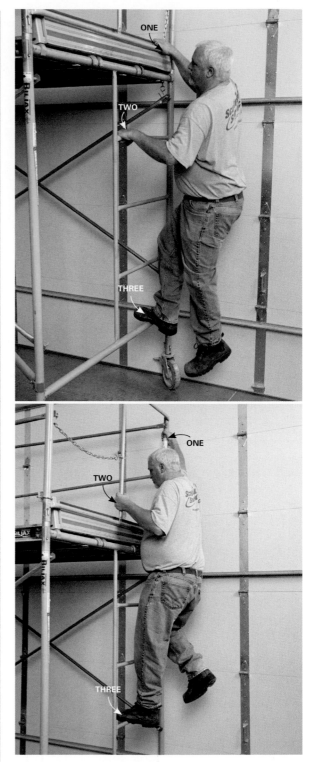

## Maintain a three-point grip

When you're climbing a scaffold, always maintain a three-point grip. That means that one hand and two feet, or one foot and two hands, should stay in contact with the scaffold at all times. Keep your body as close to the frame as possible. Leaning way out could cause the whole works to tip over right on top of you. And never climb on the cross braces; they're not designed to handle the weight.

2x4 TOE BOARD

WIRE

## Keep stuff from falling

Keep the planks clear of clutter to reduce the risk of tripping or kicking stuff onto unsuspecting souls working below. Keep your tools and supplies in buckets, caddies and toolboxes whenever possible. Install a 2x4 toe board to prevent items from falling. Hold it in place at the corners with wire. It's tempting to hang tools from the railings, but don't do it. Adding weight to the railings increases the odds that they could fail if someone leans against them. Hard hats for ground workers are always a good idea.

## Access the platform with a ladder

Use a ladder to safely and easily access a scaffold, especially when you're working with wood planks hanging over the ends. Run the ladder at least 3 ft. past the surface of the planks. Lean the ladder on the wall rather than the scaffold itself or you could tip it over when climbing up.

## Rent or buy?

If you only need to use a scaffold for a weekend, then renting is probably your best option. If you have a three-month-long project, you may want to consider buying your own scaffold. That way you'll have it for the next job. Consider storage before you buy; frames and planks take up a lot of wall space. Another option is to buy and then sell when you're done. If you enjoy wheeling and dealing, the cheapest option is to buy used and then sell it off again.

You can buy a 5 x 7-ft. frame and brace scaffold with adjustable base jacks, three planks and guardrails for $400 to $500 new or $200 to $300 used, depending on the quality. The same setup will cost about $50 to rent for a day and $95 to rent for a week. So do some math to help you decide.

CLEAT

6" TO 18" OVERHANG

## Working with wood planks

It's perfectly acceptable to work on wooden planks, but there are a few things you should know. Use at least 2x10 planks made from a sturdy wood like Douglas fir. Some softer pine boards won't hold up. Especially avoid boards with large knots.

Laminated veneer lumber (LVL) is ideal. Planks obtained from a rental center should have a stamp on the edge indicating they're safe to use. Wood planks should hang over the edge of the frame a minimum of 6 in., but don't have them overhang by more than 18 in. or they could tip if you step too close to the edge. Install a cleat to hold the planks in place.

## Don't mix and match

Combining scaffold styles can result in an unstable and dangerous platform. Just because most scaffold frames are yellow doesn't mean they're the same. There are at least five different styles of scaffold, and many have no identifying marks. The same manufacturer often builds several different styles.

To add to the confusion, the differences in tube diameters and cross brace stud locations can be small enough that the pieces "kind of" fit together. The only way to really be sure is to measure the overall frame dimensions, the inside and outside tube diameters, and the cross brace stud spacing.

DIFFERENT DIAMETER TUBES

CROSS BRACE STUD

CROSS BRACE STUD

## RISK OF ELECTRIC SHOCK

### Stay clear of power lines

You don't have to touch a power line to get electrocuted. Electricity can arc from the line to conductive materials (like scaffolds). Keep a minimum distance of 10 ft. from all power lines.

## Build a handy workbench

One way to organize your workspace is to create a workbench by installing planks at a higher level than the ones being walked on. A workbench adds a level of safety as well because you'll be less likely to trip on supplies and tools.

# 6 Outdoor Structures, Landscaping & Gardening

## IN THIS CHAPTER

# DELUXE
# DRUM COMPOSTER

It's large and loaded with features—but you can build it for the cost of a bargain model

by **Rick Muscoplat, Contributing Editor**

Drum composters convert yard waste to finished compost much faster than stationary compost bins do because they allow you to churn and instantly aerate the waste. Plus, drum composters are easier on your back. You can buy them online or at any garden center for as little as $150 for the smallest units and up to $400 for the large, fancy rigs. They all follow the same basic design—a drum on a stand. Our version is an adaptation of that using a plastic 55-gallon drum. The drum and stand together cost about the same as the low-price models, but our composter is built stronger and has more features. It takes a full day to customize the drum and build the stand. We used rivets to speed up the assembly, but screws, nuts and lock washers work too.

## Finding and customizing the drum

Ask for free used 55-gallon polyethylene drums at car washes and food processing and industrial manufacturers. Since beggars can't be choosers, you'll probably wind up with a white, green or blue drum. If that doesn't fit your backyard color scheme (paint doesn't stick well to polyethylene), contact a container firm and order the color you want. We ordered a black "tight-head" drum (top permanently sealed to the drum) for $52 from a local supplier.

Next, use a jigsaw to cut a door panel slightly smaller than the width of your wheelbarrow. The next step takes the most time and isn't mandatory, but it adds strength and stability to the entire door assembly: Bend 1/8-in. x 1-in. flat aluminum stock around the drum to form side reinforcements for the door opening. Cut the bent aluminum slightly longer than the door opening and mount it to the drum (**Photo 1**, p. 219).

Then cut flat aluminum pieces for the top and bottom of the door opening and the hinge side of the door. Mount the top and bottom door opening reinforcements in the same manner. Mount the hinges at the bottom of the door opening so the door hangs down when you empty the drum. Finish the door by adding the latches (**Figure A**, p. 218).

To make stirring paddles, cut an 8-ft. piece of 4-in. PVC pipe in half lengthwise using a jigsaw. Cut the halves to length so they're slightly shorter than the inside height of the drum. Arrange two halves back-to-back. Then drill and screw the pieces together to form one paddle unit. The back-to-back design is stronger than a single "scoop" and allows you to rotate the drum in either direction. Repeat for the second paddle unit.

## What it takes

TIME: 1 day

COST: About $115 plus the cost of the drum

SKILL: Intermediate

TOOLS: Clamps, miter saw, cordless drill, 4-in-1 screwdriver, drill bit set, jigsaw, pocket hole jig, safety glasses, rivet gun

## How it works

Waste becomes compost thanks to millions of hungry microbes, which break it down and convert it to nutrient-rich fertilizer. Those microbes need oxygen to thrive, and turning the drum daily creates fresh air pockets in the mix. You can accomplish the same thing by churning a pile of compost with a shovel, but a drum composter makes it easier. And the more thorough mixing speeds decomposition.

**ROTATE DAILY**
Screw the bung caps into the holes to prevent compost from leaking out. Then grab the handles and rotate the drum several times in either direction to stir the mixture.

**DROP, ROLL AND DUMP**
Park your wheelbarrow under the drum and open the door. As you roll the drum downward, the compost will dump right into the wheelbarrow.

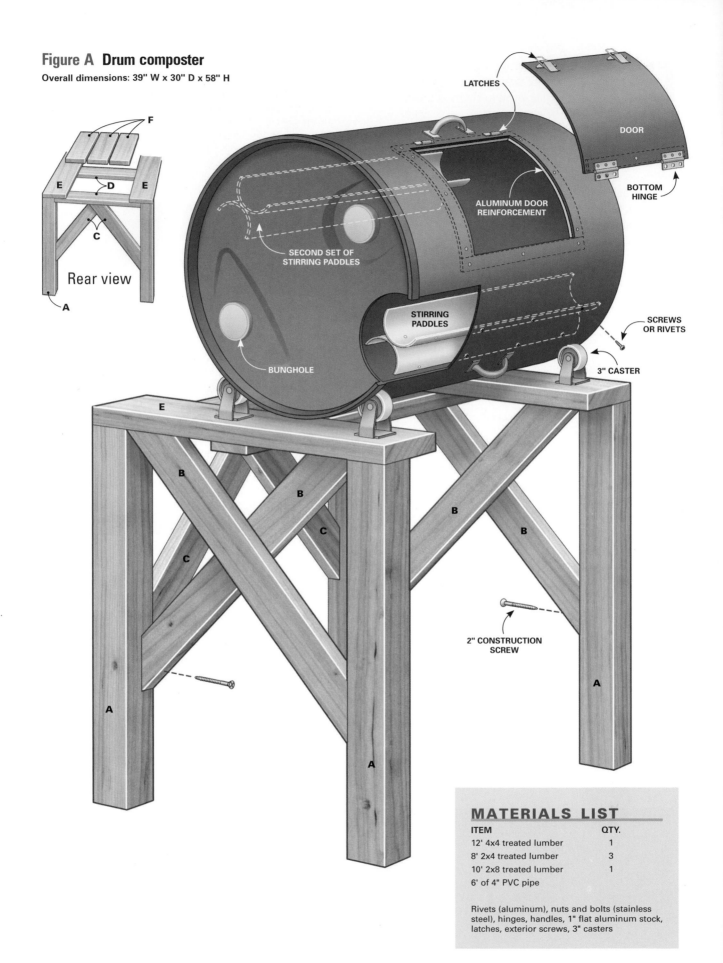

# Figure A  Drum composter

Overall dimensions: 39" W x 30" D x 58" H

F

E   D   E

C

Rear view

A

LATCHES

DOOR

ALUMINUM DOOR
REINFORCEMENT

BOTTOM
HINGE

SECOND SET OF
STIRRING PADDLES

STIRRING
PADDLES

SCREWS
OR RIVETS

BUNGHOLE

3" CASTER

E

B

B

B

B

C

C

C

2" CONSTRUCTION
SCREW

A

A

A

A

## MATERIALS LIST

| ITEM | QTY. |
| --- | --- |
| 12' 4x4 treated lumber | 1 |
| 8' 2x4 treated lumber | 3 |
| 10' 2x8 treated lumber | 1 |
| 6' of 4" PVC pipe | |

Rivets (aluminum), nuts and bolts (stainless
steel), hinges, handles, 1" flat aluminum stock,
latches, exterior screws, 3" casters

**1** **Reinforce the door opening.** Clamp aluminum strips in place so 1/2 in. extends into the door opening. Fasten the strips with rivets or nuts and screws.

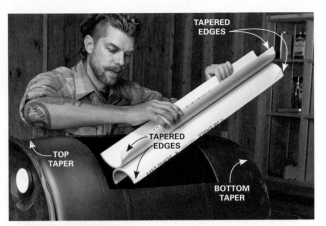

**2** **Install the paddle.** Taper the ends of the paddle to match the tapered ends of the drum. Sand the paddle with a belt sander until it fits. Install the paddle with screws.

**3** **Assemble the stand.** Screw the legs to the rails. Then install the cross braces. Strengthen with diagonal struts.

**4** **Mount the casters.** Then set a level on top of the drum and pry the drum up with a board. When the drum is level, position the last caster, mark its location and screw it into place.

Since the drum has a taper at the top and bottom, you'll have to sand the ends of the paddles to match (**Photo 2**). Mount the paddle units 180 degrees apart and secure them to the drum with screws, nuts and washers. Finally, mount grab handles around the drum to rotate it.

A tight-head drum comes with two threaded "bung-holes." Remove the threaded caps to provide ventilation.

## CUTTING LIST

| KEY | QTY. | SIZE & DESCRIPTION |
|-----|------|--------------------|
| A | 4 | 4x4 x 32-1/2" (legs) |
| B | 4 | 2x4 x 32-3/8" (side braces; cut at 45-degree angle, long point to long point) |
| C | 2 | 2x4 x 30" (back braces; cut at 45-degree angle, long point to long point) |
| D | 2 | 2x4 x 32" (cross braces) |
| E | 2 | 2x8 x 30" (drum deck) |
| F | 3 | 2x8 x 13-1/2" (deck, evenly spaced; optional) |

You may need to drill additional ventilation holes if the mixture stays too wet.

## Build the stand and mount the rollers

Cut the legs and deck boards to length according to the Cutting List. Then assemble the stand using a drill and exterior screws (**Photo 3**). Add diagonal struts to prevent front-to-back and side-to-side movement when spinning the drum.

Flip the stand upright and mount two casters so they ride in the recess around the drumhead. Then level the drum and mount the remaining two casters (**Photo 4**).

## Load, spin and dump

Load the drum with yard waste and add a compost starter to get the batch cooking (available at any home or garden center for about $10). Rotate at least once every day to mix and aerate the batch. When the compost is ready, just dump it out.

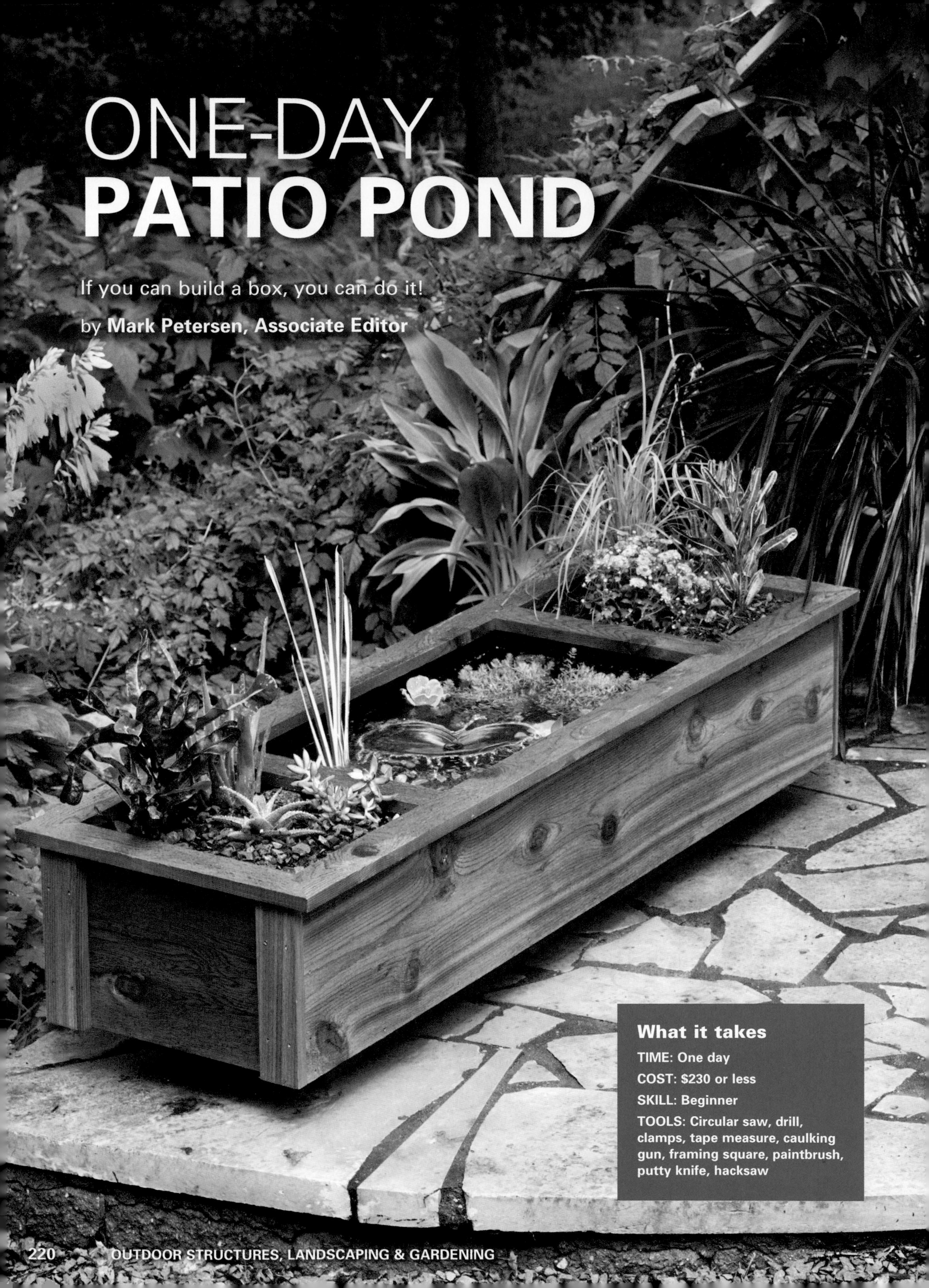

# ONE-DAY
# PATIO POND

If you can build a box, you can do it!

by **Mark Petersen, Associate Editor**

## What it takes

**TIME: One day**

**COST: $230 or less**

**SKILL: Beginner**

**TOOLS: Circular saw, drill, clamps, tape measure, caulking gun, framing square, paintbrush, putty knife, hacksaw**

When my wife wanted to dress up our patio, she brought home a few water plants from our local nursery and dropped them in a new lime green plastic planter filled with water. I was impressed with the plants, but the planter…not so much. Being careful not to criticize her buying decision, I decided to ditch the plastic and create a patio pond that would be a little more suitable for the space. I came up with a wooden container that holds both water plants and regular plants. My wife was thrilled with the final results and never even asked where the plastic container ended up.

## Join the bottom boards

Cut the two bottom boards (A and E; see **Figure A**, p. 222) to length. Cuts made at the lumber mill are usually rough, so trim the ends of all the boards before measuring.

I joined all the components with both trim-head screws and construction adhesive. Adhesive works better than wood glue on rough-sawn lumber and is more forgiving on joints that aren't super tight. Apply a bead of adhesive and clamp the two bottom boards together. Scrape off the excess adhesive with a putty knife, and clean the rest with mineral spirits.

Install temporary cleats on the smooth side of the boards, which will be the inside of the container (**Photo 1**). Hold them in place with 1-1/4-in. screws. I used cabinet screws, but other types of screws would work just fine. Don't worry about the screw holes left behind when you remove the cleats; the liquid rubber will fill them in.

## Cut the boards to size

The width of 1x12s can vary slightly, so double-check the width of the bottom before you cut the ends and dividers (B and C) to length. The rough-sawn cedar I used was 7/8 in. thick. If you're working with material that's only 3/4 in. thick, you'll have to adjust the length of the sides.

All the trim parts are made from 1x6s ripped in half. If you don't have a table saw, go to familyhandyman.com and search for "circular saw long cuts" to see a simple guide that lets you make perfect cuts with a circular saw. A few home

### A simple box with a rubber lining

I wanted a super-easy-to-build water feature, so I designed this wooden box that just about anyone can build with basic tools. What makes it work as a pond is a paint-on rubber lining. There are a few different brands of liquid rubber; I used Rubberize It! Universal Rubber from rubberizeit.com. It's ultra-stretchy and UV-stable, and it can be used on lots of materials, including wood, metal and concrete. It's amazing stuff, though expensive at about $75 a gallon.

You can use liquid rubber to fix leaky gutters and metal roofs, seal RVs and trailers, and for many other applications. Ranchers love it for sealing leaks in metal water tanks. And we love it because it can turn just about anything, even a simple wooden box, into a water feature.

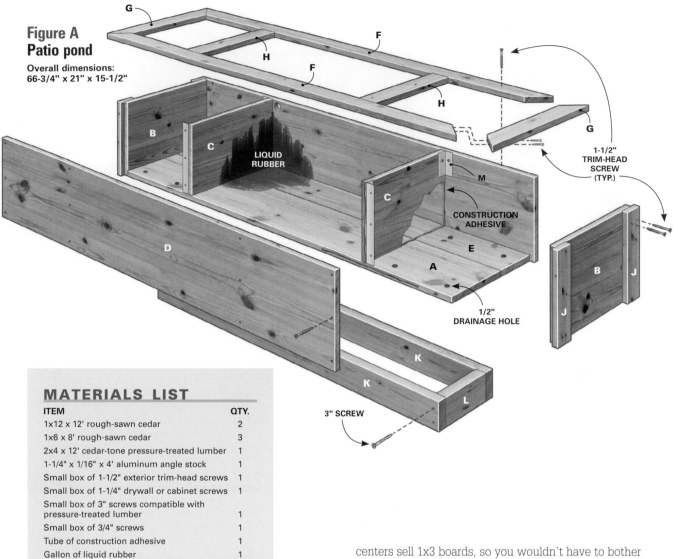

**Figure A**
**Patio pond**
Overall dimensions:
66-3/4" x 21" x 15-1/2"

G

F

H

F

H

G

1-1/2"
TRIM-HEAD
SCREW
(TYP.)

B

C

LIQUID
RUBBER

C

M

CONSTRUCTION
ADHESIVE

D

E

A

B

J

J

1/2"
DRAINAGE HOLE

K

K

L

3" SCREW

## MATERIALS LIST

| ITEM | QTY. |
|---|---|
| 1x12 x 12' rough-sawn cedar | 2 |
| 1x6 x 8' rough-sawn cedar | 3 |
| 2x4 x 12' cedar-tone pressure-treated lumber | 1 |
| 1-1/4" x 1/16" x 4' aluminum angle stock | 1 |
| Small box of 1-1/2" exterior trim-head screws | 1 |
| Small box of 1-1/4" drywall or cabinet screws | 1 |
| Small box of 3" screws compatible with pressure-treated lumber | 1 |
| Small box of 3/4" screws | 1 |
| Tube of construction adhesive | 1 |
| Gallon of liquid rubber | 1 |

## CUTTING LIST

| KEY | DIMENSIONS | QTY. | NAME |
|---|---|---|---|
| **Cut from rough-sawn 1x12 cedar*** | | | |
| A | 62-1/4" x 11-1/4" x 7/8" | 1 | Bottom |
| B | 16-3/4" x 11-1/4" x 7/8" | 2 | Ends |
| C | 16-3/4" x 10-3/8" x 7/8" | 2 | Dividers |
| D | 64" x 11-1/4" x 7/8" | 2 | Sides |
| *Widths may vary* | | | |
| | | | |
| **Cut from 1x6 rough-sawn cedar** | | | |
| E | 62-1/4" x 5-1/2" x 7/8" | 1 | Bottom |
| F | 2-11/16" x 66-3/4" x 7/8" | 2 | Face frame sides |
| G | 2-11/16" x 21" x 7/8" | 2 | Face frame ends |
| H | 2-11/16" x 15-9/16" | 2 | Face frame dividers |
| J | 2-11/16" x 11-1/4" | 4 | End caps |
| | | | |
| **Cedar-tone pressure-treated 2x4** | | | |
| K | 54" x 3-1/2" x 1-1/2" | 2 | Base sides |
| L | 8-1/2" x 3-1/2" x 1-1/2" | 2 | Base ends |
| | | | |
| **Aluminum angle stock** | | | |
| M | 10-1/4" x 1-1/4" x 1/16" | 4 | Corner bracket |

centers sell 1x3 boards, so you wouldn't have to bother with ripping at all.

## Assemble the container

Mark guidelines for the dividers with a framing square 14 in. in from the ends of the bottom. Transfer that line to the inside of the sides (D). Face the smooth sides of the dividers toward the center compartment. That will ensure more even coverage of the liquid rubber in the compartment where it matters most.

Attach the ends and dividers to the bottom with adhesive and three 1-1/2-in. exterior-grade trim-head screws (**Photo 2**). Join the sides with adhesive and screws, three in each side of each end and divider. Space the screws about 10 in. apart along the bottom. The end caps hide the end grain and strengthen the corners. Secure them with four screws and adhesive. Cedar isn't as prone to splitting as harder woods, so I predrilled holes for screws only in areas where a knot was in my way.

Install four aluminum angle brackets (**Photo 3**). Cut them to size with a hacksaw or a jigsaw fitted with a bimetal blade. Drill two holes in each side, and secure them with adhesive and 3/4-in. screws.

Assemble the base with two 3-in. screws into each joint. I found it easier to center the base when the container was upside down. Hold it in place by driving in four screws at an angle. Flip the whole thing over and secure the base to the container with 3-in. screws driven down through the bottom of the container.

After removing the temporary cleats, drill four 1/2-in. drainage holes in the corners of the outside compartments and one in the middle. If you plan to install a water pump, drill a 1-1/2-in. hole for the cord. I used a hole saw. Figure out which side of the container has the best-looking wood grain and drill the hole on the opposite side about 3/8 in. down from the top edge.

## Poor man's pocket hole

If you're a regular weekend woodworker, you really ought to get yourself a pocket hole jig. But if you don't have one, here's a quick and easy trick that works well on soft woods like cedar: Start by laying out the face frame, rough side down, and marking two guidelines at each joint. Then drill 1/8-in. holes through the end grain at an angle so the drill bit pops out about 3/4 in. to 7/8 in. down from the end of the board (Photo 4). At that length, a 1-1/2-in. trim-head screw will travel about 3/4 in. into the adjoining frame section. If you mess up and drill at a funky angle, you can always drill another hole a little bit over, and no one will be the wiser because it's on the underside of the face frame.

## Build the face frame

Assemble the sides and the ends of the face frame with two 1-1/2-in. trim-head screws and adhesive (Photo 4). Keep downward pressure on both trim boards while driving in the first screw. A wood clamp on the seam works well as a third hand. Before installing the face frame dividers, measure diagonally from one corner to the other both ways to make sure the frame is square. If the frame is a little out of whack, adjust the frame until it's square, and clamp it to your workbench to hold it square.

**1** **Build the bottom.** Glue the bottom boards together with construction adhesive, and install three temporary cleats to hold them together until the project has been assembled.

TEMPORARY CLEAT

**2** **Install the dividers.** Fasten the dividers to the bottom, and then add the sides. Join all the parts with both adhesive and trim-head screws. Scrape any excess adhesive with a putty knife.

CONSTRUCTION ADHESIVE

TRIM-HEAD SCREWS

**3** **Add corner brackets.** Cut aluminum angle stock to create corner brackets. Drill four holes in each bracket, and secure them with adhesive and screws.

CORNER BRACKET

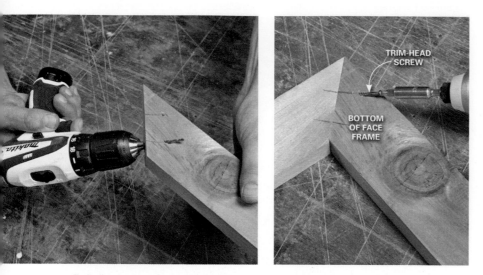

## Apply the liquid rubber and wood finish

Tape off the top edge of the container, the power cord hole and the drainage holes on the bottom. Brush the rubber on thick into the corners, seams, screw holes and defects in the wood (Photo 5). It takes three heavy coats to make a watertight seal and at least three hours between coats. I applied only one coat in the two outside compartments because they'll be filled with soil rather than water. I also applied just one coat on the very top edge of the container. Avoid blocking the drainage and cord holes with rubber by mopping the excess out with a cotton swab or rolled-up paper towel. The rubber needs to dry for a few days before it's ready for water.

Rough-sawn cedar isn't supposed to be smooth; hence the name. So resist the urge to sand, and embrace the imperfections. I applied a cedar-tinted wood finish made by Sikkens, but any exterior stain or clear finish would work.

**4** **Build the face frame.** Join the face-frame parts so that the new screws will be invisible. First, drill pilot holes through the end of one part (left photo). Then just hold the parts together and drive in screws (right photo).

**5** **Apply the liquid rubber.** Glob a thick coat of the liquid rubber into all the seams, corners and defects in the wood. Apply one coat on the outside compartments and three on the middle.

## Finish up and add water

Once the finishes are dry, clamp the face to the container and fasten it with adhesive and 1-1/2-in. trim-head screws spaced every 10 in. or so (Photo 6). Set the screws flush with the surface of the wood to keep water from pooling.

A water pump isn't necessary but does help the water stay fresh. Some pumps have suction cups to hold them to the bottom, but the rubber-coated wood may not be smooth enough for them to stick. I laid down a small chunk of Plexiglas at the bottom and stuck the pump's suction cups to that. Floating water plants with exposed roots will clog the pump filter, so only use potted plants, or plan to build some sort of additional screen or filtration system. A pump that moves 120 gallons per hour is plenty big enough for this situation.

Now it's time to fill up your new creation with water and plants. If the local nursery doesn't carry water plants, you can order them online. Search online for "buy aquatic plants" to locate sources.

**6** **Secure the face frame.** Clamp the face frame into place and hold it down with adhesive and trim-head screws. Leave the screw heads flush with the surface to avoid pockets where water can pool and penetrate the wood.

# MODERN
# DECK BUILDING

Expert tips for great looks that will last decades

## by **Mark Petersen, Associate Editor**

There are tons of new decking products on the market, and building methods continue to evolve and improve. To keep up with the changes, we traveled to builders' shows and deck expos to meet with tool and product manufacturers and get advice from top-notch deck builders. Here are some of the best tips and products we found.

### Smart spacing

These yellow deck board spacers can be used to space boards either 1/8 in. or 3/16 in. apart. Our experts like large spacers like these because they're easy to grab and pull out, and less likely to fall down between the boards. They're also highly visible, which makes them less of a trip hazard. You can find the Johnson DeckMate spacers at home centers or online for about $5 each.

## Decision tool

Besides picking the color of the decking, you'll have to decide on the color of the fascia boards, railings, spindles, hardware, posts and caps. And those aren't easy decisions, especially when all you have to go on is a brochure with tiny color swatches. AZEK has a new, free app for the iPad that can help. Check it out at azek.com or the App Store on iTunes. The app allows you to change the color and texture on several different stock deck scenes, and once you find the combination that suits you best, there's a place to keep notes so you won't forget and have to start all over.

Visualizers like this are super handy, but our experts still recommend a hands-on experience before you make your final decision. Go to the supplier and check out a sample of the actual product. Pick it up and feel the texture. If there's a display, take off your shoes and walk around on it.

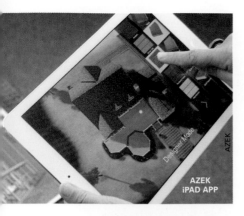

AZEK
iPAD APP

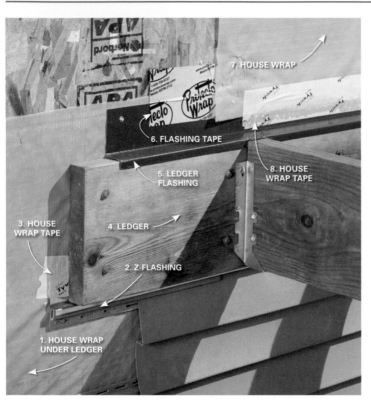

7. HOUSE WRAP

6. FLASHING TAPE

5. LEDGER FLASHING

8. HOUSE WRAP TAPE

3. HOUSE WRAP TAPE

4. LEDGER

2. Z-FLASHING

1. HOUSE WRAP UNDER LEDGER

## Best way to flash a ledger board

Deck ledger boards are a common source of water infiltration, and it can be years before you discover the damage caused by water finding its way behind the ledger and into your home. The process below may seem a little excessive, but the extra time spent following these steps may save you thousands of dollars in repairs.

1. Install house wrap on the wall several inches higher than where the top of the ledger board will be.
2. Install a Z-flashing approved for pressure-treated lumber where the bottom of the ledger will be.
3. Cover the top of the Z-flashing with house wrap tape.
4. Fasten the ledger board over the Z-flashing.
5. Install flashing approved for pressure-treated lumber on top of the ledger.
6. Cover the top of the flashing with window/door flashing tape.
7. Install house wrap over the flashing.
8. Fasten the house wrap to the wall with house wrap tape.
9. Install the siding…finally!

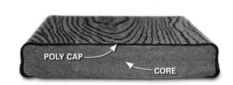

POLY CAP

CORE

## Tougher decking

Just a few years ago, most manufactured decking was "composite," typically a combination of wood fibers and polymers. Composite was a big improvement over wood, but today most manufacturers offer something even better: "capped" or "shelled" decking.

The core of capped decking is similar to composite or made from cellular PVC, but that core is covered with a layer of denser, tougher polymer. That means better resistance to scratches, stains and fading. Brands include AZEK, TimberTech and Trex. It costs about $5 to $10 per sq. ft. Paying more usually gets you a thicker or tougher cap, plus deeper texturing and blended coloring for a more natural look. The decking shown above, Trex Transcend, is made from 95 percent recycled material and includes a 25-year fade and stain warranty.

## Better than lags

Structural screws work great for hanging a ledger board and fastening thick framing members. The main advantage of structural screws over traditional lag screws is that they don't need a pilot hole, which cuts the installation time in half! The Strong-Drive TIMBER Screws shown here have a low-profile head and are driven in with a large Torx bit. An 18-volt impact driver or 1/2-in. drill should be enough to get the job done.

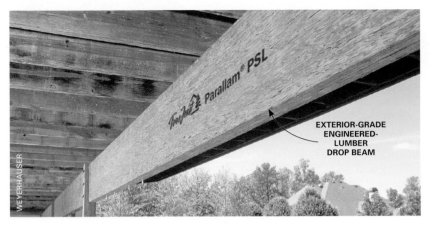

## Longer spans, fewer posts

Engineered lumber has been used inside buildings for years because it's stronger and straighter than regular lumber. And now there are versions for outdoor use. It may not be cost effective to frame an entire deck with engineered lumber, but installing an engineered-lumber drop beam is a great way to reduce the number of posts and footings needed to support a deck. The one shown here is made by Weyerhaeuser.

## Hide ugly ends

The ends of manufactured deck boards are ugly, and you don't want to leave them exposed. There are a couple ways to hide them. The easiest solution is to raise the fascia board so the top is flush with the top of the decking (Photo A). But keep in mind that most fascia/skirt boards are 11-1/4 in. wide, which means they aren't wide enough to fully cover both the deck boards and a 2x12 joist.

Another way to hide the ends is to install a border/perimeter board around the outside edges of the deck (Photo B). This method can really dress up your deck, especially if you choose an accent color for this board. The downside of a perimeter board is that it requires extra framing underneath.

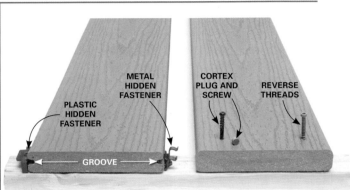

## Fastening options

Screwing through the face of the boards is by far the fastest, easiest and most structurally sound method of fastening deck boards. Modern deck screws have reverse threads to suck the decking down tight to the joists and specially designed heads to prevent mushrooming. Some face-screwing systems, like the Cortex system from FastenMaster, allow you to countersink the screws and fill the holes with plugs made out of the same material as the decking. Installing the plugs is time consuming, but the fastener locations are almost invisible.

Boards with grooves on the sides can be held down with hidden fasteners. Hidden fasteners are self-gapping and easy to install, and you can't beat them if you want a nice, clean, fastener-free look. Each decking manufacturer has a recommended fastening system, but our experts avoid the kind that require fastening from underneath. They also prefer fasteners that don't require removing half the deck in order to replace one damaged board in the middle.

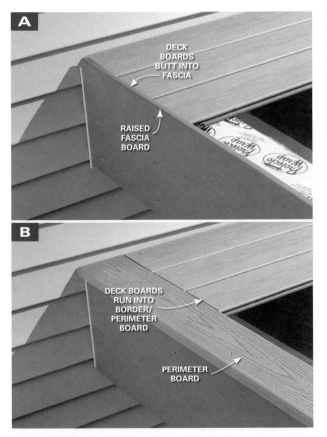

## Blocking keeps decks flat and square

Manufactured decking isn't as stiff as wood decking, so it allows joists to bow. And that leads to a wavy deck surface. To help keep joists flat, our experts always attach blocking perpendicular to the joists. They also install diagonal blocking to keep the entire frame from racking.

Use narrower lumber (2x8 blocking on 2x10 joists) so the blocking looks less conspicuous from a distance. Once everything is secure, our experts run a string on the top side of the joists and plane down the remaining high spots.

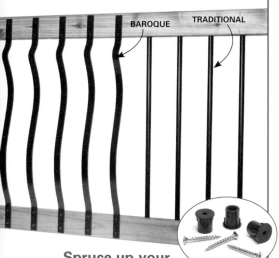

## Spruce up your existing deck

New metal balusters can give your existing wood deck a sleek, modern feel. These two options are made by Deckorators. The Baroque balusters are simply screwed to rails. The round Classic balusters are held in place by hidden connectors that require no hole drilling. Deckorators balusters don't need to be painted or stained, which is probably the most tedious deck maintenance task there is. The Classic is sold in 10-packs; connectors are sold separately. The Baroque is sold in 5-packs that cost about the same as a 10-pack of Classic and connectors. Search online for sources.

## Good-looking, maintenance-free posts

One way to spruce up posts is to cover them with a maintenance-free material. AZEK makes a PVC Column Wrap that's super easy to install. Simply glue together three sides, slide them over the post, glue and clamp the last side in place, and then never worry about painting or staining again. AZEK Column Wrap is available for 4x4, 6x6 and 8x8 posts; prices vary based on post size and height. Order it at home centers and lumberyards that carry AZEK products.

## Stronger decking

NyloDeck is unlike most decking on the market. It's made from 100 percent recycled carpet fibers. It cuts and installs like other decking products, but it's much stiffer. Unlike most other manufactured decking, it can span joists spaced 24 in. on center and can be installed at a 45-degree angle over joists spaced 16 in. on center. That comes in handy when you're resurfacing an existing deck frame. The extra stiffness also helps constrain new treated lumber, which tends to twist and warp. NyloDeck doesn't eliminate the need for blocking between the joists, but it does help prevent a wavy-looking finished product. NyloDeck is similar in cost to the better grades of capped decking (p. 226). To learn more, go to nyloboard.com.

DEMOLITION HAMMER

DIAMOND PIER FOOTING

## No-dig footings

Our experts gave up concrete deck footings a couple years ago. Instead, they've been using the Diamond Pier foundation system. To install a Diamond Pier footing, just drive in four pipes with a demo hammer. That eliminates a ton of digging and concrete work.

The standard deck model costs about $125. Most home centers and lumberyards that carry this product will also have breaker hammers you could borrow or rent. Check out the videos at pinfoundations.com. The Diamond Pier system is relatively new, and you need to make sure it's approved in your area.

## MEET THE EXPERTS

PRECISION DECKS
OR OUTDOOR

**Bob Januik and Matt Norden, owners of Precision Decks, let us know what's new in the world of decks. They've been building decks for 20 years and are constantly trying new methods and materials.**

RUBBER BUMPER

STARBORN INDUSTRIES

## Perfect screw sinker

When you're screwing decking, this Smart-Bit Deck Screw Depth Setter is a great tool to make sure all the screws are set at a consistent depth. The type of bit can be changed to match the screws, and the depth of the screws can be adjusted. It also has a free-spinning collar with a rubber bumper to prevent marring. They cost about $20 online.

## Avoid rot with flashing tape

Pressure-treated lumber that stays wet will eventually rot. Flashing tape keeps water from getting trapped between doubled-up joists. If you're resurfacing an existing deck frame, tape over any joists that have a lot of holes from the previous nails or screws. Buy black tape if you can find it; shiny silver and white tapes may be noticeable between the gaps in the decking. The tape shown

FLASHING TAPE

will be covered by the perimeter deck board. Flashing tape is available in 50-foot rolls at home centers.

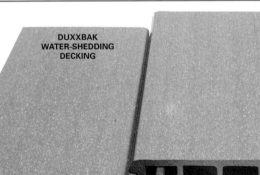

DUXXBAK
WATER-SHEDDING
DECKING

## Water-shedding deck

DuxxBak decking is a unique composite decking that doesn't allow water to pass between the deck boards, keeping the area under the deck dry. A dry space under the deck is a great place to continue your deck party during a rain shower, or to create some useful dry storage.

In order to channel the water away, the decking needs to run perpendicular to the house, so remember to install the framing joists parallel to the house. And make sure the substructure has enough slope to carry the water away. Go to greenbaydecking.com to find more information on DuxxBak and locate a dealer. Expect to pay about the same as the better grades of capped decking (p. 226).

# REPLACE A SPRINKLER HEAD

It's easy to damage a sprinkler head—but it's easy to replace one, too

by **Rick Muscoplat, Contributing Editor**

I t's pretty easy to damage a sprinkler head with your mower if the head sits too high. And we're convinced that snowplow operators intentionally shear off sprinkler heads along the curb just for the entertainment value.

No matter how your sprinkler head got damaged or quit working, there's no need to call the irrigation company to do the repairs. This is a DIY job from start to finish. All you need is a new head, an assortment of different-length poly cutoff riser fittings and parts to build a homemade flushing tool. You can get all the parts for less than $15 at any home center. You'll also need a garden spade, poly sheeting, a wet/dry shop vacuum and a saw. Here's how to attack the job.

## How to buy replacement sprinkler heads

A replacement sprinkler head doesn't have to be the same brand as the broken head. But it does have to be the same type: pop-up (stationary, rotor- or gear-driven rotor) or impact. And the new head must also match the inches-per-hour (iph) or gallons-per-minute (gpm) delivery rate of the old head. Plus, the spray pattern and throwing distance must also match. If you install the wrong head, it can over- or under-water that section of your lawn or garden and possibly cause other heads in that same zone to underperform. So you'll need all the specs from the broken head before you buy a replacement.

Locate that information on the nozzle, the top of the head (if it's still there) or on a label stuck to the body of the head (see "Remove the Broken Head" at right). If you can't find the specifications, at least find the brand and part number. Then look up the

specs on the manufacturer's website. If you strike out on the specs and part number, take the old head to an irrigation service company and ask for a matching replacement head.

Buy a replacement head at a home center or online. The replacement head will most likely come with an assortment of snap-in nozzles, so you can adapt the head's delivery rate, spray pattern and throw rate to fit your needs.

## Remove the broken head

Lay down plastic sheeting next to the broken sprinkler head. Then use a garden spade to cut an 8-in. circle around the old head. Pry out the sod and set it aside. Then dig down and around the old head, placing the dirt on the poly sheet (**Photo 1**). When you reach the water line, unscrew the broken head.

If the head is located at the low spot of a watering zone, chances are the hole will fill with water, and mud will get into the water line. Suck the mud out with your shop vacuum. (The water line gets flushed later.)

## Set the new head height

If the old riser fitting came out with the old head, remove it and screw it onto the new head. Then test-fit the new head by screwing it into the water line. The top of the head should be flush with the ground, not sticking up into the grass. If it's not the right height, grab a new poly cutoff riser (about $1 each at home centers) with multiple threaded sections and cut it to the correct length (**Photo 2**). It may take a few tries (and a few risers) to get the height just right. Once you get the proper height, remove the head and flush the line using the steps shown here.

## Build a flushing tool and flush the water line

No matter how careful you are, dirt is going to fall into the water line fitting. If you can't remove all the dirt with your shop vacuum, you'll have to flush it. Build a flushing tool with 3/4-in. PVC pipe and the fittings (a couple bucks in parts at home centers) shown in **Figure A**. Then flush the water line (**Photo 3**). Finish by sucking the water out of the flushing tool (Photo 4).

## Install the head and backfill

Screw the new head into the flushed water line and begin backfilling the hole. Align the head so it sits straight in the hole as you tamp the dirt with your hand. Finish the job by replacing the grass. Water immediately to reestablish the grass roots.

**1** **Scoop out the dirt.** Slice the garden spade straight down the sides of the hole to give you room to maneuver. Then lift the dirt up, out and onto the poly sheeting.

**2** **Cut the riser to length.** Slice through the multiple-thread poly cutoff riser using a metal-cutting blade for a smooth cut. Deburr the cut edge with a knife. Then install the riser on the head, screw the head into the water line and check the height.

**3** **Flush the line.** Screw the flushing tool into the water line and aim it into the street or away from your work area. Turn on the water for that zone and let it run for about 30 seconds.

## Figure A
## Build a flushing tool

Cut a length of 3/4-in. PVC pipe into two 18-in. sections. Glue a 3/4-in. x 1/2-in. MPT fitting to one end of a pipe and a 3/4-in. x 3/4-in. MPT fitting to the other. Then glue a 3/4-in. x 3/4-in. MPT fitting to the second piece of pipe. Connect the two pipes with a 3/4-in. x 3/4-in. FPT elbow.

**4** **Vacuum out the remaining water.** Slide the vacuum hose nozzle over the vertical pipe and suck out all the remaining water.

**5** **Install the head and backfill.** Screw the riser fitting into the irrigation tube, then the sprinkler head. Backfill with dirt and sod.

# A BETTER LAWN WITH FEWER CHEMICALS

This may change the way you think about lawn chemicals

by **Joe Churchill, Contributing Editor**

**M**ost homeowners overapply pesticides and fertilizer to their lawns. Coming from a guy who sells lawn supplies, that may sound strange, but it's true: Homeowners tend to look for a chemical solution to lawn problems when they should be thinking about *healthy grass* instead. When a lawn is healthy, it resists disease. If it isn't sick, it doesn't need "drugs" and extra care.

Here are 10 tips to help you keep your lawn healthy. Whether you want to reduce chemical use or eliminate it altogether, following these tips will help your grass, your wallet and the environment.

## Adjust your expectations

Lawn chemicals do work, and it's difficult to get that flawless "golf course look" without them. So if you plan to eliminate or drastically reduce chemical use, you may have to accept imperfections. Expect a dandelion or two and areas that will be a little less green at some times of the year. That said, you could still expect your lawn to look good—probably as good or better than most of your neighbors' lawns.

## Water less

One of the biggest mistakes made by lawn owners who have a sprinkler system is overusing it! Too much water is costly, wasteful and bad for your lawn. Water early in the morning, not during the afternoon when it's hot or when it's windy. More of that precious water will make its way to the roots.

Space irrigation cycles as far apart as possible. Let the grass wilt and turn a little blue before watering again. The less you water, the deeper those grass roots will go to look for it. This is a good thing! Overwatering discourages roots from penetrating deep into the soil. They are encouraged to stay close to the surface where the moisture is. A lawn with shallow roots dries out quicker. Not good!

## Mow regularly

Mowing is a chore that's easy to put off—the grass will still be there in a couple days. But delay is bad for your grass. The taller it gets, the more you'll cut off when you finally mow. And the more you cut off, the more you'll "shock" the grass. That weakens each individual plant and leads to other problems later on. It also opens up the turf canopy and allows weeds to bully their way in.

Rule of thumb: Never remove more than one-third of the leaf blade each time you mow. And keep your lawn mower blade sharp. A clean cut reduces the chance of common lawn diseases making their way into the leaf tissue. Your lawn will look much better too.

## Raise your mower

Taller grass means a healthier lawn. It shades the soil surface, keeps the soil from drying out and reduces watering needs. Shaded soil also makes it harder for weeds to get started. If you raise your mowing height, you may even find that the taller grass chokes out existing weeds. For northern lawns, 3 in. is a great target height. For warm climates, 1-1/2 to 2 in. is best.

## Remove thatch

Thatch is a layer of slowly decomposing grass stems, roots, clippings and debris that accumulate at the soil surface over time. It can build up in your lawn and virtually choke it to death. Excessive thatch buildup is commonly found in lawns that have been overfertilized or overwatered and have never been aerated. Thatch buildup of 3/4 in. or more will restrict water and nutrient penetration into the soil (think thatched roof) and can harbor disease organisms that can increase the need for pesticides. Slice open a section of turf. If the thatch is more than 3/4 in. thick, take action.

Regular core aeration (see tip above right) will slow thatch development. However, it won't do much to remove existing thatch. This can be done by renting a power rake, which will "lift" the thatch from the soil surface. This thatch residue can then be raked by hand and removed. Dethatching is hard work, so it's smart to prevent buildup in the first place. The best way to do that is to avoid overwatering and overfertilizing.

## Aerate the soil

"Aerating" simply means making holes in the ground by removing plugs of soil. And it's the single most important task you can perform to maintain a healthy, good-looking lawn. Nothing else comes close! It relieves compaction caused by foot traffic and creates extra pore space in the soil, allowing air, nutrients and water to enter. All of that helps roots to thrive.

Aerate your lawn at least once a year, preferably in the fall. Do it two or even three times each year if you can. The more, the better. You can rent a lawn aerator at any equipment rental store for about $60 for an afternoon. Get one that will remove plugs of soil rather than one that pokes holes in the ground.

THATCH

## Add compost

Top-dress your lawn with high-quality compost. Compost can bring depleted or damaged soil back to life, resulting in stronger root systems and happier plants. One teaspoon of compost contains a billion beneficial microorganisms that help create better soil structure and texture, which improves nutrient, water and air retention.

To apply compost, spread it over your lawn with a shovel, aiming for a layer 1/4 to 1/2 in. thick. Then work it into the turf with a rake. It's best to do this after aerating. Most garden centers sell bagged compost. But to cover an entire yard, it's better to buy in bulk from a garden center. Quality compost for a typical lawn will cost $150 to $350. Don't worry about buying too much—leftovers will benefit your garden and shrub beds.

## Fertilize just enough

Regular composting doesn't replace fertilizing. Your lawn will still require food once in a while. And testing your soil (every two or three years) is the best way to know when and how much fertilizer your grass needs. It will help you determine nutrient deficiencies and excesses, so you won't pay for or apply fertilizer you don't need. Don't fertilize because you think your lawn needs it. Contact your local university or garden center for help with soil testing.

There's no need to fertilizer more than twice a year. An organic fertilizer applied after core aeration will maximize plant and soil health. Like compost, organic fertilizers help feed beneficial organisms and replace valuable nutrients in your lawn. Most organic fertilizers are very safe to use nearly any time of the growing season. I prefer meal-based organics containing bonemeal, blood meal, fish meal and feather meal; however, organics made with poultry litter and biosolids work too.

## Reseed

Instead of applying costly pesticides, sow quality grass seed. Reseeding your lawn every year will help maintain good turf density and make it very difficult for weeds to take hold and grow. In fact, some grasses actually release a beneficial toxin into the soil that acts like a natural preemergent herbicide, preventing weeds from germinating.

Reseeding with genetically improved varieties will also boost your lawn's performance. Many newer grasses require less fertilizer, watering and mowing compared with the older grasses that are most likely in your lawn. If you haven't reseeded in the past 10 years, you're long overdue. Simply use your fertilizer spreader to broadcast seed immediately after core aerating. Those soil plugs lying on your lawn's surface will dry out while you do this. After you've spread the seed, break up these cores with a rake. The combination of seed and pulverized soil will backfill your aerator holes, creating perfect seed-to-soil contact.

## Trim trees

Grass is a sun-hungry plant. By strategically removing a few branches or carefully trimming lower limbs, you'll give it more sunlight. This can also improve air circulation, which helps cool your lawn during hot, humid conditions and reduces lawn diseases. In many cases, your trees and shrubs will look better too. If you love your trees and shrubs just the way they are, consider replacing grass with shade-tolerant ground covers or decorative mulch. Remember: You can't have both deep shade and lush grass.

# HandyHints®

## HIGH-RISE BIRD FEEDER

We live close to a natural habitat for deer and find that they enjoy our bird feeder as much as the birds do. To keep the food away from the deer, we drove a steel stake into the ground and attached an extendable painter's pole to the stake. We then attached the bird feeder to the other end. Now we can lower the bird feeder, fill it and raise it to keep it "for birds only."

–Dick Seils

PAINTER'S POLE

## GARDEN/GARAGE TOOL CADDY

I had some leftover wood and plastic lattice from a fence I was building. Rather than toss the scraps, I decided to use them to build a caddy to organize my garden shovels, hoes and brooms. I installed casters, so it scoots easily into a corner of my garage.

–Philip J. Gruber

OUTDOOR STRUCTURES,
LANDSCAPING & GARDENING

# DECK REVIVAL TIPS

## A fresh finish makes weathered wood look like new

by *The Family Handyman* Editors

Remember how great your deck looked when it was new? Well, you can restore that look with a new finish. The basic process is simple: Remove the old finish with chemical stripper, wash the wood with a cleaner (often called a "brightener") and apply a new finish, which may be a stain, sealer or waterproofer. You'll spend at least eight hours on this project, spread over a couple days. Here are some tips for faster, better results.

## Make repairs first

If you have cracked or rotted deck boards or railings, replace them before you strip the deck. Putting new wood through the same stripping, cleaning and staining process as the old wood will produce a better match when the job is done. Even you may not be able to tell the new wood from the old.

## Save time with a pressure washer

To prep a deck for a fresh coat of stain, you'll have to clean it and strip away the old stain. You can get great results with a stiff brush and elbow grease, but a gas or electric pressure washer will save you hours of labor. Most pressure washers have a tank or intake tube that will add stripper or cleaner to the water as you spray. You can rent a pressure washer for a day at a rental center.

Keep in mind that a pressure washer can damage wood. Start gently in an inconspicuous area, at a setting no higher than 1,000 psi, and hold the wand at least 12 in. from the wood. Increase the pressure or hold the wand closer if needed, but check for gouging and "fuzz" before you move on to the rest of the deck.

## Protect plants

Some deck cleaners and strippers are formulated to be harmless to plants. But refinishing pros tell us that these products are often less effective than stronger cleaners. And since protecting plants is quick and easy, there's no need to avoid the most effective products. Just give nearby plants a good soaking and then cover them with 2-mil plastic sheeting. On a sunny day, plastic covering can "cook" your plants, so keep the cover-up time to a minimum. (See the Great Goof on p. 238 for a real-world example!) Spread the plastic right before you begin to clean, and remove it immediately after.

## Scrape before you strip

Stripping off the old finish is the slowest—and most tedious—part of deck refinishing. And since you never know how well a stripper will work until you try it, do a little experiment: Apply some stripper to a small area where the old stain is in fairly good condition. While you're waiting for the stripper to loosen the stain, hit another area with a paint scraper. Don't try to scrape off all the stain; just get most of it off. Then use stripper to remove the remaining stain on the scraped area. You just might find that a combination of light scraping followed by stripper is much faster and easier, especially on areas where the stain is in good shape.

## Rinse everything, then wait

Whether you're using a pressure washer or elbow grease, be sure to thoroughly rinse all the wood after you're done stripping off the old stain. That not only washes away any leftover debris but also neutralizes stripper residue. Also rinse down any nearby surfaces that the stripper may have drifted onto.

After the final rinse, wait for the wood to thoroughly dry. Drying times depend on the weather, but expect to wait at least 48 hours. If it rains, you'll have to wait another two days. That's frustrating, but dryness is critical. Most stains won't penetrate or adhere well to damp wood. If you rush the job, the new stain will flake off and you'll have to repeat the whole project. **Exception:** Some stains can be applied to damp wood. One example is Thompson's WaterSeal Waterproofing Stain.

## Stain railings first

Work from the top down, starting with the rail, followed by balusters and posts. Rollers and foam paint applicators are great tools for applying stain fast. But also keep a paintbrush handy; you'll need it to smooth out runs and drips. If you drip onto the deck (you will!), immediately brush the drips to avoid spotting.

## GreatGoofs®

### Don't fry your shrubs!

I got up early one Saturday last summer to paint the large gable end of the house before the afternoon heat. Below the gable were a group of variegated aucuba bushes (my wife's favorites), so to protect the leaves from paint drips, I draped them with a plastic drop cloth. I climbed the ladder and started painting. After five hours I was finished, and so were the plants! I pulled the plastic away from the bushes, and yikes, they looked like they had been hit by a flamethrower. The plastic had created a solar tent, overheating and killing the bushes. Several hundred dollars later, the new bushes are doing fine!

–Dwight H. Covington

## Spray stain

If you have lattice or other hard-to-coat surfaces, put some stain in a spray bottle. To avoid runs, set the spray at a wide pattern and apply a light coating; you can always add more stain if the color is too light. Keep a paintbrush handy to smooth out runs.

# A FINE FINISH FOR OUTDOOR WOOD

Tips for using spar finishes

by **Tom Caspar, Contributing Editor**

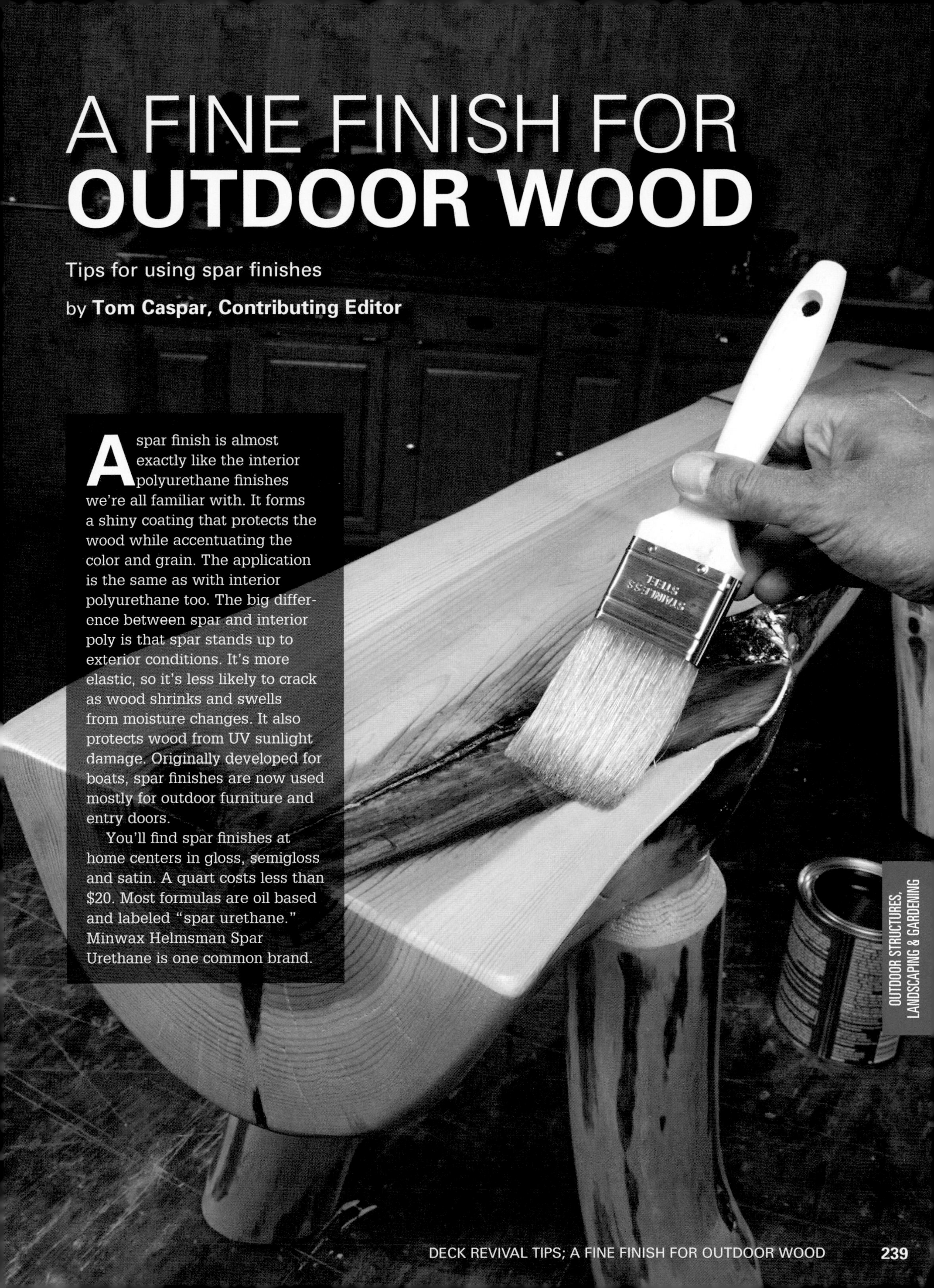

A spar finish is almost exactly like the interior polyurethane finishes we're all familiar with. It forms a shiny coating that protects the wood while accentuating the color and grain. The application is the same as with interior polyurethane too. The big difference between spar and interior poly is that spar stands up to exterior conditions. It's more elastic, so it's less likely to crack as wood shrinks and swells from moisture changes. It also protects wood from UV sunlight damage. Originally developed for boats, spar finishes are now used mostly for outdoor furniture and entry doors.

You'll find spar finishes at home centers in gloss, semigloss and satin. A quart costs less than $20. Most formulas are oil based and labeled "spar urethane." Minwax Helmsman Spar Urethane is one common brand.

## Seal the legs

The end grain at the bottom of legs wicks up water like a thirsty sponge, providing a perfect home for the fungi that cause wood to rot. Sealing the end grain with spar (or any other finish) often fails because the end grain is so porous. Exterior wood glue fills the pores and seals out water much better. Brush on one coat, let it soak in and dry, then put on a second coat for good measure. If you slop any glue onto the visible sides of the legs, wipe it off and resand the spot before finishing.

## Keep legs high and dry

Even when wood legs are sealed (see tip above left), they shouldn't stand directly on wet or damp surfaces. Plastic glides provide the perfect moisture buffer. They're sold in packs of four at home centers and hardware stores.

## Load and wipe off

To maximize the amount of finish your brush can carry, dip it in the can about a third of the way. Lift out the brush a few inches, then jab it toward the can to release excess finish. Dab the end of the brush on a white cotton rag to remove any finish that may have puddled there. Hang on to the rag as you work in case you need to wipe off excess finish inside a corner or around an edge.

## Work from the bottom up

When you start brushing the first coat of a spar finish, begin at the bottom of your project and work your way up. If you get any runs or drips as you go, they'll fall on a finished surface and you can deal with them when you're ready. If runs or drips fall on an unfinished surface, wipe them up right away so their edges don't leave a shadow line. **Tip:** Run screws into the ends of the legs to serve as standoffs. This way, you can start brushing at the very bottom of each leg.

## Check for drips

After you're done brushing a section, aim a light at it to check for drips. Hold the light at a low angle so the surface looks glossy. Even tiny runs, drips and skips will be easy to see.

## Dab at drips

If you spot a drip, stab at it with a dry brush, a technique called "stippling." (To temporarily dry your brush, just wipe the tips of the bristles on a paper bag.) Brushing out a drip that has started to dry makes a gooey mess. Stippling is less likely to leave permanent blemishes. And if it does, the imperfections will be smaller and easier to sand flat after the finish dries.

## Spray the final coat

Spar in a spray can is convenient and provides a smooth, flawless finish. But it costs about $9 per can, and a mid-size project might require five or 10 cans. So here's an economical approach: Brush on two or three coats, then after final sanding, spray on a final, perfect coat.

# PERFECT PERGOLA

Stunning but simple, elegant but economical

by **David Radtke, Contributing Editor**

I designed this pergola with simplicity and economy in mind, but not at the expense of good looks. The pergola is made from standard dimensional lumber, so you just cut the parts and screw them together—no special skills required. To keep the cost down, I used pressure-treated lumber, which looked great with two coats of semitransparent stain.

I sized the pergola for small gatherings of family and friends. With an eye toward daytime comfort, I spaced the roof slats to block some sun but still let in enough rays for warmth.

You can build this project in about two weekends if you have an agreeable helper. I spent just under $1,300 on materials. The concrete floor, which is optional, added another $500. Your floor could be flagstones, paver bricks or even a ground-level deck.

## Survey the site

Be sure you have a fairly level spot in your yard. Slopes can be subtle and a bit deceiving, so bring a level attached to a long, straight 2x4 out to the yard as you

### Big, but not complicated

If you think this pergola is beyond your skill level, take a closer look. It takes time and muscle, but it's really just a bunch of standard lumber parts screwed together. The trickiest part of the job—positioning the posts—is almost goof-proof with simple plywood plates (see Photo 3). Most sheds and even fences are more complicated than this project!

OUTDOOR STRUCTURES, LANDSCAPING & GARDENING

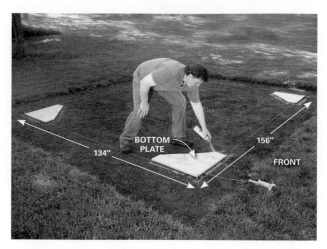

**1** **Mark out the perimeter.** Cut the sod away and mark the perimeter of the pergola with stakes and string. Check the layout by taking diagonal measurements; equal measurements means the layout is square.

**2** **Position the postholes.** Align the post bottom plates with the strings and then outline them with spray paint.

check site locations. Our site sloped by about 3-1/2 in., which worked out well. I made sure the slab would be just above the grade of the yard at the higher end, which then left the lower area as a "stepping off" the slab point. If you have a challenging yard, you may need to level an area by first terracing with a short retaining wall.

## Prep the site

If you're building in a grassy area, you'll need to remove the turf. You can rent a kick-style sod cutter, but if you're over 22 years old, you'll probably agree that renting a gas-powered sod cutter (about $60 a day) is well worth the cost. You can remove the sod in less than two hours and still have a good chance of getting out of bed the next day. If you don't have a spot that could use fresh turf, make plans to get rid of a full pickup load of sod.

## Prep the lumber

Every stack of treated lumber contains some beautiful wood and some ugly stuff. Take the time to pick through the pile and select good material—your project will look much better. When you get the lumber home, you'll be eager to start right away. But I strongly recommend that you let the lumber dry for a few days. Stack it with spacers so air can reach all sides of each board. Then stain it before building. Staining this pergola after assembly would be a slow, messy job. I applied two coats of Behr Semi-Transparent Waterproofing Wood Stain (No. 3533).

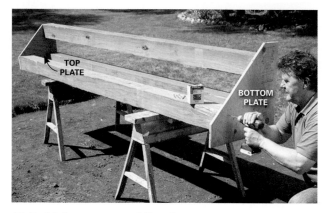

**3** **Build the post assemblies.** Screw plywood plates to the posts. Joining the posts this way saves you the hassle of positioning and plumbing them individually.

## Setting the posts

You'll need to mark out a perfectly square layout for the posts. To start, position two strings exactly perpendicular to each other using the 3-4-5 triangle method (in this case, your measurements will be 9, 12 and 15 ft.). If you're not familiar with this trick, search online for "345 triangle." Once you get two lines squared, the other two will be easy. But double-check your layout with diagonal measurements (**Photo 1**) before you mark the posthole locations (**Photo 2**).

To keep the post groupings positioned precisely, I cut plates from treated plywood and fastened them to the posts (**Photo 3**). That way, you can position, plumb and brace each assembly of three posts as if they were one post (**Photos 4 and 5**).

Bracing the assemblies takes several trips up and down the ladder. Start by screwing some horizontal 1x3 braces onto the tops of the posts. Make sure the post assemblies are spaced the same on the top as they are on the bottom. With the spacing established, you can brace the groups diagonally to the ground with stakes (**Photo 5**). Keep at it until it's close to perfect.

### What it takes

**TIME:** Two weekends; the floor will be another weekend or two
**COST:** $1,300
**SKILL:** Intermediate
**TOOLS:** Circular saw, drill, level, standard hand tools

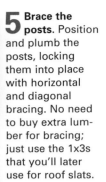

**5** **Brace the posts.** Position and plumb the posts, locking them into place with horizontal and diagonal bracing. No need to buy extra lumber for bracing; just use the 1x3s that you'll later use for roof slats.

**6** **Fill the post-holes.** Mix concrete and fill in around the post assemblies. Let the concrete harden at least one day before removing the bracing.

12" DEEP HOLE

**4** **Set the posts.** Place each post assembly in its hole. You'll need at least one helper for this job. Be careful so the sides of the hole don't cave in.

**7** **Install the headers.** Position the headers so they'll be at least 80 in. from the floor of the pergola. Screw them to the posts, then cut off the posts flush with the headers.

FRONT HEADER

TEMPORARY BRACE

Use a tub or wheelbarrow to mix the concrete, then toss it into the hole (**Photo 6**). The mix isn't critical because you don't need to trowel a finish onto it. Just make sure you get it packed into the holes evenly around each grouping. I used about four bags per hole, but get a few extra bags just in case.

## Fastening the headers

The next day you can install the headers (**Photo 7**). Overlap the corners as shown in **Figure A**, p. 246. I removed my braces at the top, one at a time, as I leveled and installed each outer side header and then finished with the front and back. Be sure to take the thickness of your slab into consideration as you measure the distance to the bottom of the headers. Leave at least 80 in. between the slab and the header. Taller people may want to nudge it up a couple inches.

Once the outer headers (B and C) are in place, cut the posts flush with the top of the headers, I used a framing square to mark them and a circular saw to cut as deep as I could. I then used a handsaw and when my arms felt like they were ready to fall off, I used a 10-in. blade in my reciprocating saw. Next, cut and install the inner 2x10 headers at the front and back and then the rafter supports (E) cut from 2x8s. Rip the 2x8s to 6-1/2 in. at a 7-degree angle. The slightly wider 6-1/2-in. edge should go toward the inner side of the pergola. The rafters will rest on this support and extend to the outer side headers (C).

## Figure A
**Post and header assembly**

B

D

E   C

C

D

B

A

**4" COATED
LEDGER
SCREWS**

150"

128"

**Overall
dimensions:
153" x 131" x 89-1/4"**

FRONT

**Our floor is a
concrete slab.
But flagstone,
paver bricks or even
a ground-level deck
would work just as well.**

## Figure B
**Post detail**

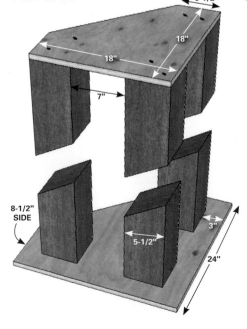

5-1/2"

18"

18"

7"

8-1/2"
SIDE

3"

5-1/2"

24"

| CUTTING LIST | | |
|---|---|---|
| **KEY** | **QTY.** | **SIZE & DESCRIPTION** |
| A | 12 | 5-1/2" x 5-1/2" x 10' treated pine (posts) |
| B | 2 | 1-1/2" x 9-1/2" x 153" treated pine (front and rear headers) |
| C | 2 | 1-1/2" x 9-1/2" x 128" treated pine (side headers) |
| D | 2 | 1-1/2" x 9-1/2" x 150" treated pine (inner front and rear headers) |
| E | 2 | 1-1/2" x 6-1/2" x 113-1/2" treated pine (side rafter supports) |
| F | 1 | 1-1/2" x 9-1/2" x 131-1/2" treated pine (ridge beam) |
| G | 10 | 1-1/2" x 3-1/2" x 74-7/8" treated pine (common rafters) |
| H | 4 | 1-1/2" x 3-1/2" x 74-7/8" treated pine (gable rafters) |
| J | 30 | 3/4" x 2-1/2" x 139" treated pine (roof slats) |
| K | 2 | 1" x 2-1/2" x 12" treated pine (ridge cover plate) |

*Note: The dimensions given here may vary slightly—measure before you cut!*

## Figure C  Roof detail

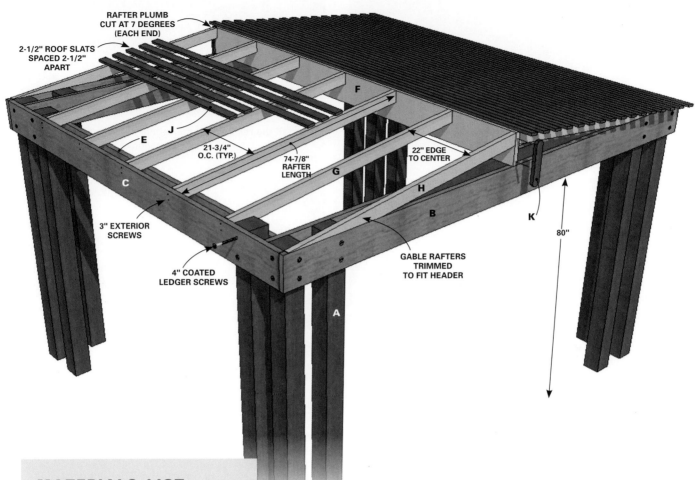

RAFTER PLUMB
CUT AT 7 DEGREES
(EACH END)

2-1/2" ROOF SLATS
SPACED 2-1/2"
APART

F

J

E

21-3/4"
O.C. (TYP.)

74-7/8"
RAFTER
LENGTH

22" EDGE
TO CENTER

G

C

H

B

K

3" EXTERIOR
SCREWS

4" COATED
LEDGER SCREWS

GABLE RAFTERS
TRIMMED
TO FIT HEADER

80"

A

### MATERIALS LIST

| ITEM | QTY. |
|---|---|
| 6x6 x 10' treated pine posts | 12 |
| 4' x 4' sheet of 3/4" treated plywood | 1 |
| 2x10 x 14' treated pine | 4 |
| 2x10 x 12' treated pine | 3 |
| 2x8 x 10' treated pine | 2 |
| 2x4 x 7' treated pine | 14 |
| 1x3 x 12' treated pine | 30 |
| 5/4x6 x 2' treated pine (ridge cover plate) | 1 |
| 1/4" x 4" coated deck ledger screws | 48 |
| No. 8 x 3-1/4" self-drilling exterior wood screws | 60 |
| No. 8 x 1-5/8" self-drilling exterior wood screws | 210 |
| Concrete for footings (80-lb. bags) | 16 |
| Concrete for slab | 3 cu. yds. |
| 1/2" rebar, 16' lengths | 8 |
| 2x6 x 16' | 4 |
| 1x4 x 2' stakes | 24 |

### MEET THE BUILDER

**David Radtke is a designer, illustrator, remodeler and cabinetmaker in Minneapolis.**

## Figure D  Footing and slab detail

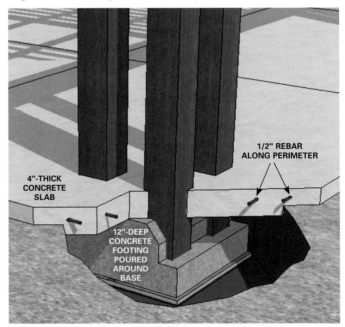

1/2" REBAR
ALONG PERIMETER

4"-THICK
CONCRETE
SLAB

12"-DEEP
CONCRETE
FOOTING
POURED
AROUND
BASE

**8** **Set the ridge beam.** Mark the center of the front and back headers and then screw the ridge beam to the headers.

**9** **Install the rafters.** Cut the rafters to fit flush with the top of the ridge beam and 3/16 in. above the outer headers. Screw them into place.

**10** **Mark the gable rafters.** Tack a 2x4 to the end of the ridge beam and then align it with the header and in the same plane as the other rafters. Scribe each end of the 2x4 to create a pattern for the other gable rafters.

**11** **Install the slats.** Screw the roof slats to the rafters using a spacer to position them. Make sure each slat overhangs the gables by about 5 in. Then, after all the slats are in place, mark the ends with a string and trim them off.

## Building the roof

Measure the distance at the center of the pergola (**Photo 8**) from front to back at the top of the headers. Cut the 2x10 ridge beam (F) to this length and drive screws at an angle into the headers. Measure from the top edge of the ridge to the inner edge of the side header (C) on each side, starting at the midpoint of the ridge and the header. Cut the rafters to fit. Ideally it should be 7 degrees, but if your ridge is cupped slightly you may need to adjust the cut. Because my ridge was slightly cupped, I had 6-degree cuts on one side of the ridge and 8-degree cuts on the other side. Install the rafters and fasten them with screws (**Photo 9**).

The gable rafters (H) are the same as the common rafters except they sit atop the front and rear headers, so they need to be scribed (**Photo 10**) to fit. Fasten these to the ridge beam by toe-screwing at an angle or by screwing through the opposite side of the ridge at a slight angle into the rafter (this method give a cleaner installation and less chance of a protruding screw). Finally, screw through the side headers into the rafter ends, making sure your spacing is even.

I cut 2-1/2-in.-wide roof slats from 1x6 material because it was better quality than the 1x3s available at the lumberyard. Start installing the slats parallel to the ridge and work your way down each side. Overhang the front and back of each course about 5 in., then you can string a line and trim them once they're all installed. Use a 2-1/2-in. spacer as you screw each row to the rafters (**Photo 11**). Check your progress every fifth course to make sure you're staying perpendicular to the rafters and that you'll finish with a full-width slat at the end.

Once all the roof slats are fastened and trimmed, cut the ridge covers (K) and nail them over the exposed end grain at each end of the ridge beam. I mitered the ridge cover tops to fit tightly under the roof slats.

## Finishing up

If you stained the lumber before assembly, all you have to do now is coat any unstained ends of parts. Be sure to stain the top ends of each post to reduce water absorption and cracking. For extra insurance, I coated the post tops with stain followed by exterior paint. If you plan to pour a concrete floor as we did, go to familyhandyman.com and search for "concrete" to find several articles about working with concrete.

## Add plants and privacy

For privacy and greenery, I built a trellis on one side of the pergola. If you want the feel of an outdoor room, you could add trellises on two or three sides.

My trellis is simply 1x4s and a 2x4 joined with 1-5/8-in. screws. I built it on the pergola floor, then stood it up and screwed it to the posts. I sized the planter boxes to hold 6-in. plastic pots and made them 25 in. long, but you can make them whatever length will work.

### Figure E  Privacy trellis

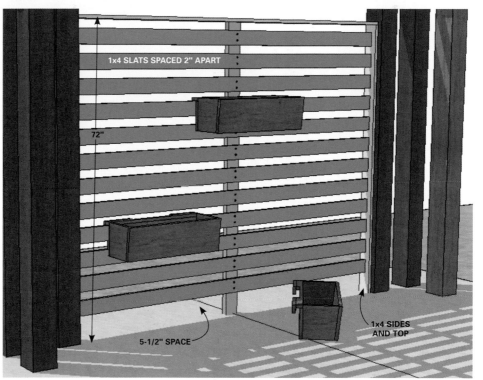

1x4 SLATS SPACED 2" APART

72"

5-1/2" SPACE

1x4 SIDES AND TOP

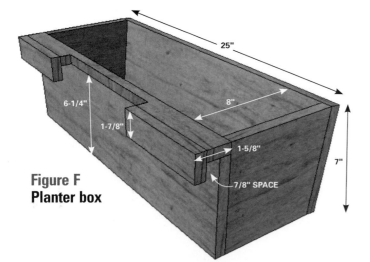

### Figure F
### Planter box

25"

6-1/4"

1-7/8"

8"

1-5/8"

7/8" SPACE

7"

## MATERIALS LIST
### Privacy trellis and planter box

| ITEM | QTY. |
|---|---|
| 1x4 x 8' treated pine | 15 |
| 2x4 x 8' treated pine | 1 |
| 1x8 x 10' cedar (per planter box) | 1 |
| No. 8 x 1-5/8" self-drilling exterior screws | 50 |
| 1-3/4" galvanized nails (for planter box assembly) | 1 box |
| Exterior construction adhesive (for planter assembly) | 1 tube |

## CUTTING LIST  Privacy trellis

| KEY | QTY. | SIZE & DESCRIPTION |
|---|---|---|
| A | 2 | 3/4" x 3-1/2" x 71-1/4" (vertical sides) |
| B | 1 | 3/4" x 3-1/2" x 92" (horizontal top) |
| C | 1 | 1-1/2" x 3-1/2" x 71-1/4" (center support) |
| D | 12 | 3/4" x 3-1/2" x 90-1/2" (horizontal slats) |

# TIPS FOR A DECK REMODEL

### Refresh your old deck without starting from scratch

by **Gary Wentz, Senior Editor**

O ur friends in the deck business tell us that "re-deck" projects are keeping them busy these days: They tear off the old wood decking and repair the deck's framing if needed. Then they install new decking, using low-maintenance composite deck boards. Usually, they install new railings, too. The home-owner gets a deck that looks completely new, without paying for new footings or framing. If that sounds good to you, check out these tips for a DIY re-deck.

## Don't limit your choices

You can stop by a home center and buy a load of in-stock composite decking. But don't restrict your selection that way. Instead, visit the materials desk and look at samples of what you can special-order. Or visit a showroom store that specializes in decking (search online for "decking supplies").

You'll see a wide range of prices, sometimes as low as $4 per sq. ft. and as high as $12. At the low end of the price range, you'll get solid coloring and a smooth texture or unconvincing imitation wood grain. Spending more will get you streaked coloring and textures that closely mimic real wood. You can also get a much tough-er, stain-resistant surface by choosing composite that's "capped" with a layer of PVC (see "Tougher Decking," p. 226)..

**AZEK VINTAGE COLLECTION**

## Brace before tear-off

On many decks, the decking plays a big role in keeping the entire structure square. So add a diagonal brace under joists before you tear off the old decking. That will lock the joists in place and hold the deck square as you pull off the old boards and lay new ones. Leave the brace in place after you've installed the new decking; it will reduce side-to-side sway and make the deck feel more solid.

2x4 BRACE

## Include splice boards

Decks are often larger than the longest deck boards available. The usual solution is to join the boards end-to-end, scattering the splices randomly across the deck. That's fine, but here's a better way: If your deck is 24 ft. long, for example, buy 12-ft. boards and run a "splice board" down the middle of the deck. The splice board will require some extra framing to support it and the adjoining deck boards, but the neat look is worth the trouble.

SPLICE BOARD

## Tear-off techniques

If your decking is nailed down, just pry up the boards. Here's a common approach: Pry up one end of each board with a flat pry bar, then use a big pry bar to do most of the work. If your deck is screwed down, tear-off will take more time. Remove all the screws you can with a drill/driver. When a stripped screw head prevents that, try to pry up the board. If that fails, you can drill into the head with a 1/4-in. bit. That will detach the head from the screw and allow you to pry the board off.

## Add pizzazz with a pattern

Because it's available in various colors, composite decking makes borders and patterns easy. For design ideas and color combinations, visit manufacturer websites. The colors shown here are Harvest Bronze and Walnut Grove from AZEK's XLM line.

## Flatten the joists

Most composite decking isn't as stiff as wood, so it won't bridge uneven joists as well. And that can mean a wavy deck surface. One pro we talked to always stretches a string across the joists and shaves down high spots with a planer. That adds an hour to the project but pays off with a flatter, better-looking deck.

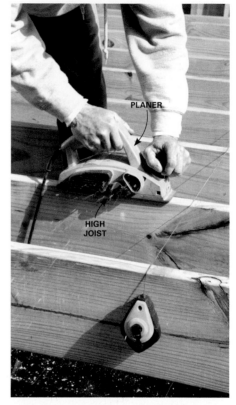

PLANER

HIGH JOIST

## Add stair stringers

Most composites require that stair stringers be spaced no more than 12 in. apart ("on center"). But your existing stringers are probably 16 in. apart. To solve that problem, remove the center stringer or stringers (you can leave the side stringers in place). Mark out as many new stringers as you need, using a removed stringer as a pattern. Cut the new stringers and install them all—old and new—at the correct spacing.

OLD STRINGER

NEW STRINGER

# Get Smart About Watering

## DRIP IRRIGATION SYSTEMS

### Save time, save water and pamper your plants

There's an easier way to keep your plants watered, even when your life gets busy or you're away from home—a simple, automated drip irrigation system. These systems are affordable and easy to set up. In small yards, you can complete the job in a day for about $150. Not only will your plants thrive, but you'll also spend less time dragging around hoses and setting up sprinklers.

■ Drip systems deliver moisture straight to the roots instead of blasting water through the air, where much of it evaporates or lands where it isn't needed. That uses a lot less water—up to 70 percent less compared with overhead watering.

■ Automatic watering is also good for plants because it's consistent, eliminates fluctuations in soil moisture and discourages diseases and fungal growth.

# Get Smart About Watering

DRIP IRRIGATION SYSTEMS continued

## THE BASIC SYSTEM

Drip irrigation systems have been around for years, but the early versions were clunky to install and prone to clogging and leaking. Newer systems are affordable, customizable and leak-proof, and they go together easily. System components vary slightly among manufacturers, but generally, you hook up the faucet assembly at the hose bib and run the 1/2-in. main line around your landscape. You can buy main line with prepunched emitter holes or punch your own holes and install in-line emitters. Or you can use leak-proof connectors to run 1/4-in. tubing to where you need it and attach the watering device of your choice. A basic system goes together in just an hour or two and is easy to expand. There are many excellent videos and other resources online to help you plan your system.

These drip systems are pressure compensated, so the water flow is even throughout the length of the tubing. The different emitters and adjustable spray heads let you vary the amount of water based on the weather and plant needs. There are drip watering systems for all sorts of different landscape elements including trees, vegetable gardens, containers and hanging baskets. You can even convert underground sprinklers to drip water systems. The primary differences among them are the kinds of emitters/watering devices they use.

**Battery-operated timer**
One 9-volt battery will last an entire season. $30 to $50 depending on the model.

**Backflow preventer**
Prevents dirty garden water from flowing back into your household water lines.

**Screen filter**
Traps particles that could clog the emitters. May be separate or part of the backflow device.

**Pressure regulator**
Lowers the incoming water pressure to a level the drip system can tolerate; 25 to 30 psi is standard.

**Hose adapter**
Connects water source to the main line.

**1/2-in. main line**
Don't exceed 200 ft. of tubing in a single circuit.

**Elbow fitting**
Connects sections of hose to one another or other components.

**Preinstalled emitter**
Spaced every 6 to 12 in.; good for straight rows of plants and for shrubs.

**Hole punch**
Makes ports in the main line to connect watering devices and 1/4-in. tubing.

**1/2-gph pressure-compensating dripper**
Ideal for flat and hillside terrain and heavy clay soil.

**Hose end clamps**
Closes off the end of the main line.

## Where to buy drip irrigation systems

You can find kits and individual components online and at home centers, garden centers and plumbing suppliers. A basic kit that waters up to 20 containers or a 75-sq.-ft. area costs $25 to $50 and comes with everything you need except the timer. Higher-quality kits may cost $70 or more.

**1/4-in. barbed tee**
Allows branching to 1/4-in. from 1/2-in. lines.

**Assorted emitters**
Adjustable emitters, also called shrubblers and drippers, can apply as little as 1/2 gph or as much as 10 gph. The right number, type and size of emitters depend on plant type, soil and weather conditions. The yellow flag dripper shown can be taken apart and cleaned.

**1/2-in. universal coupler**
Allows you to cut out damaged tubing and install new line.

**Tubing stakes and adjustable sprayer**
You can mix and match watering devices, but don't use more than 150 gallons per hour (gph) on a single circuit.

**Goof plugs**
Plug unneeded holes when you change the placement of your tubing, watering devices or landscaping.

**Tee fitting**
Creates branch lines to expand and customize the system.

**1/4-in. micro tubing**
Good for containers, zoned areas and customizing your system. Comes in a variety of colors to help hide it. Don't exceed 50 ft. of 1/4-in. tubing in a single circuit.

**1/4-in. barbed connector**
Connects 1/4-in. micro tubing to the main line.

# Get Smart About Watering

## Installation and design tips

■ Soak the tubing in warm water or lay it out in the sun for a little while to soften it and make it easier to work with.

■ Hold the hole punch at a right angle to the tubing when you punch a hole for an emitter or a connector. This makes a round hole that will seal tightly around the barb of the emitter.

■ Flush out the system before installing emitters or other watering devices to clear it of any debris.

■ Create your lateral lines (1/4-in. tubing and emitters) before hooking them up to the main line.

■ If you have plants with drastically different watering requirements (like trees and containers), you can add or subtract the number of emitters or sprayers for each plant or, even better, break the system up into zones of plants with similar needs.

## Expert tips for container irrigation

Container gardening expert Rosalind Creasy is a writer, lecturer and landscape designer. She is the author of the 10-book "Edible Gardening" series. She also wrote "Edible Landscaping," for which she won the American Horticulture Society Book Award.

Creasy says automatic drip irrigation is perfect for containers because they dry out so quickly and require daily watering in hot weather. She's been using drip irrigation for more than a decade to grow an extensive selection of flowers and edible plants in containers at her northern California home. She says these online retailers—urbanfarmerstore.com, harmonyfarm.com and gardeners.com—are also good sources of information on installation, watering schedules and equipment options.

Here are some of Creasy's tips for using drip irrigation for containers:

■ The goal is for the center of the plant's root-ball to be damp but not soggy. Set a timer to water containers twice a day for five to ten minutes, depending on the plant and weather conditions.

■ You can also stick a soil moisture probe ($25 online and at garden centers) 6 to 8 in. into the container to check for wetness.

■ Watch the plant for signs that it needs water.

■ Don't rely on rain for watering because mature plants shed water off the side of the container.

■ Choose adjustable emitters and sprayers with flow control so you can adjust the water pattern for individual plants as they grow.

■ For hanging baskets, run the 1/4-in. tubing up posts, under eaves or in the joint between two walls.

■ Consider adding a fertilizer injector to the faucet assembly so you can feed your plants while you water. These are available online (they start at about $30) and are installed downstream from the backflow preventer.

■ Install a good filter and change it every few months or at least once a season, especially if you have alkaline or mineral-rich water.

RAINDRIP

# WATERING TIPS for sprinklers, hoses, and systems

Proper watering is the single most important thing you can do to keep your lawn in tip-top shape. And even though lawn watering is pretty simple, there are tricks and tips that can help you save time and money. Here are 10 of our best tips for watering quickly and efficiently to maintain a strong lawn.

## Watering wisdom

■ Adjust your watering to the conditions. Different areas of your lawn will have different watering requirements. The key is to make note of this as you water so you can tailor your watering. For example, south-facing hills may require more water; areas under trees, less.

■ Keep watering in a drought. Don't believe the common wisdom that grass goes dormant in a drought. If you don't provide your grass some moisture in a drought, it will die.

■ Water in the morning if possible. The grass can benefit from the water all day long. Plus, watering in the evening may encourage the growth of harmful fungi.

## Buy an impact sprinkler on a tripod

Impact sprinklers are even more versatile if you buy one that's attached to a tripod (**photo above**). These are great for large areas because the extra height increases the distance the sprinkler will throw water. There are other benefits too. You can easily adjust the spray pattern with less stooping, and you can direct the spray over the top of bushes and flower gardens. And finally, the adjustable legs allow you to level out the sprinkler on uneven ground. Look for tripod impact sprinklers at home centers and garden centers.

# Get Smart About Watering

## Using well water?
## Run all your sprinklers at once

Constant starting and stopping will prematurely wear out your well pump. If you're using a well to provide water for your lawn, try to connect as many sprinklers as possible to maximize water flow. This will keep the well pump running continuously and increase its life span.

## Add a remote hose connection for easier watering

If you're constantly dragging long lengths of hose from the house to the far corners of your yard, consider adding a remote faucet instead. Depending on how much time and expense you want to put into it, this can be as simple as a length of garden hose connected to a fence with pipe straps (photo above), or an underground pipe complete with a vacuum breaker at the house. (Go to familyhandyman.com and search for "outdoor faucet" to see how.) Either way, you'll save a ton of time and effort by not having to deal with long hoses.

## Check soil moisture to determine watering time

Common wisdom for establishing the correct length of time to water is to place a pie pan in the yard and note how long it takes to fill 1/2 in. deep. But the expert we talked to prefers a more accurate method that takes soil conditions into account. Heavier soil doesn't absorb moisture nearly as fast as loose or sandy soil, so it needs to be watered longer.

After an extended warm, dry period (dry soil is the key) set up your sprinkler and set a timer for 30 minutes. Then turn off the water and check the soil for moisture depth. Do this by pushing a shovel into the lawn and tipping it forward to expose the soil. See how deep the water has penetrated. Moist soil will be darker. Your goal is to run the sprinkler until the water penetrates 3 to 4 in. into the soil.

If the water has not penetrated far enough, restart the watering and continue to keep track of the time. Check again in another 15 minutes. With trial and error, you'll eventually arrive at the optimal length of time to water for your soil type and water pressure.

SOIL MOISTURE LINE

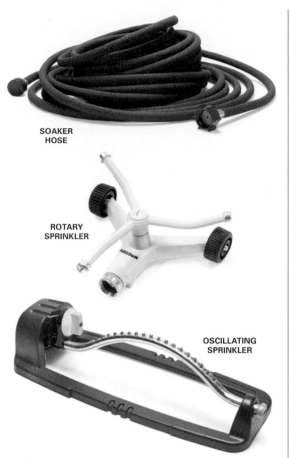

SOAKER
HOSE

ROTARY
SPRINKLER

OSCILLATING
SPRINKLER

## Choose the best sprinkler

Impact sprinklers are a great all-around choice because they're so adjustable and generally waste less water. But there may be better sprinklers for small, difficult-to-water areas.

If you have just a small circular area to water, the round watering pattern of a rotary sprinkler is perfect. Long, narrow spaces like boulevards are easiest to water with flat soaker/sprinkler hoses.

For square or rectangular areas, it's hard to beat an oscillating sprinkler. It's not the most efficient design, but the spray pattern makes it easy to water all the way into the corners.

## Water in the fall

Your lawn still needs water in autumn, even though the leaves are changing, the growing season is winding down and your grass isn't growing fast. Fall watering helps your lawn recover from summer stress and gain strength for the winter ahead. Also, if you fertilize in the fall, watering is necessary for the fertilizer to dissolve and soak into the ground where it's needed. So don't put your hoses or sprinklers away until the ground starts to freeze.

LIGHT
MIST

SEEDED LAWN

## Water grass seed carefully

Seeding is a great way to grow a lawn or patch a bare spot. The key to success is proper watering. For seeds to germinate and grow, they must be kept constantly damp until the seedlings establish roots. Once the seeds sprout, a dry period of even a day will likely kill the new sprouts, and you'll have to start over.

Seeds covered with fabric or mulch or mixed with a mulch-like product stand a better chance. But even with this protection, you should water lightly at least once or twice a day during hot or windy days. Sprinkle the seeds with a light mist until they sprout. A hard spray or big droplets of water will wash the seeds away or make them clump together. After the seeds sprout, keep watering once a day until the grass is ready for its first mowing.

# Get Smart About Watering

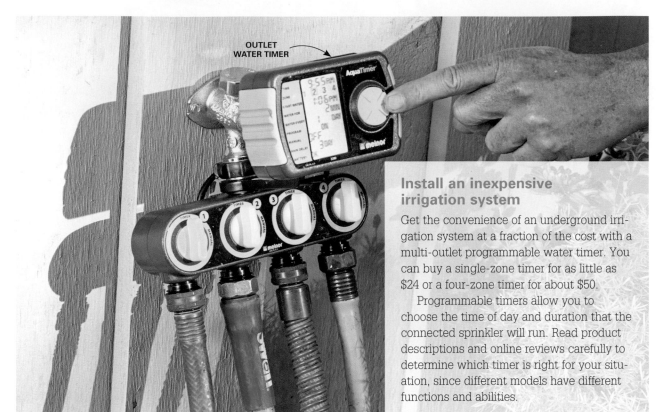

OUTLET
WATER TIMER

## Install an inexpensive irrigation system

Get the convenience of an underground irrigation system at a fraction of the cost with a multi-outlet programmable water timer. You can buy a single-zone timer for as little as $24 or a four-zone timer for about $50.

Programmable timers allow you to choose the time of day and duration that the connected sprinkler will run. Read product descriptions and online reviews carefully to determine which timer is right for your situation, since different models have different functions and abilities.

## Save water with an impact or rotary sprinkler

Sprinklers that spray water high into the air or break up water into a mist are very inefficient, especially if you're watering when it's hot and dry. A large percentage of the water will simply evaporate before it ever reaches the grass. Impact and rotary sprinklers, on the other hand, can be adjusted to keep the water nearer the ground; the water comes out in streams or large drops that fall quickly to the ground without evaporating. You'll save water and money using an impact or rotary sprinkler whenever possible.

ROTARY
SPRINKLERS

IMPACT
SPRINKLERS

# 7 Vehicles & Garages

## IN THIS CHAPTER

# DEALING WITH
# DEAD BATTERIES

The old methods aren't the best for modern vehicles

by **Rick Muscoplat, Contributing Editor**

You probably keep jumper cables in your vehicle so you can solicit a jump if your battery dies or offer a jump to a fellow driver. But jumping batteries on cars built after 2000 might not be so smart. That's because newer vehicles contain as many as a dozen computers and even more digital devices. Jump-starting with cables connected to a running vehicle can create a voltage surge large enough to fry expensive computers in either vehicle. And, since most of these components communicate on a shared data bus, surge damage to just one computer or digital device (even a radio) can disable the entire data bus, preventing the vehicle from starting and costing hundreds to diagnose and repair. Think about that: You can cause expensive damage to your own car simply by providing a jump to someone else.

Here's the bottom line: Dealing with a dead battery in a modern vehicle requires new equipment and techniques. We'll get you up to speed on the latest jump-starting methods and show you what new equipment you need to safely jump-start and replace an automotive battery.

## Avoiding voltage spikes

When you connect jumper cables from a running vehicle to a dead battery, the alternator in the running vehicle instantly puts out maximum charging voltage. That can create a voltage spike of up to 15.5 volts in both vehicles. And it's that voltage spike that can fry computers and digital devices.

One way to eliminate the voltage spike is to leave the engine off in the donor car. That will prevent frying computers in the donor car. But if the car won't start right up, don't grind away to the point that you end up with dead batteries in both cars!

Jump-starting with a jumper pack (also called a booster pack or a juice pack) is a better alternative. The battery inside the jumper pack provides the boost to the dead battery at a safe voltage. When used properly, it's the safest way to protect the electronics in the dead vehicle while providing enough boost to get the engine running.

To use a jumper pack, first turn off all lights and electrical accessories in the dead vehicle. Next, connect the cables the same as you would ordinary jumper cables—positive clamp to the positive battery post and negative clamp to a metallic engine component or chassis grounding point. Then try starting the vehicle. Follow the jumper pack's instructions for maximum cranking times. If the jump works, you're all set. If not, you tried your best and didn't damage any electronics.

## Choosing a jumper pack

Big-box retailers and auto parts stores sell jumper packs and emergency and recreational portable power packs. Even though both have battery cables and clamps, they're two different animals. Emergency and recreational portable power packs are designed to provide low power for long periods to get you through a power failure or provide portable power for picnics, camping or tailgating. They may start a vehicle with a slightly discharged

## Power pack vs. jumper pack

Emergency portable power packs and jumper packs look alike, but they're built with different batteries. A power pack battery is designed to provide low power for long periods, while a jumper pack battery is designed to provide maximum power for short periods to start a deeply discharged vehicle battery. A power pack can usually provide enough power to jump a slightly discharged vehicle battery, but that can shorten the life of the unit.

**Uses for an emergency portable power pack**

- Power port sockets for recharging phones and tablets during a power failure.
- Inflate a spare tire.
- Light up a work area.
- Jump a slightly discharged vehicle battery.

**Uses for a jumper pack**

- Jump-start a dead battery.

## Peak amps vs. cranking amps

Many manufacturers list a peak amp rating on their pack. But it's not a reliable indicator of battery power. Instead, check for the pack's cranking amps (CA) rating. To arrive at the CA rating, the battery is discharged for 30 seconds. The number of amps the battery delivers during that period while still maintaining at least 1.2 volts per cell is its CA rating. The higher the CA, the better the battery.

AC CORD

AC WALL TRANSFORMER

POWER PORT ADAPTER

## Keeping it charged

If your jumper pack is equipped with an internal charging mechanism, plug an AC extension cord into it and connect to any receptacle. The internal charger is the easiest to use but the most costly to repair if it fails. If an external transformer ever fails or you misplace it, simply order a new one from the manufacturer. Some units come with a power port adapter used for emergency charging.

## Maintain computer memory when changing a battery

Replacing a battery in an older vehicle is simple; remove the cables and hold down and swap in the new battery. But if you're changing a battery in a vehicle built after 2000, a jumper pack and power adapter cables are good tools to have on hand. That's because newer vehicles require backup power (a minimum of 12 volts) to maintain the "learned" calibrations for the electronic throttle body, anti-pinch windows, power sliding door, HVAC actuators, theft-deterrent radio and security system. If you don't provide backup power, the vehicle will "forget" the calibrations when you disconnect the old battery. Then, when you connect the new battery, the vehicle may not start or may run so poorly that it has to be towed to a shop. Some vehicles require costly ($150 and up) dealership-only recalibration with a factory scan tool. Others will run poorly until they eventually relearn.

You can avoid all those recalibration issues by providing backup power to the vehicle while you change the battery. Use your jumper pack with a special cable (SOLAR ESA30 OBD II Memory Saver Connector). Find the OBD II diagnostic port on your vehicle (usually under the dash on the driver's side) and push the D-shape connector onto the port. Plug the other cable end into a jumper pack or emergency and recreational portable power pack. Then remove the battery cables (negative cable first) and insulate each one with electrical tape or shove them into a nonconductive cover to prevent shorting.

### Connect the backup power
Let the engine sit for at least 15 minutes to allow the computer modules to power down. Then find the OBD II diagnostic port on your vehicle (usually under the dash on the driver's side) and push the D-shape connector onto the port. Then plug the other cable end into a jumper pack or emergency and recreational portable power pack.

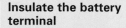

### Insulate the battery terminal
Remove the negative cable first and insert it in a nonconductive cover, like a leather glove. Repeat on the positive terminal. Then replace the battery and install the negative cable last.

battery, but they may not pack enough punch to jump-start a seriously discharged battery or start a vehicle that's flooded. Packs meant for jumping, on the other hand, have batteries that'll deliver a lot of power for short periods and are the ones to buy if emergency battery jumps are your intended purpose.

Here's how to choose a jumper pack. First, ignore the pack's peak amp rating. Peak amps doesn't indicate the pack's ability to start a vehicle. Instead, look for the unit's cranking amps (CA) rating. You need a minimum of 225 CAs to start a four- or six-cylinder engine. (One jumper pack that meets these specs is the Clore JNC300XL with 225 CA). If you have a larger engine or want more power, find a pack with 400 or more CAs. (Two choices at amazon.com are the Clore ES5000 with 400 CA, and the Schumacher PSJ-3612 with 470 CA.)

## Keep the pack charged

Jumper packs require regular recharging. You can't charge a pack, throw it in your truck for six months and expect it to work when you need it. Recommendations vary, but count on recharging a jumper pack at least once every 30, 60 or 90 days. If you don't keep the pack charged, its battery will degrade to the point that it won't accept or hold a charge. Then you'll have to buy a new battery, which costs almost as much as a pack. However, if you maintain it properly, it'll last for several years.

Jumper packs must be recharged at a very low rate (usually less than 1 amp) for long periods (usually 24 hours). The units come with a wall transformer or an AC extension cord (as shown on p. 263) that plugs into an internal transformer. Some packs also come with a power port adapter cable for emergency charging. Since a port outputs almost 12 amps (12 times the recommended charging rate), always follow the manufacturer's instructions to avoid overheating the internal battery. Finally, never connect a jumper pack to the battery on a running vehicle or to an automotive battery charger. The high charging rate will destroy the jumper pack battery.

Maintaining a jumper pack is a hassle. They're not the perfect alternative to jumper cables, just the safest. So it really comes down to this: You can drag the pack inside and charge it periodically, or you can take your chances with jumper cables. If you forget to recharge your jumper pack, you're out about $125. If you fry an electronic component while using jumper cables, you're looking at a minimum of $500 for a tow, diagnostic fee, labor and parts. The choice is yours.

## Test your battery and charging system

You can check the condition of the battery, starting and entire charging system with a computerized battery tester. One choice is the SOLAR BA9. Besides testing voltage, it tests internal resistance and the condition of the starter and alternator. This one works on conventional SLI batteries, as well as gel and absorbed glass mat (AGM), so you can also use it on motorcycle and lawn and garden equipment.

# GreatGoofs

### Dignity vs. the garage door

A story in *The Family Handyman* inspired me to tune up my overhead garage door. I set up my stepladder and prepared to lubricate the bearings and pulleys directly over the door. For some weird reason, I had the garage door opener remote resting on top of the ladder. You can guess what happened next: I bumped the remote button with my elbow. The door opened and swept me off the ladder on its way to the full open position. Surviving the fall with only a couple of bruises to my body and my dignity, I set the ladder back up, closed the door and unplugged the opener before going back to work.

–Bob Busch

### Cut the lights

When I built my house, I wanted a tall garage door opening to accommodate our full-size trucks. That meant I had to mount the garage door track just a few inches from the ceiling. The installation went without a hitch. The first time I hit the garage door button, the door opened perfectly, rolled smoothly along the rails—and sheared off my ceiling lights!

–Ernie Smith

VEHICLES & GARAGES

# ONE-DAY GARAGE STORAGE SYSTEM

An incredibly easy solution for a cluttered garage

by **David Radtke, Contributing Editor**

This storage system is made mostly from wire shelving and plastic-coated particleboard (called "melamine"). Those two simple materials, along with some clever engineering, provide three big benefits:

**Quick, simple construction.** If you can make a few easy cuts (which don't have to be perfect), drive some screws and brush on a little paint, you can build this system in a weekend. If you're an experienced DIYer, you might even be done in a day.

**Fits any space.** The system is made up of separate units, so you can build just one, cover an entire wall with several units or leave spaces between units.

**Versatile storage.** Aside from wire shelves, the system includes optional hanging spaces for clothes and outdoor gear, plus oversize upper shelves for bulky stuff. As your needs change, you can easily remove or reconfigure the shelves.

## What it takes

**TIME:** 1 or 2 days

**COST:** About $100 per unit

**SKILL:** Beginner

**TOOLS:** Circular saw or jigsaw, drill, clamp, level, stud finder, bolt cutter

**1 Cut the sides.** Cut one melamine board at a 45-degree angle and use it as a pattern to mark the others for cutting. Mark your cutting line on a strip of painter's tape—the tape reduces chipping as you cut.

**2 Position the shelf supports.** Mark where the edge of each shelf support is located and mark a centerline for screw locations. Drill three 9/64-in. screw holes for each support.

**3 Fasten the shelf supports.** Drive 1-1/4-in. screws through the sides and into the shelf supports. A clamp makes this step much easier.

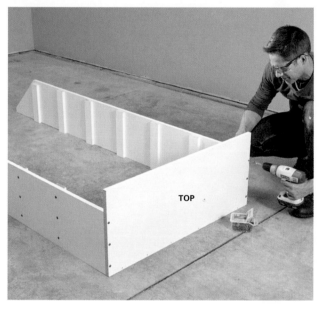

**4 Assemble the unit.** Drill holes in the top, then drive cabinet screws to fasten the top to the sides.

## Build the units

To get started, cut all the parts (see Cutting List, p. 271). The coating on melamine tends to chip when you cut it. For cleaner cuts, use a 60-tooth carbide circular saw blade and apply painter's tape over the cut (**Photo 1**). Melamine is slippery stuff, so clamp it in place before cutting. Set the depth of your saw blade at 1 in. Chipping won't be a problem when you cut the solid wood parts (B and D). When you cut the supports for the lowest shelves (B1), note that they're shorter than the others. To avoid slow, fussy painting later, paint the wood parts before assembly.

Our shelf spacing is 12 in., but any spacing you choose is fine. Lay pairs of sides (A) next to each other when you mark shelf support locations. That way, you can be sure that the supports will match up after assembly. Drill screw holes (**Photo 2**) and then fasten the shelf supports (**Photo 3**).

Pick out a flat spot on the floor and attach the top (C) to the sides (**Photo 4**). Then tilt the assembly up a few inches and slide wood scraps beneath it so you can add the rails (D) with 2-in. screws (**Photo 5**).

With the unit completely assembled, sand the exposed

**5** **Install the rails.** Drill screw holes in the sides and fasten the three rails. You'll need to raise the unit off the floor in order to screw the top and bottom rails.

**6** **Paint the cut edges.** For looks and moisture protection, apply two coats of paint. If you slop a little paint onto the melamine surface, just wipe it off with a damp rag.

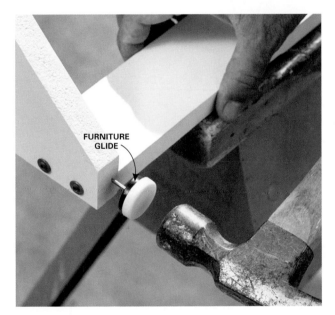

**7** **Add glides.** Nail plastic furniture glides to the bottom of the sides to keep them from resting directly on damp surfaces, especially concrete.

cut edges of the melamine using 150-grit sandpaper, then paint them (Photo 6). Finally, hammer on some furniture glides (Photo 7) and the unit is ready for installation.

## Install the units

If you have finished walls, locate the wall studs with a stud finder and mark them with masking tape. Get some help to lift the assembly up to the wall and hold it in place (Photo 8). Our floor had a row of concrete blocks that protruded from the wall about 1-1/2 in., so we rested the glides on them. The blocks were level but the floor had a slight pitch

**8** **Install the first unit.** Mark the stud locations with painter's tape and set the first unit in place. To ensure that the unit is level and square, check both the top and one side with a level.

VEHICLES & GARAGES

toward the door, so this saved us the hassle of having to allow for the slope of the floor.

With the assembly against the wall, you can shim underneath to level it (if necessary) and then plumb the sides with a level. Screw it to the wall studs with 2-1/2-in. screws (**Photo 9**).

If you're willing to spend $25 or so on a bolt cutter, cutting the wire shelves will be quick and easy (**Photo 10**). Bolt cutters are sized by length; 24 in. is a good choice. When the shelves are cut, set them in place and "clip" them to the wall (**Photo 11**). Also secure the shelf fronts with coaxial cable staples (**Photo 12**), which are available in the electrical aisle at home centers. Remove the nails that come with the staples and use 4d nails instead. To store balls or other items that tend to roll off shelves, install a shelf or two upside-down. The lip on the front of the shelf keeps stuff in place.

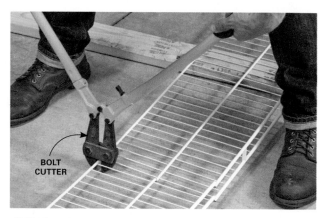

**9** **Add as many units as you like.** With the first unit installed square and level, you can simply butt the next unit against it. Screw all units to studs at the top and bottom rungs.

**10** **Cut the shelves.** A bolt cutter is the best tool for cutting wire shelving to length. A hacksaw or a metal-cutting blade in a jigsaw will also do the job.

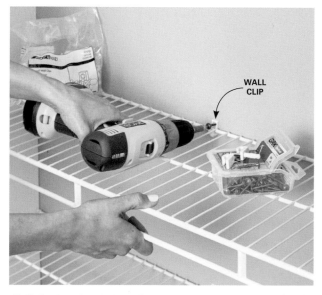

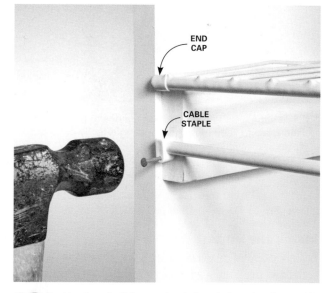

**11** Anchor the shelves. Fasten each shelf to the wall with at least two clips. When you want to fasten the clip to a stud, simply cut off the drywall anchor part of the clip and drive a screw through the clip.

**12** Fasten the shelf fronts. Lock the shelves in place with coaxial cable staples. End caps give the shelves a finished look.

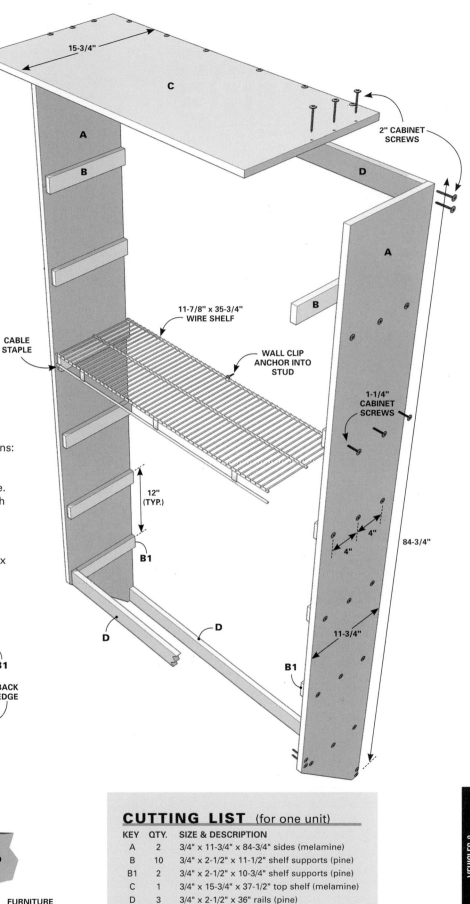

## Figure A
## Shelf unit

**Overall dimensions: 11-3/4" deep x 37-1/2" wide x 85-1/2" tall (top shelf is 15-3/4" deep)**

15-3/4"

C

A

B

D

2" CABINET SCREWS

A

B

11-7/8" x 35-3/4" WIRE SHELF

WALL CLIP ANCHOR INTO STUD

CABLE STAPLE

1-1/4" CABINET SCREWS

12" (TYP.)

B1

84-3/4"

4"

4"

4"

11-3/4"

B1

D

D

D

## MATERIALS LIST
### (for one unit)

| ITEM | QTY. |
|---|---|
| 3/4" x 11-3/4" x 8' melamine shelf board | 2 |
| 3/4" x 15-3/4" x 37-1/2" melamine shelf board | 1 |
| 3/4" x 2-1/2" x 8' pine boards | 3 |
| 12" x 12' wire shelving | 2 |
| Wire shelving wall clips | 12 |
| Wire shelving end caps | 12 |
| Coaxial cable staples | 12 |
| Cabinet screws (1-1/4", 2", 2-1/2"), 4d (1-1/2") nails | 1 pkg. ea. |
| Furniture glides | 2 |
| White paint | 1 qt. |
| 150-grit sandpaper | |

*All of these materials are available at home centers.*

## CHOOSING SCREWS

We used No. 8 "cabinet" screws throughout this project for three reasons:

■ The large "washer" heads design looks much neater than a bugle head countersunk into the melamine surface.
■ The washer heads won't pull through the particleboard.
■ The coarse threads hold well in particleboard.

Cabinet screws are made by GRK, Spax and other manufacturers.

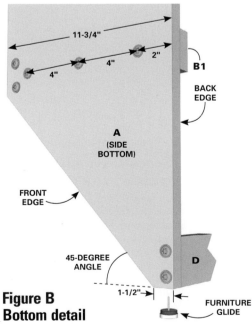

11-3/4"

2"

4"

4"

B1

BACK EDGE

A

A (SIDE BOTTOM)

FRONT EDGE

45-DEGREE ANGLE

D

1-1/2"

FURNITURE GLIDE

## Figure B
## Bottom detail

## CUTTING LIST (for one unit)

| KEY | QTY. | SIZE & DESCRIPTION |
|---|---|---|
| A | 2 | 3/4" x 11-3/4" x 84-3/4" sides (melamine) |
| B | 10 | 3/4" x 2-1/2" x 11-1/2" shelf supports (pine) |
| B1 | 2 | 3/4" x 2-1/2" x 10-3/4" shelf supports (pine) |
| C | 1 | 3/4" x 15-3/4" x 37-1/2" top shelf (melamine) |
| D | 3 | 3/4" x 2-1/2" x 36" rails (pine) |

# SURVIVING A FLAT TIRE

## The owner's manual doesn't cover everything!

by **Rick Muscoplat, Contributing Editor**

**Y**our car or truck owner's manual shows you how to change a flat tire, assuming a best-case scenario. But the real world includes all kinds of surprises: lug nuts that won't budge, a wheel that's rusted to the hub or a spare tire that's so under-inflated, it's useless. In other words, even if you know how to change a flat tire, chances are pretty good you'll run into problems you're not prepared for. Don't think you're out of the woods just because you have road-side assistance. Because if you get a flat tire in an area with no cell phone coverage, or the service is so backed up that it'll be hours before they get to you, you just might have to change your tire yourself.

To help you survive a flat-tire ordeal, we've collected these tips. Some we've taken from our own ugly encounters, and others we've learned from our readers.

## Space-saver spares require extra caution

So slow down! The spare-tire manufacturers are serious about their 50-mph maximum speed limit. Get your flat tire repaired or replaced right away because space-saver spares are designed to run for only 50 to 70 miles.

LARGEST SPOKE

## Don't break your plastic wheel covers

Carmakers use two methods to secure plastic wheel covers: spring clips and screw-on plastic lug nuts. If you don't know which type is on your vehicle, try turning one of the plastic nuts with the socket end of your tire iron. If it rotates, you have the screw-on type. Unscrew all the plastic nuts and lift off the cover.

If the nut doesn't turn, you have the snap-on style. Those have to be pried off, and that's where some people get into trouble. If you jam the tapered end of your tire iron into a weak area on the cover, you'll break it to pieces. So be sure to pry behind one of the larger spokes and twist until the cover pops off.

KEYED SOCKET

KEYED LUG NUT

## Do you know where your keyed socket is?

To avoid theft, many cars have one special lug nut on each wheel that requires a special "keyed socket" to loosen it. If you can't locate the key when you have a flat tire (or another driver in the family isn't aware of it), it won't be possible to remove the wheel. You'll have to use Fix-A-Flat (see p. 274), call for roadside service or have the vehicle towed to a shop. That can cost upward of $200. So make a point of keeping the key in a safe place, like the glove box, that is known to everyone who drives the car.

PLUG INTO POWER PORT ON DASH

## Pack a tire inflator

If you don't routinely top off the air pressure in your spare tire, don't be surprised if it's severely underinflated when you need it. Driving on a severely underinflated full-size spare is unsafe, and driving on an underinflated space-saver spare is downright dangerous. Solve that problem by keeping a plug-in tire inflator in your vehicle at all times (one choice is the Slime 12-Volt Digital Tire Inflator, No. 40022). Start the engine, plug the unit into your power port and bring the spare tire up to the recommended pressure (found on the decal inside the driver's door area) before installing it on the hub.

## Removing a stuck wheel

If you don't rotate your tires every 5,000 miles, your wheels may be bonded to the hub by rust. One of our readers suggested a way to knock the wheels loose.

With the lug nuts loosened about three-quarters of the way, grab the spare by the center hole and use it as a battering ram. Swing it horizontally with all your might so it strikes the stuck wheel at the 12 o'clock position. Repeat the blows at the 3 o'clock and 9 o'clock positions until the wheel breaks free from the hub.

## Fix-A-Flat can get you out of a jam!

If you're not confident that you or the driver can change a flat tire, buy two cans of aerosol tire sealer from any auto parts store (Fix-A-Flat is one well-known brand) and keep them in the vehicle. The cans are sold in several sizes for compact, standard and truck-size tires. Tire sealants work on tread punctures 3/16 in. or less in diameter. They won't work on side-wall punctures, blowouts or any other catastrophic failures. You've got little to lose by trying sealant.

You can greatly increase your chances of a successful seal if you can find the puncture site and move the vehicle until the leak is facing down. If you see the culprit, don't remove it; it'll help seal the hole. If the can is frozen, thaw it with the defroster or floor heater vents until the contents move freely when shaken. Then fill the tire following the directions on the can. If the rim doesn't lift off the ground after using a second can, the puncture is too large to be sealed and you'll have to call for help.

Top off the air pressure as soon as possible. If you have a tire inflator on hand, do it now. This is a very temporary fix, so get the tire repaired professionally ASAP. Tire sealant must be removed within three days or 100 miles, whichever comes first. Inform the tire shop that you've used tire sealant so no one breathes in the propellants (not flammable, but not healthy either). The shop may charge extra for cleaning the sealant from the tire.

### What's the deal with tire plugs?

Many DIYers think they can permanently repair tire punctures with just a plug. They're wrong. A tire plug is just half of the repair. The tire's interior liner must also be repaired with a patch, and that means a trip to the tire store. Skip the patch and you risk a catastrophic blowout.

### Assemble a mission-critical kit

Whether you change your tire yourself or rely on a tire sealant, keep these "mission-critical" items in your vehicle at all times.

**Wheel chocks.** Keep your car from falling off the jack, especially on slopes.

**Plug-in flashlight.** Dark nights can make it impossible to see what you're doing.

**Gloves.** Good to have all year long, but critical for handling cold metal in subzero temps.

**Tire inflator.** You'll need this to fill low spares and top off tires repaired with Fix-A-Flat.

### Spare your limbs when installing the spare

Truck and SUV tires are really heavy. Some DIYers sit on the ground with their knees under the wheel so their legs can help with the lifting. That's a great way to lose a limb or two if the vehicle falls off the jack (which happens more often than you think). Instead, raise the vehicle just enough to get a 1-in. clearance between the tire and the ground.

Rotate the hub until one of the studs is in the 12 o'clock position. Roll the spare tire next to the vehicle and position it so the holes line up with the studs. Then grab the wheel by the rim, lift it up and hang the tire on the top stud. Then align the rest of the holes with the studs and push it on.

### Save your back when loosening lug nuts

There's no way you can loosen the lug nuts once you raise the vehicle—the tire will just spin. Instead, break loose—but don't remove— the lug nuts while the tire is still on the ground. To save your back, place the tire iron on each lug nut so the handle is in the 9 o'clock position. Place both hands on the tire iron and push down with all your might. If that doesn't work, use a downward bouncing motion with your weight to break the nut loose.

# AIR-CONDITION
# YOUR GARAGE

Don't put up with a
sweltering garage any longer

by **Rick Muscoplat, Contributing Editor**

**W**renching on a car or doing a project in a sweltering garage is no fun. The heat and humidity
slow you down, make you grumpy and increase
your frustration. Air-conditioning your garage solves those
problems and doesn't cost a fortune. You can buy a TTW
(through-the-wall) unit for about $700. Window units cost
a bit less, so consider going that route if you have a suitable window. Window and TTW units are the same except
for installation. A window unit comes with hardware and
sealing gear for mounting it in a window, while a TTW
unit requires a separate sleeve that fits into a wall opening
that you frame into the wall.

If you start the installation in the morning, you'll be
enjoying cold air by mid-afternoon. A ceiling fan helps circulate the air and eliminate hot spots, but if the A/C unit
keeps you cool enough, you can skip the fan. We'll show
you how to pick the right size unit for your garage and
how to install it in the wall.

## Consider insulating first

If you plan to use your garage A/C only occasionally, you
don't have to install insulation. It'll just take longer to
lower the temperature to a comfortable level and the A/C
compressor will run for longer periods, costing you more
in electric bills. However, you can dramatically speed up
the cool-down time and increase cooling effectiveness
by hanging drywall on the ceiling. That reduces the size
of the area to be cooled and helps the cool air circulate.
Install a vapor barrier first, in case you decide to add attic
insulation later on. But if you plan to frequently use the
garage A/C, it's well worth insulating and finishing the
entire space.

## Then size the A/C unit

Measure the area of your garage (length times width) to
determine the total square footage, then consult the chart
on p. 277. Apply the adjusting factors at the bottom of the

**1 Cut the stud.** Cut through the center stud, leaving a space 3 in. taller than the rough opening height of the A/C sleeve to allow room for the top and bottom plates. Knock the cut piece sideways to break it loose from the sheathing and siding nails.

**2 Frame the sleeve opening.** Nail top and bottom plates to the center and adjacent studs. Then add a short jack stud to frame the opening to the proper width.

**3 Cut through sheathing.** Test-fit the sleeve before cutting out the sheathing with a reciprocating saw.

## Other A/C options for your garage

We didn't cover portable A/C units in this story. They're an option but not a very good one. Portable units use cold air from the room to cool the condensing coil and then exhaust that air to the outdoors. The negative pressure this creates inside the garage draws in an equal amount of hot humid "make-up" air from outside. The portable unit then has to cool that make-up air and the cycle repeats over and over, wasting 30 to 50 percent of the rated capacity of the unit. Overall, portable units don't come close to the efficiency of a window unit or a TTW unit.

If you want the very best cooling option and are willing to dig deep (expect to pay about $4,000), contact an HVAC company and get quotes on a split system. Those are heavy-duty units that can quickly cool your garage and maintain the temperature even under the hottest conditions.

chart. Then shop around for the best price on the A/C unit and a matching through-the-wall sleeve (an additional $100 to the cost of a window unit)

## Pick a location and cut the opening

A/C units have weak circulating fans, so don't locate one on the end wall of a large, rectangular garage. Instead, locate it in the middle of the longest wall and aim the airflow toward the garage door. If you're installing a window unit and it's located on the end wall of a rectangular garage, plan to install circulating fans to help move the cold air to the other end.

Next, check the sleeve installation instructions for the rough opening size. Some manufacturers want a 1-in. clearance on the sides and top of the sleeve. Plus, the distance from the ceiling is critical. Don't place the opening directly below the top wall plate. That'll result in rapid compressor cycling and inefficient cooling. Locate the top of the sleeve opening about 24 in. down from the ceiling (or as shown in the sleeve installation instructions). Then remove drywall (if any) in that location to expose the studs. Cut the center stud to allow for the thickness of the new top and sill plates. The biggest task is reworking the siding. In most cases it's best to remove as much siding as needed before cutting the opening in the sheathing and then to trim and re-side around the opening. Follow the manufacturer's instructions to mount and secure the sleeve to the framing.

Run electrical cable to the location and install the receptacle. Most 120-volt units require a dedicated receptacle on either a 15- or 20-amp circuit breaker (no extension cords allowed). A unit sized from 9,000 to 12,000 Btu will typically run on a 20-amp, 120-volt circuit. But you'll have to install a 220-volt circuit for larger units.

## Add circulation fans

A through-the-wall A/C unit will dump most of its cool air right into the center of the garage, creating hot spots around the sides. To get more uniform cooling, add a ceiling fan to suck hot air from the ceiling corners and blow it down to the floor. Use a floor fan on the opposite side to blow the newly warmed floor air up toward the A/C unit intake.

### A/C sizing for an insulated garage

| Typical garage size | Square feet | Btus for TTW or window unit |
|---|---|---|
| 2-car (18' x 20') | 360 | 9,000 |
| 2.5-car (22' x 22') | 484 | 12,000 |
| 3-car (20' x 32') | 640 | 14,000 |

**Adjusting factors:**
- Buy the next larger size if your garage isn't insulated.
- Add 10 percent if the garage is exposed to direct sunlight.

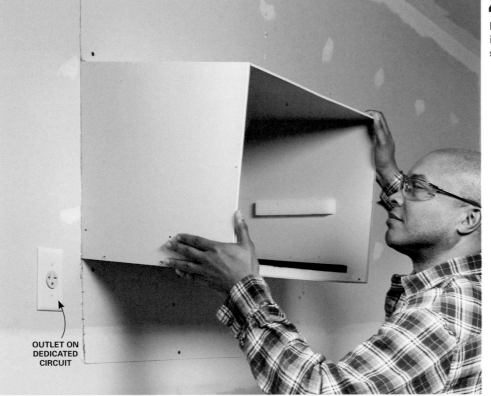

**4 Install the sleeve.** Secure the sleeve brackets (if equipped), install filler strips and secure the sleeve.

OUTLET ON DEDICATED CIRCUIT

## CLOSING THE GAP

Keep mulch from clogging the tailgate opening of your truck. Use a
PVC pipe to fill the
gap. When I'm not
using the pipe, I
store it behind the
front seat.

–Francis Itaya

## SLIDE-PROOF RAMPS

If your vehicle ramps slide forward as you drive onto them, secure them
to a piece of plywood. I used 3/4-in. plywood, some 2x4
blocks, lag screws and bolts. Now as I drive onto the
plywood, the weight of the car holds the ramps in place
so they don't skid away on contact. Drill a hole in the plywood so you can hang the ramps on the wall.

–Wayne Clark

## CARGO HOOK

Packing and unpacking my truck with
the tonneau cover in place got a whole
lot easier when I put a utility hook on the
end of a broom handle.Now I just push
things in with the handle and retrieve
them with the hook.

–Mel Gibbons

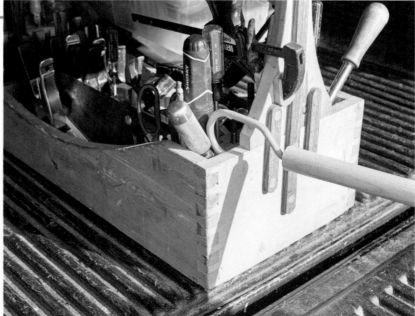

# FIX
# RUST SPOTS

Don't let your ride deteriorate into crumbles

by **Rick Muscoplat, Contributing Editor**

As long as vehicle body panels are made from steel, they're going to rust. Sure, you can lower your risk by applying paint protection film to chip-prone areas like the front edge of the hood, and by frequently washing off road salt and waxing your vehicle regularly. But even then, you're still going to get rust spots. If you ignore them, they'll spread and turn your sheet metal into Swiss cheese in no time. However, if you deal with rust early, you can stop it from spreading and squeeze a few extra years out of your vehicle.

Rust repair isn't hard, but it is time-consuming (mostly waiting for primer and paint to dry between steps). Plan to spend about $100 on supplies like sandpaper, primer,

masking tape and poly sheeting, a tack rag, polishing compound and touch-up paint and clear coat. Choose a calm, overcast day and block out the full day to fix the most common rust spots on the hood and doors. Here are the steps.

## Buy paint and supplies

You can buy automotive touch-up paint in pints and quarts to use in a spray gun, in aerosol cans, or in roller ball applicators. Even if you know how to use a spray gun, mixing automotive paint with a reducer to match the temperature and humidity conditions can be mighty tricky. We don't recommend it. Instead, buy aerosol cans for larger

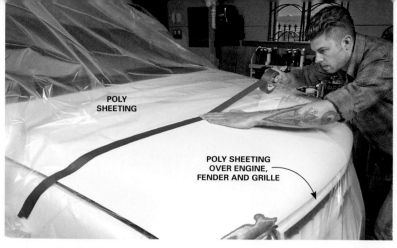

POLY
SHEETING

POLY SHEETING
OVER ENGINE,
FENDER AND GRILLE

**1** **Mask off the repair area.** Tape the leading edge of poly sheeting a few feet away from the repair so you'll have room to blend the touch-up paint into the good areas.

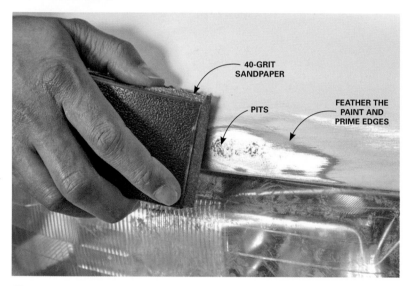

40-GRIT
SANDPAPER

PITS

FEATHER THE
PAINT AND
PRIME EDGES

**2** **Remove the rust.** Sand through the rust spots, down to bare metal. Then enlarge the sanded area so you'll have space to feather the edges. Switch to 120-grit sandpaper to feather the edges of the repair area. Complete the feathering with 220 grit.

**3** **Clean with detergent.** Clean the entire unmasked area with a grease-cutting dishwashing detergent, followed by clean rinse water. Let it dry. Then wipe the area one more time with a lint-free cloth to remove any remaining dust or lint.

repairs and roller ball applicators to fix scratches.

In order to buy the perfect color match for your vehicle's factory paint, you'll first need to find the car manufacturer's paint code. It can be in a variety of places on the body, in the engine compartment or trunk, or other places. Use either of these online resources to find instructions on how to locate your paint code: automotivetouchup.com/paint-code.htm or duplicolor.com (slide the "Explore Projects" graphic over "Fix a Scratch or Chip" to access the paint finder).

Most late-model vehicles were painted with base coat/clear coat paint. The base coat contains just the pigment and binding resins—the clear coat is just the gloss. You'll need equal amounts of both. You'll also need an epoxy self-etching primer to bite into the bare metal and a lacquer primer to hold the paint. We used paint, primer and sanding supplies from automotivetouchup.com for this repair. The Dupli-Color brand is available at most retail auto parts stores, car dealers and online retailers. Or, you can buy automotive paint locally from a professional auto body supplier.

Next, buy 40-, 600- and 1,000-grit sandpaper, a sanding block, grease and wax remover, poly sheeting, painter's tape, a tack rag and a microfiber cloth.

## Mask the vehicle

Protect the entire vehicle from paint overspray with poly sheeting. If you're painting the hood, spread poly sheeting over the engine and fenders. In door areas, cut poly sheeting to fit the door opening and tape it to the jamb. The final masking must be a foot or two away from the repair area (Photo 1).

## Sand, feather, and clean

Crack off any blistered paint with a scraper. Then sand the rust using 40-grit sandpaper (Photo 2). Then feather the paint edges. Use a tack rag to remove particles from the unmasked area. Then clean the sanded area (Photo 3) and apply the paint manufacturer's prep solvent.

If the rust has created pits in the metal (Photo 2), you can fill them now with body filler or wait until the epoxy primer dries and apply multiple coats of filler primer.

**4** **Apply epoxy primer, then filler primer.** Spray the filler primer in heavier coats to cover the entire repair area. Move the can away from the surface slightly and blend it into the surrounding painted area.

**5** **Sand the primer.** Starting with wet 600-grit sandpaper, smooth the primer and feather the edges. Then switch to wet 1,000-grit sandpaper to final-sand the entire repair, including the blended areas.

**6** **Apply the colored base coat.** Start at the bottom of the repair and apply the color coat in left-to-right rows, overlapping each pass by about one-third. Build the color slowly into the repair and surrounding areas in two to three coats, allowing about 10 to 15 minutes between coats.

**7** **Spray on the clear coat.** Apply several coats of clear coat, allowing the recommended drying time between coats. Gradually work the clear coat into the surrounding painted areas to achieve a smooth blend line.

## Prime the surface

Self-etching epoxy primer provides a strong bond to bare metal, so use it as your first coat. Spray two to three medium coats, allowing the recommended wait time listed on the label (usually 15 minutes) between coats. Wait a full hour for the epoxy to dry to the touch (longer if it's humid outside). Sand the epoxy primer with wet 1,000-grit sandpaper. Wash with clear water and let dry. Wipe the dried epoxy primer with a lint-free cloth and apply two to three heavier coats of lacquer filler primer (**Photo 4**), allowing drying time between each coat. Let the lacquer primer dry until it's dry to the touch—at least one hour— before sanding.

Sand drips and sags with 320-grit sandpaper. Then final-sand the entire repair area (**Photo 5**).

## Spray the base coat

Holding the spray can about 12 in. away from the surface, spray the repaired area (**Photo 6**). The slower you build the color coat, the better it'll look under the clear coat. Allow the base coat to dry, until it's dry to the touch, at least 60 minutes. Don't sand the base coat (especially metallic colors) unless you've created sags. In that case, sand lightly and then respray the touched-up areas.

## Add the clear coat

This is the hardest part because all clear coats run easily and that will ruin the look of your paint job. If you create a run in the clear coat, you'll have to let it dry for at least 48 hours before attempting to fix it with fine-grit sandpaper and polishing compound. Then you'll have to respray the sanded area. So practice spraying on a scrap piece of cardboard to get a feel for the nozzle and the speed of application.

Clean the painted area one last time with a tack rag. Then apply the first layer of clear coat so it looks wet (**Photo 7**).

Let the clear coat dry for several hours before driving the vehicle and at least 48 hours before buffing.

## Buff the repair

Using an old cotton T-shirt or microfiber cloth and buffing compound, hand-buff the repaired area. Don't use a polishing machine for this. Wait at least 30 days before waxing.

# Well, *that's* embarrassing!

## Domestic situation

Nighttime is no time for exterior repairs, but I couldn't sleep with that loose piece of trim slapping against the house. So despite the wind and rain, I grabbed a hammer and crawled out the window onto the roof—wearing only my tighty-whitey underwear. Before I could even begin the repair, my wife woke up and closed the window. As soon as I heard it shut, I scurried back to the window and tapped. No response, so I whispered, no response, louder, no response ....

A light went on next door and I could hear our phone ringing. It was the neighbor calling and sheepishly asking if we were having marital problems. (Why else would I be on the roof in my underwear, begging to be let in?) Finally, the window opened and I slipped in, cold and soaked, still tormented by that slapping trim.

–Jim Lyle

## No way out

I was relocating the shower in a bathroom that was built over a crawl space. To gain access, I cut a hole in the subfloor and slithered down between the joists with all my materials and tools. The floor would be an easy patch since I was retiling anyway. After I spent a few hours down there soldering copper pipes and gluing ABS drain lines, the new plumbing setup was perfect. Then it dawned on me that my beautiful new plumbing job blocked my way out through the opening. Unless I took the whole thing apart, I was trapped! I didn't have the heart to rip it all out, so I used my cell phone to call my son. I cooled my heels down there for an hour until he showed up and cut another hole in the floor to let me out.

–Jim Bianchini

## Free facial

Just days before Hurricane Sandy was to hit New Jersey, I was helping my husband install a "water jet sump pump backup system" in my parents' basement. In the event of a power outage, it works off the water pressure of the house. My husband asked me to hold on to the PVC pipe so he could cut out a piece with his reciprocating saw. While I held it, he made the first cut. When he made the second cut, nasty brown water started gushing out of the pipe and hit me full in the face.

Being the dutiful wife, I held on tight! It took him a few seconds to realize what was happening. He had forgotten to unplug the pump. After pulling the plug, he looked at me with a worried expression, but I began laughing

hysterically. I was soaked with that disgusting water from head to toe. At least the project turned out as planned—after Sandy, they had no water in their basement.

– Jill Gallery

## Stranded and phoneless

One evening after my wife and daughters left the house for a few hours, I enlisted my four-year-old son to help me inspect our brand new roof. I got the ladder out and climbed up on the roof as my son watched from the ground. Not a minute after I was up there, our hyper puppy wrapped its leash around the bottom of the ladder and yanked it down, narrowly missing my son. He was fine, but I was stranded.

I hollered down to my son to get my phone so I could call a neighbor. "Throw the phone to Daddy as hard as you can!" As the phone flew through the air in what looked like slow motion, I realized his arm wasn't quite strong enough to get the phone to the roof—and it shattered on the concrete below. I had to be patient and wait on the roof until someone who could help walked by. Needless to say, I'll keep my phone in my pocket the next time I venture onto the roof.

–David Duncan

# INDEX

Visit *familyhandyman.com* for hundreds of home improvement articles.

# ACKNOWLEDGMENTS

## FOR THE FAMILY HANDYMAN

| | |
|---|---|
| Editor in Chief | Ken Collier |
| Senior Editors | Travis Larson |
| | Gary Wentz |
| Associate Editors | Jeff Gorton |
| | Mark Petersen |
| | Jason White |
| Senior Copy Editor | Donna Bierbach |
| Art Directors | Vern Johnson |
| | Marcia Roepke |
| Photographer | Tom Fenenga |
| Production Artist | Mary Schwender |
| Set Builder | Josh Risberg |
| Office Administrative Manager | Alice Garrett |
| Production Manager | Leslie Kogan |

## CONTRIBUTING EDITORS

| | |
|---|---|
| Elisa Bernick | Rick Muscoplat |
| Spike Carlsen | David Radtke |
| Tom Caspar | Larry Roepke |
| Joe Churchill | Jim vonMeier |
| Tim Johnson | |

## CONTRIBUTING ART DIRECTOR

Ellen Thomson

## CONTRIBUTING PHOTOGRAPHERS

| | |
|---|---|
| Paul Nelson | Gary Sundermeyer |

## ILLUSTRATORS

| | |
|---|---|
| Steve Björkman | David Radtke |
| Christopher Mills | Frank Rohrbach III |

## OTHER CONSULTANTS

Al Hildenbrand, electrical
Rune Eriksen, electrical
Tim Johnson, electrical
John Williamson, electrical
Les Zell, plumbing

For information about advertising in
*The Family Handyman* magazine, call (646) 293-6150

To subscribe to *The Family Handyman* magazine:
- By phone: (800) 285-4961
- By Internet: FHMservice@rd.com
- By mail: The Family Handyman
Subscriber Service Dept.
P.O. Box 6099
Harlan, IA 51593-1599

We welcome your ideas and opinions.
**Write:** The Editor, The Family Handyman
2915 Commers Drive, Suite 700
Eagan, MN 55121
**Fax:** (651) 994-2250
**E-mail:** editors@thefamilyhandyman.com